To Mike:

A great Texas
Naturalist like you is
sure to enjoy this Texas
adventure. Read it with my
invitation — to visit your second
in Texas anytime it fits your p...

Dave Brown

July 28, 1992

**Adventures with a
Texas Naturalist**

Adventures
with a
Texas Naturalist

ROY BEDICHEK

Illustrations by WARD LOCKWOOD
Foreword by H. MEWHINNEY

UNIVERSITY OF TEXAS PRESS
AUSTIN

Requests for permission to reproduce material from this
work should be sent to Permissions, University of Texas
Press, Box 7819, Austin, Texas 78713-7819.

International Standard Book Number 0-292-70311-2
Library of Congress Catalog Card Number 61-12914

Fourth Paperback Printing, 1988

To my father, a gentle philosopher, who, by both precept and example, taught me, a little savage, to love animals.

Foreword

"Mister Bedi," while he was still among us, loved to quote the poets and the philosophers, more especially the Greeks. Might we not as well begin this ceremony—for it is as much a ceremony as when an Arapaho Indian or an Upper Palaeolithic mammoth hunter cut off a finger in memory of his dead—by quoting with him?

> Here lapped in hallowed slumber, Saon lies,
> Asleep, not dead: A good man never dies.
>
> Callimachus (Symonds)

> For the whole earth is the sepulchre of famous men; they have a memorial not only in their own country but in foreign lands also, graven not on stone but in the hearts of men.
>
> Pericles (Jowett's *Thucydides*)

> He was beginning to grow cold about the groin, when he uncovered his face, for he had covered himself up, and said—they were his last words—he said: "Crito, I owe a cock to Asclepius; will you remember to pay the debt?" "The debt shall be paid," said Crito; "is there anything else?" There was no answer—
>
> Plato, the *Phaedo* (Jowett)

And now that thou art lying, my dear old Carian guest,
A handful of grey ashes, long, long ago at rest,
Still are thy pleasant voices, thy "Nightingales," awake,
For Death, he taketh all away, but them he cannot take.

                                        Callimachus (Cory)

Hast thou named all the birds without a gun?
Loved the wood-rose, and left it on its stalk?

                                        Emerson

Very old are the woods;
And the buds that break
Out of the brier's boughs
When March winds wake
So old with their beauty are—
Oh, no man knows
Through what wild centuries
Roves back the rose.

                        De la Mare

Collige, virgo, rosas—
                        Ausonius

Perhaps we loved Roy Bedichek mostly because, in an age
of small and incomplete men, he was a full and ripened man.
He loved nature first, as Landor put it in the famous quat-
rain, and, next to nature, art. Art, for Mister Bedi, was something that began with Homer and not with Aldous Huxley,
or Ernest Hemingway, or Erskine Caldwell. Nature was the
world around him: the hen that laid more flavorsome eggs
because she could run loose and catch grasshoppers rather
than being kept in a box and fed on stuff that came out of
a sack, the cowbird trying to lay her egg in a flycatcher's
nest, the flint weapon point lying on the creek flat where the
Indian lost it, the scarce flowers and grasses that escaped
extinction because they were growing on a railroad right-of-
way and not in an overgrazed and gullied pasture, all that
complex of interrelationships among sun and water and soil
and the plants that feed on the soil, the animals that feed on

the plants, the other animals that feed on animals, and man, who feeds on everything as the greatest predator and destroyer of them all. To read Mister Bedi's essays on these matters is to study ecology transformed into poetry. It enlarges a man's awareness of the world around him, much like reading Darwin's famous essay on earthworms, with the added benefit that Mister Bedi was a more graceful artist than Darwin.

Thus, although Mister Bedi was an accomplished and observant field naturalist—ornithologist, mammalogist, botanist, ecologist—and although the essays in this book have much to tell about the birds, mammals, and flowers of Texas, they have a larger message than that, just as Wordsworth's poem about the daffodils is something more than a taxonomy for the genus *Narcissus*.

Mister Bedi was a man who could look at a rose, even at that lovely nuisance from China, *Rosa bracteata*, that has damaged so many pastures on the Gulf Coast, and remember what Homer, and Herodotus, and Ausonius, and Herrick had written about roses.

That quality made him a larger man than most of his contemporaries.

For it is the curse of this century that most men, no matter how clever or accomplished, have little background either in nature or in art. They have never milked a cow, dug a post hole, skinned a squirrel, or heard the dogs tree a coon. They have never read Homer, or Herodotus, or Plato, or even Xenophon.

When Mister Bedi died in 1959 that little weekly the *Texas Observer* devoted one entire issue to his memory, and a number of us—all devoted lovers of Mister Bedi, though not necessarily of one another—were invited to write something about him.

One man, at least, was too sorrowful to write a word. Some of the essays were splendid. But what I remember best about that memorial issue is a series of tiny incidents that would have appealed to the salty-cynical streak that so often showed up suddenly in Mister Bedi.

I had quoted, without marks and without acknowledgment, one of the lines from Emerson quoted above and said that Mister Bedi could name all the birds without a gun.

Four different times in the weeks that followed, four different friends of mine—all of them admirers of Mister Bedi— came up to me and told me that I had written the most beautiful sentence in the paper.

Likely enough, it really was the prettiest sentence. But the man who wrote it was Emerson.

Bear in mind two things, if you will: All four of those friends are subtle and intelligent people, all four are well read and well informed in the modern sense, all four are good enough judges of poetic language—and good taste in language is much rarer than good taste in painting or music— to admire that lovely sentence. But not a one among them had ever read Emerson. Much less would any one among them have ever read the *Phaedo*.

And right there you have the predicament of modern man. He knows as little of Emerson, or Ausonius, or Homer as he knows of the wild rose itself. More than any Esau who ever lived before him—not that he has ever opened a Gideon Bible and read about Esau while waiting in a hotel room for his girl friend—he has traded away his inheritance for a bowl of bean soup. He is the fellow who buys this trash that was being advertised in the newspapers last Christmas: a carving knife with a miniature electric motor in the handle and a miniature saw in the blade, guaranteed to slice the turkey neatly, whether or not the man himself has skill enough with a pocket knife to trim his fingernails; a pair of binoculars with a built-in transistor radio, so that the fellow can sit in the stands and watch one football game while listening to a broadcast about another one.

If he considers himself an outdoors man, this is the fellow who goes deer hunting in the fall. Of course, it is not often that he shoots another hunter, being so little skilled in taxonomy as to have mistaken *Homo sapiens* for *Odocoileus virginianus*. For the most part, he merely sits in a miniature sitting room built up in a tree, with a carpet on the floor and with an electric heater to keep him warm. He is armed with a .270 rifle, fitted with a telescopic sight. He knows for pretty much of a certainty that his buck will keep the appointment, for the buck has been coming there every day for the previous six weeks to eat cottonseed cake out of a self-feeder. Not that the men of our era, as distinguished from the women, enjoy any monopoly on these short cuts to prowess in hunting or to familiarity with the arts. I sat lately in the apartment of a charming little blue-eyed girl who is an accomplished writer of short stories, more or less in the manner of Eudora Welty, and is intensely and indeed almost exclusively interested in literature or at least in what she conceives to be literature. There were five or six hundred books on the shelves in the sitting room. Not, of course, that these were the only five hundred books the blue-eyed girl had ever read; but they were the specific five hundred that she liked well enough to buy with her own money and to keep on the shelves of her sitting room. Well, I looked at the titles, one by one. Exactly one book among the five hundred had been written before the year 1900 A.D., and that one was *The Brothers Karamazov*. No Homer, no Plato, no Shakespeare, no Anthology, not even an anthology of English verse. Lord help us, not even a Bible.

Lately, again, I sat in another apartment during the course of what was intended as an evening of literary talk. I fell into a random discourse with a young engineer from Greece, here in Texas to learn how to set up a carbide plant in Calcutta, I believe he said. The young fellow said he could read ancient Greek pretty well and I asked him his opinion of Xenophon as a narrative stylist.

At this point it developed that the handsome blonde young woman seated next to me on the sofa, possessed of an undergraduate degree in philosophy, intensely interested in contemporary verse, and now engaged in writing what she described as a novella, had never even heard of Xenophon. The engineer and I, mildly surprised, checked her out, spelling it for her—X-e-n-o-p-h-o-n. No; she had flat never heard of him. Nor, indeed, had she ever heard of the Ten Thousand, of their once famous retreat, of the cry of Thalassa! Thalassa!, of Cyrus the Younger, or, naturally, of Cyrus the Elder. She had little interest in ancient history, she explained. These two encounters reminded me of some opinions expressed lately by J. Frank Dobie, who with Mister Bedi and with the historian Walter P. Webb, formed for so many years a sort of intellectual triumvirate in Texas. Indeed, Mister Bedi wrote this very book—by no means his first formal piece of prose, but his first full-sized book—at the age of seventy or thereabouts, after ending a long career of directing the Interscholastic League, while quietly ensconced on a ranch owned by Mister Walter.

Mister Frank expressed a low opinion of twentieth-century American literature in the preface to a sort of Dobie Anthology, dedicated to his dead friend. Among other things, he said:

> Reading Hazlitt, Herodotus, Chaucer, Shakespeare, Boswell, Montaigne, and certain other emitters of luminosity never palls. . . . I am so grounded in respect for the English language as used by noble writers for more than five hundred years that I have never been contemporaneous with more than four or five writers whom I admire. My contemporaries have lacked amplitude, wit, Johnsonian horse sense, play of mind, and other virtues common to predecessors still waiting to be enjoyed. Most modern American writing in the "best seller" lists is so loosely—often sloppily, ignorantly, hideously—composed that it has no appeal for a craftsman disciplined to lucidity and the logic of grammar, bred to a style "familiar but by no means vulgar," and harmonized from infancy with the rhythms of nature.

And, indeed, how many men are there in modern Texas who can enjoy going out into the country, not to shoot a baited deer, but to lie on the ground beside a campfire at night, waking to watch the Dipper wheel around the Pole

Star and to listen to the whippoorwills? (Mister Bedi would have said they were actually "chuck-will's-widows," but when I was a boy we called them "whippoorwills.")

Dobie was saying that our contemporaries lack wit, amplitude, and Johnsonian horse sense. Bertrand Russell, a notable non-Christian, said apologetically not long ago that what this age chiefly needs is old-fashioned Christian love—what little of it there ever was. But perhaps what it really needs is what Roy Bedichek so conspicuously had—a sense of man's background in the woods, pastures, and streams around him and in the writings by great artists that began nearly three thousand years ago and are still so much nobler than the books being written in this century. Perhaps, if not Christian love, at least a love of something, a willingness to take one's own emotions seriously, a willingness to shed tears, as Odysseus shed them when his old dog, lying on the dunghill, recognized him after the twenty years. It is astonishing that so many modern novels are merely dreary recitals of multiple fornications, which neither the characters nor the author can manage to take seriously. When Amnon, in the Bible, raped his sister, at least both of them took the matter seriously.

But this is enough of preface. We can best remember Roy Bedichek, we can best sacrifice the cockerel that he now owes to Asclepius, by reading his book. Or, in the other metaphor—that borrowed from Callimachus—these essays are Roy Bedichek's nightingales. And they are still awake. We can listen while they sing.

H. MEWHINNEY

Acknowledgments

The year's leave of absence from my regular duties which gave me the opportunity to write this book was made possible by a fund contributed by Texas people, collected and administered by the Texas Historical Association. W. P. Webb and J. Frank Dobie, both lifelong friends of mine, have given me not only encouragement but valuable suggestions, as well as detailed textual criticisms of certain chapters.

Kathleen Blow, Loan Librarian in the University of Texas, has reduced the number of errors herein by digging up authentic information for me from the vast resources of a really great library.

One cannot write at any length about Nature in Texas without occasional use of Spanish words and phrases and without reference to the lore of the Spanish-speaking Indians. My wife, who is a specialist in the field, has aided me greatly with her accurate knowledge of both the lore and the language of this nature-loving and artistic element of our population.

THE AUTHOR

Contents

Introduction

I begin this "year's leave" hoping to reduce to some order quite a lot of notes which, at the moment of their jotting down, seemed to me to have more than temporary interest. At my elbow is a huge wastepaper basket and, near by, a fireplace to relieve the container as congestion occurs. When all is said and done and published I know that I shall regret not having made more generous use of these facilities.

My friends call it "going on leave," or "temporary retirement," and treat me as if I were on a vacation. "You have plenty of time now," they say, "so why don't you" . . . And here follows an array of thus-and-sos—"now since you have nothing else to do you can read," or "fish," or "travel," or "garden"—in short, do whatever my adviser of the moment would like himself to do.

The sights, sounds, odors, and, especially, the *feel* of this place stimulate in me memories so warm and intimate that taking up residence here seems more like a homecoming than an escape.

I first thought of going away, but feared the distracting influences of an unfamiliar environment. Why not travel a bit—take to the open road? I have a camp car especially equipped to back up my scorn of hotels, tourist camps, and other commercial accommodations. But I resisted this allurement, feeling sure that I would get more done of the thing I wanted to do by facing a typewriter and staying put until the job was finished. I therefore chose to settle myself in the section of Texas in which I feel most at home. Better work in proved territory, I concluded, than end up, as so many wildcatting oil drillers do, with a dry hole. I was never much of a gambler.

The time and the place settled, I next prescribed for myself a year alone, or, at least, as nearly alone as was practicable. "My mind to me a kingdom is" whose government is thrown out of order—sometimes into a state of anarchy—by too frequent contacts with my kind. When I took up the receiver to answer that last call on January 31, my face had none of the smiling complacency which rests upon faces chosen to embellish the advertisements of the telephone company. The excited voices of news casters trying to incite me to action for which I have no stomach, shouting headlines, and circular appeals from do-good organizations, all left me cold. The morning mail looked like it weighed a ton.

"But surely you want somebody around." No, no one at all. "Not a cook?" Certainly not. I am a cook of parts myself, and no cook in the world is as anxious to please his master as I am to please mine. Besides, with what face can a mere boardinghouse philosopher give suggestions on cooking, dishwashing, and housekeeping generally, advance notice of which is hereby given?

"No one to clean up—not even once a week?" No, again. I can redd up this room in less than ten minutes, not, it is true, to meet the critical eye of a rival housekeeper, but to satisfy "minimum essentials." The unsympathetic observer might call the operation "a lick and a promise."

No, indeed, no. No one to cook, no one to clean up, wash the dishes, and put the things away. My little household duties amuse me and furnish a refuge in reality, which the visionary needs. "Doing my own chores" gives me a sense of independence and of satisfaction in doing my share of the dirty work of the world. If everyone cleaned up his own messes there would be no household drudges. "Act only on that maxim whereby thou canst at the same time will that it should become a universal law." This rule of conduct is greatly simplified in solitude.

"But company?" Never fear, you have plenty of that; and I like it, since it comes in moderation. I find that if you make yourself sufficiently inaccessible, you set up a screen which lets through only the most desirable particles. To this writing I have not been subjected to a single bore. My one door has not yet opened upon an uninteresting or an unwelcome guest.

When the cotton was laid by in June, we used to make a covered-wagon trip due west from the edge of the great blackland prairies where I was reared to a point on the Colorado River eighteen miles west of Lampasas. Following the first night's camp on the Leon and continuing our journey, we soon gained sight in the morning sun of broken hills covered with cedar and live oak. To my eyes, which rarely saw a tree except in yards and in creek bottoms, this vast stretch of tree-covered country was a new world opening up like a veritable miracle.

Nor have these eyes by greener hills
Been soothed, in all my wanderings.

We stayed about a month, returning home in time for early cotton picking.

As we left the Leon going west out of Belton for our next camp on the Lampasas River, we were traversing the Edwards Plateau, a rugged area whose wet-weather creeks ran in "riffles" over polished boulders, or stayed awhile in blue "holes," or plunged recklessly from ledge to ledge of clean limestone shelving. I was accustomed to dirt "tanks" and to Deer Creek, Elm Creek, and the Cow Bayou, all sluggish and slimy, often clogged with debris, tributaries of the Brazos, whose drowsy current, after it leaves the hill country, always reminds me of dirty dishwater. So hills and trees, clear streams with splashing waterfalls, bluffs which to a prairie lad seemed mountainous, all presented a fresher world, and certainly nearer a boy's idea of heaven than the summer's dust and winter's mud of my native blackland. This great plateau comprises about one eighth of the area of the entire state; and, although I have lived most of my life around its edges, my heart has been in the highlands. Hence I chose the Edwards Plateau for my year of stock-taking. A friend offered me sanctuary in a great rock house on a small ranch of his in Bear Creek Valley, which is an indentation of the escarpment dividing the plateau from the prairies eastward. It is several miles from a highway, situated, as the plains editor said of his home town, "in the center of the surrounding country"—a goat-and-deer country, rich in browsing, and, viewed extensively on a clear day, near and far, mottled with the contrasting greens of cedar and of several species of oak—billowy rise after rise growing ever more purplish and smoky in the distance until they finally blur vaguely into an indefinite horizon.

The house was built near a century ago as a school for boys, is L-shaped, fronts south, is two stories with limestone walls three feet thick, giving it more the appearance of a fortress than of a school or residence. Mine is a second-story room, twenty-two by twenty-three feet, with four windows, each as wide as a barn door: two south, exposing Bear Creek Valley with Friday Mountain just beyond, and two north, looking up a slope crowned by pioneer stock pens, log cribs, and sheds scattered about among giant live oaks. This room has three walls of limestone,—roughhewn blocks, presenting countless irregular nicks and niches, slopings, and miniature precipices. The other wall is a flimsy partition against which I have put bookcases to cover just as much of it as possible.

I found myself concerned with the looks of my room. I didn't want it spick and span, and still it must not look as if a willful wind had just passed through. My ideal was a kind of picturesque disorder.

The most conspicuous piece of furniture is a table, round and of solid oak, which a ranger confiscated in a gambling hideout a few years ago where it accommodated an eight-hand game of poker, leaving plenty of room for action in case action became necessary. I placed a large student's lamp in the center, with books crowding gently toward it as if to keep warm on winter nights. The "bookcases" against the wooden wall are oak-stained apple boxes stacked atop one another clear to the ceiling. My vegetable man gave me most of the boxes, and I bought the remainder in the open market at ten cents a piece. The typewriting table accommodates an ancient Oliver (No. 5), a book or two, a manuscript holder, and a stack of paper. The chairs (except for one sacred, expensive, newfangled, cleverly adjustible typewriter's chair) are rawhide bottomed, oak-framed, and built by an artisan whose workshop is somewhere in the woods near Apple Springs, Texas.

For curtains and couch cover I had sewed into shape eight-ounce duck called "cotton sacking," which goes well with yellowed limestone. The floor, worn with a century of use, is wavy from the warping of the six-inch material used in its construction. I wish I might have been successful in collecting a cheerful rag carpet with which to replace two dismal and disintegrating rugs now spread down the central portion.

A knothole in the ceiling annoyed me considerably until one day, lying on my couch, I saw framed in it a canyon wren peering down inquisitively. I didn't move an eyelash, and presently he flew to the mantelpiece, hopped along from one end of it to the other, inspected the typewriter table, and flitted over to the center table on which he spent some time going over books and pamphlets for fish moths. After a short visit to a low stand he exactly retraced his steps—big table, little table, mantelpiece, and on out through the ceiling. He gives me a going over every once in a while, and I have become reconciled to the knothole.

Cooking equipment and food supplies are relegated to one corner and introduce a discordance which I have not yet been able to remedy. Perhaps this sour note in the symphony of my interior decorations cannot be sweetened at all.

We have become so accustomed to specialized rooms that one generalized to the extent this one is seems to present irremediable disharmonies.

But why this concern over looks? Am I not pursuing a mere tradition, a shadow without substance in making all this to-do about setting myself up to write a book in the field of natural history? Why shouldn't I have sensibly and matter-of-factly cleared out a room in my own house in the city, put a "don't-disturb" sign on each door, disengaged the telephone, and gone to work? I don't know, but I couldn't. I tried it. I couldn't shuck off the character I had in the city. Out here it slips off, and I find myself posing as a student, as a fireside philosopher, as a secluded naturalist, as a man maybe with a message—at any rate as a person determined to write some kind of a book.

Set solidly in the west wall of my room, opposite the books, is an institution that ties me to an ancient past and gives me —an infinitesimal human unit—a comfortable sense of belonging and continuity with my kind,—connects me lovingly with precedents. I find that living by a properly constructed fireplace, in a rock room, pleasantly isolated, is like camping outside, inside. The mystic circle of the campfire is reduced to a semicircle, but in return for the bisection there are not a few compensations.

There comes no blast howling out of the north, whipping your fire this way and that; no rain beating down upon you; no glare of the noonday sun, or other whimsies of the weather to visit discomforts upon the flesh. There are no pre-caveman inconveniences. The campfire brought inside these roughhewn walls completes a cave replica.

The fireplace was born in a cave many thousands of years before any kind of a house was built. To this day little country boys trench out a rough half-flue in the bank of a ravine, build a fire there, and sit around it in a semicircle, watching the flames lick up their improvised half-chimney, and cracking nuts pilfered from a nearby pecan bottom. Grown a few years older, these same boys hollow out a cavity in the bank, dig a hole from the surface above to connect with it, and the fireplace is born again. When the first caveman found a fissure in the overburden of his cave, and, with a little punching, gave his fire a draft, he revolutionized indoor living, since the first air-conditioning unit was then in operation. The sour corners of the cave became suddenly as sweet as the winds of heaven. Noisome odors vanished; food kept better; and an access of energy came to the human denizens through better oxygenation of their blood—a magic purification which my own fireplace is performing for me here and now. The pioneer mason built it to draw just right, by gentle suction, moving all the air of the room in a constant flow, yet not so rapidly as to take all the heat out: *flow* but no *rush*, replenishment without haste.

Far from being brought into the house, as above carelessly suggested, the house was originally built around the fireplace. The genealogy of the latter is longer by some ages or eons.

People unhabituated to this institution are prone to violate its etiquette. I have known those who hover over the stone flagging, hearth broom in hand, to sweep it clear of every ash or cinder happening to fall out upon it. And there is, unhappily, the nervous individual who sits hunched out of his chair, jabbing coals loose from the body of the wood where they belong. And it's bad fireplace manners to be too sensitive to a little smoke, especially to the savory smoke of good oak wood, or mesquite, or juniper, since a whiff is as incense in the nostrils of the orthodox. I used to know an old woodsman whose final preparation for striking camp was to hold his hands in the smoke to scent them up for sniffing later. I have found that the odor doesn't last long enough to bother with it; but if a commercial chemist will provide a fixative for the perfume of burning oak or mesquite, I can assure him of at least one customer.

Electric or steam heat, furnaces—indeed, central heating of all types—divorce man from the presence of fire; but he is bound to it by unbreakable ties. Half the hunting craze of the city man is at bottom the yen for a campfire. Something, he knows, has been left out of his life. We have lived on intimate terms with an open fire so long that our souls freeze without it. And what a sorry device is the "log" of the gas fireplace! It's as pathetic as the doll complex outlasting childhood.

More than any other of my chores, washing dishes disturbs my pose; and I soon found myself studying the whole dishwashing problem. I dismissed paper dishes, since they are no good except for the sandwiches and the fodder of an afternoon picnic. The Fabian tactic of "putting things to soak" (especially pots and pans) is merely humoring a cowardice which attacks the human will while it is rocked into somnolence by the sluggish pulsations of an organ concerned with the task of rendering recently ingested food absorbable.

When my fireplace had accumulated a supply of good clean ashes, the pot-and-pan annoyance was considerably relieved. Roasting peanuts, potatoes, and eggs in the campfire is a part of the lore of boyhood. I was surprised, however, to find the wide range of food which yields graciously to this primitive method. Cabbage, cauliflower, broccoli, indeed, all commercial species of the cabbage tribe, except collards, may be disinterred from a two-hour burial in the fireplace, steaming and savory, with every jot and tittle of the original vitamin and mineral content readied for assimilation. Roasting ears, apples, sweet potatoes, beets, carrots, all succumb deliciously to the steady heat of properly banked coals and ashes.

It's simple. Wrap your vegetable about in plenty of tough, wet paper, nest deeply in a hollowed-out bed of coals and hot ashes, cover and tamp, and go on about your work. Two or three hours later rake your dinner out of the hearth, disengage the parched wrappings, transfer to plate, season to taste. After your meal, sweep up the hearth, wash plate, knife, and fork, and take a nap.

There are some watery vegetables—celery, tomatoes, asparagus, and, of course, greens of every kind—which I couldn't make conform to this method; but they stew, and stewing doesn't dirty a pot anything like baking. If one is alone, there's nothing to keep him (as I found out) from eating a stewed vegetable out of the pan in which it is cooked. This neat device sidesteps the dirty plate.

Some carnivorous reader may be curious about the meat. Well, when I have a carnivorous guest, I broil the steak if he has been thoughtful enough to provide one. On occasion I tried roasting in hot ashes, but with disappointing results, owing, I think, to lack of practice. Ordinarily, I avoid messing things up with meat by practicing vegetarianism, and find my physical strength unimpaired, my mental vigor not more subnormal than when I had meat once or twice a day, and my prejudices as vindictive as ever. One can get along without meat easily enough.

Half the dishwashing battle is won by not putting it off. Use military strategy. Strike at once, suddenly, sans mercy. He who hesitates in front of a pile of dirty dishes is compounding trouble. Tiny bits of food are taking a deadly grip; liquids are drying up, leaving sedimentary deposits; grease is caking; sticky things like melted cheese, and gummy things like peach preserves, are throwing up barricades of defense against assaults of steel wool and dishrags, foamy with soapy water.

Whether or not this book is any good, I am already compensated by having regained a sense of the flow of time. There are now few moments mutilated with flurried haste. The incubus of some neglected task has loosened its hold, and I feel no longer the internal disquietude of something hanging fire which it was my duty to straighten out a week or two ago. Rhythm comes of timing the items of one's routine to conform to those of the natural day.

Whence comes the deliberation and aplomb of out-of-doors people the world over, savage as well as civilized? The American Indian is recorded as grave, slow, measured in speech and manner. The frontier Texan figures in fiction and in factual descriptions with a "drawl" and as a man of few words. Of course, now, with a generation of urbanization, as much chatter falls from the composite mouth of Texas as from that of any other state, excluding only those of disproportionate metropolitan populations. Outdoor living not only softens speech but slows its tempo, reflecting quieter nerves and mental reactions surer if somewhat slower on the trigger.

It is because Nature herself is deliberate. Ninety-nine per cent of her performance is gradual. To take a single instance out of those hundreds ready at hand: what a large percentage of urbanized populations miss beginning the day under the spell of the silent, pervasive, leisurely preparations of the heavens to receive the sun!

Adventures with a
Texas Naturalist

1. Fences: Fields and Pastures

I have been looking over a two-hundred-acre plot of fenced land and trying to compare the life it now supports with that which it had been supporting for thousands of years when the first white man occupied it a hundred years ago. This land has been living upon its own fat and finally upon its own vitals, consuming its capital instead of the interest alone, as it did in the year 1846 and before.

In spring and early summer the abandoned field of fifty acres is blanketed with povertyweed (*Filago nivea*); in later summer and early fall with Mexican tea, a species of croton which even the hungry goats refuse to eat. Judging from the native vegetation growing on an adjacent highway, there were no less than a hundred different species of flowering plants and shrubs, as well as a dozen different grasses thriving here before the pasture land was intensively grazed, the field was fenced, and the first plow disturbed its long-accumulated humus. Relatively few vegetable species have survived, which means that the variety of animal life, also, has been proportionately reduced. Variety has been sacrificed during the past hundred years to produce cotton, corn, oats, and to graze sheep, goats, and other domesticated animals.

In the two hundred acres under fence there are now about a hundred chickens, fifty turkeys, twenty head of neat cattle, three or four horses, and little wild life to speak of, but even this domestic stock is not supported from the land upon which it is confined. From year's end to year's end the food which nature supplies from the depleted soil has to be supplemented with store-bought provender, grown elsewhere, processed, sacked, transported great distances, and at last dished out as an individual purchase and hauled twenty miles. It is this elaborate organization which permits animal life to subsist at all upon these famished acres, and which gives many people in similar circumstances the illusion that the land is providing something besides space in which the animals may move around.

It is true that even in prepioneer times fire restricted the variety of life on prairies and plains for the benefit of grazing animals valuable to the Indians such as the antelope and buffalo; but annual autumn fires had no such disastrous effect upon natural life as fencing has had, since the *flow* of grazing life was unimpeded and the fertility of the land itself little impaired.

In pre-Columbian times, on the creek skirting this tract, there were a couple of beaver dams which multiplied the number of species, both animal and vegetable, manyfold. With the extermination of the beaver, floods have swept their old check dams away and scoured banks and channel bed. Swollen to madness by the increasing runoff from its tilled watershed, the little stream ground and tore away all obstructions, year after year, until the channel throughout its length from hills to river valley is swept clean as a floor. Present owners, or some of them, along its course are constructing concrete dams at a cost of from $500 to $1,000 per dam to take up again the work which the beavers left off seventy-five years ago. I think they are locking the door after the horse has been stolen. They may be able to recover some kind of horse, but not the superior animal that escaped.

As the period of abuse lengthened, the creek grew temperamental and had spells of refusing to run at all during long summer droughts, drying up into stagnant pools which are death-traps for aquatic life. Thus blow followed blow during successive years, destroying here a link and there another, loosening and letting fall whole chains of interdependent life. The decline was so gradual that it was long unnoticed; and even now it requires the perspective of a whole century to bring before the mind's eye the full extent of the catastrophe.

In pre-Columbian times deer and other browsers wandered across this acreage, taking mast in the fall or nibbling tender shoots in the spring, but wounding nothing to its hurt. Opossums, coons, skunks, snakes, fish, frogs, beaver, predators and preyed-on, and man himself had reached an equilibrium when the first fence appeared; and year after year there had been no diminution in the amount of life or, what is more important, in the variety of life immediately dependent upon the creek and the acres along its borders. Instead of the fifty-odd turkeys now liberally subsidized, this plot of ground in prepioneer times served merely as a part of the range for flocks of wild turkeys who stayed not long unless there happened to be a pest of insects and then they not only stayed but brought in reinforcements until the pest was effectually checked. Mobile life flowed in and concentrated only when an excess of other life justified such concentration. Thus monopoly by any one form of life was prevented, and less fortunate forms were tided over and given a chance to recuperate. Nature, left alone, multiplied forms: from the infinite number of mutations called forth, a few are continually chosen to slake the eternal thirst for variety. She abhors not only a vacuum, but monotony also. Free and unlimited fencing has interfered with the healthy circulation of natural life, congested and confined it in pockets, restricted its channels, and developed conditions analogous to varices and hardened arteries in the human circulatory system. In the present instance, the fence has frustrated nature, and nature retaliates with povertyweed and Mexican tea.

As the wild turkeys took the part of the threatened against the overwhelming force of insect numbers, so with other vital adjustments. In the free circulation of life there is always moderation, nothing too much, no robbing or senseless gorging. The acres now under fence were as rich at the end as were at the beginning of any period, a year or a hundred thousand years. As for human life, this plot of ground supported the minute fraction of an Indian. If "one" is made the numerator of this fraction, the denominator will, I think, run into at least six figures. But whatever the size of the denominator, it can be multiplied by one thousand to get the fraction of an Indian this same plot of ground would now support with fences down, present population removed, and domesticated life permitted to seek its own competitive level. This is a fundamental, permanent, irremediable impoverishment, differing from the devastation of war, which, being wrought mainly upon the works of man, is by man quickly repaired. It is all recorded statistically. Cold columns of figures set forth the facts, but no Isaiah, or other poet of desolation, has burned the truth into the public mind. The "plan of salvation" presupposed a "conviction of sin" and this necessary basis has not yet been laid.

The curse which has blighted these two hundred acres has been multiplied a thousand or a million times. Texas, topographically considered, is an inclined plane tilted suggestively toward the Gulf of Mexico which still has in its yawning chasms room for unlimited consignments of soil fertility. In periods of excessive rainfall the regurgitations of a dozen bloated rivers spill over the continental shelf. In droughty seasons, sweepings of vast erosions are blown by violent winds clear from the high plains miles out to sea.

Natural life in North America has been more profoundly affected by fencing than by any other of man's devices, ancient or modern, for it is the fence which has enabled him to multiply at will those species which minister to his wants, while suppressing plants and animals which do not. From the walling about of a desert water hole by Arab or Hebrew nomad to the throwing of a prefabricated net of barbed and other wire over the great plains and prairies of North America, the fence has fenced off or fenced in certain natural life from one resource or another that it must have to survive, and has given priority to other forms favored by the fence maker.

There have been times and places where a ditch-and-bank was the only fence possible. A ditch is still a fence in English law. Trimmed shrubs have provided effective barriers in other times and climes. Hesiod speaks of "the wall of a fenced court." How much that is obscure in the human record on Crete would be revealed if we could compile a history of fencing there from the first rude walls, ditches, and embankments down to fencing with finned bombs at the close of World War II.

The rail has passed into proverb in the more generously wooded sections of the country, the hedge into the psychology of England; the wall, in sacred literature, is used in a thousand metaphors; and though they now serve no purpose, the picket and the paling still appear in cities as a cultural survival from rural life. A hundred years ago on Cape Cod schools and meeting-houses were protected with tight board fences against encroaching sand "to preserve the plot within level and hard." The fence of adobe performs a similar function for homesteads in the southwestern deserts today. In pioneer New England, cedar rails brought from the coast of Maine cost so much that communities abandoned sheep-raising because it required four rails to turn sheep, while cattle may be turned with two. They finally got down to a one-rail fence and then split the rail! In fisher villages of New England toward the middle of the last century fences were made of hogshead staves or of whalebone driven into the sand. I have seen a fair fence, and quite ornamental at that, made out of automobile license plates.

Texas is certainly the most fence-conscious state in the Union, and I am one of the most fence-conscious individuals in it. A fence-war burst upon my childhood with a shock I can still feel. At sundown I saw stretching for miles across the gently rolling and virgin prairie a lately completed barbed-wire fence, four shining strands of galvanized Glidden held up by cedar posts peeled and weathered to the shade of old ivory and set solidly eight feet apart. It was the first real fence I had ever seen, and I had watched the workmen building it, wide-eyed with wonder. But at that, it was an interest mingled with fear instilled by half-heard murmurs against fencing up the country. Men sitting around the general store on Saturday afternoons didn't like it a bit. One day at sundown I took a long look at the wonderful fence and went to bed thinking about it. Next morning at sun-up I rushed out to have another look. During the night a frightful transformation had occurred. Each tightly stretched strand had been cut between each pair of posts, and the wire had curled up about them, giving the line as it led away into the sun a frizzled appearance, as of a vicious animal maddened so that every particular hair stood up on end. I was speechless. I couldn't for the moment call anyone to come and see what had happened.

As a result of this fence-cutting, an old, smoldering feud flamed up in the community. There were duels with pistols, and there were mysterious riders at night, moving along in such close formation that you could hear stirrups popping against each other as a group approached in the darkness. Law and order, however, finally prevailed; the fence was rebuilt.

Then there was a period of big pastures. The prairies were still virgin. There were endless swells of greenery in spring stretching away to the horizon in every direction, parched in summer, brown and sere in autumn and winter. There was still riding-room, space to follow a pack of greyhounds chasing jack rabbits. But every time a dog ran afoul of one of those cursed fences and split his noble back from neck to tail, my hatred flamed up against them. I sympathized with the fence cutters, no matter how much I heard them condemned by my elders.

The more extensive fences, that is, field-and-pasture fences, in the rougher portions of the Edwards Plateau,

were of stone or rail before Glidden's time, and the building
of the stone fences was a task for Hercules. Some idea of the
cheapness of labor in that period may be gained by the
knowledge that it was profitable to enclose five-dollar-an-
acre land in a fence weighing not less than a ton per linear
yard. Besides, the stone was often hauled a mile or two and
much of it required chipping to make it serve. It is true
that there was a little offset in the cost of this enormous

task, since some of the land selected for fields had to be
cleared of loose stone anyway.

A few of these fences have been kept in repair and still
serve, but most of them are tumbled down along property
lines, aged aristocrats abased at the feet of a usurping
skeleton, an upstart in the hierarchy of fences. Sometimes
one finds a fence-museum out in the cedar brake; a stretch
of disintegrated stone fence paralleling an old rail fence
rotted down, while alongside these relics of other eras runs
a string of shining barbed-wire fence, five strands stretched
tight and stapled to stalwart posts firmly tamped into two
feet of dirt or rock.

Yes, "I sympathized with the fence-cutters."

I didn't know then how true my instinct was. Wire fences meant not only the doom of the greyhound and the sport of chasing jack rabbits, but of natural vegetation at a time when there was no generally diffused knowledge of its conserving function, no science to mitigate or put off the disaster, and no social consciousness to impel the use of such science even had it been available. Topsoil muddying creeks and rivers caused little comment; great gashes in the earth appeared, wounds from which it will never recover, but no one cried out against this havoc. Soon there was five-cent cotton, tenantry, women worked to death, and undernourished children reared in shameful ignorance. It has been estimated that Texas has paid thirty million tons of humus-laden soil for every bale of cotton she has ever marketed.

Much has been said and written of man's inventiveness in destructive devices outpacing his sense of responsibility, but the inventions and appliances of peace are often just as disastrous and for the same reason. There was no serious discussion of the social implications and of the sensible use of barbed wire, as the terrific assault began—only general jubilation over the solution of the fencing problem and glorification of "the wondrous, wondrous Age."

Samson and Hercules must assemble the material for a stone fence, but mere brute strength is not enough. There is an art involved, the art of chinking. I was taught this by a robust Italian farmer who builds even now the best stone fences in the country. They are worth going miles to see: solid, massive, rising out of the earth with the grace of a natural growth, and following the contours of the land like a garment designed and tailored to a perfect fit. Delaney's fences won't harbor a field mouse, they are so closely and perfectly chinked. Smooth as a mortared wall, each stone is set in right obedience to the laws of gravitation which cooperate in holding it in its place instead of working with stubborn and unresting will to pull it down. They are built without mortar, but they are built " 'gainst the tooth of time and razure of oblivion."

The art of chinking is an ancient one, even here in the new world. Walls of loose stone built by aboriginal tribes of Arizona, notably on the Fort Apache Indian Reservation, reveal the principle but not the touch of the master chinker. Nevertheless, after ten centuries the walls of Kinishba stand firm.

The stone fence grows more beautiful with age. Wood, even cedar, eventually decays; wire fences are ugly to begin with and become progressively more unattractive; iron fences, besides having a military aspect, rust, and paint only makes them more offensive. Wordsworth spoke with regret of the introduction of "iron palisades to fence off family burying grounds," as they destroyed much of the rustic simplicity of a churchyard where he himself had taken pains to protect certain yew trees with a "substantial oak fence." The weathering of stone fences, the look of age, venerable and nerve-quieting, is time-created. Without losing evidence of their human origin, they finally come to harmonize with natural features of the landscape, pleasing also because they are plainly indigenous. Another generation or two may clear away surviving segments of these fences, as the last generation has sawed up the priceless red-cedar logs of pioneer cabins in the same area.

> That which each man loved
> And prized in his peculiar nook of earth
> Dies with him or is changed.

Sections of these noble fences, especially those available to highways, should be preserved, not only because they are beautiful in and of themselves, but because their testimony is significant of a period which will grow in historical importance, century by century, as long as present civilization endures. The blocks composing these structures are crumblings off the great limestone ledges, vertebrae of the hillsides, quarried by the swelling roots of a vegetation starved for any pitiful little pocket of moisture or bit of nourishment stingily stored in natural creases and seams of rock.

Fences of cedar also survive, both worm and stake-and-rider, antedating in some cases the fences of stone. I know a stake-and-rider fence nearly a hundred years old with hardly a blemish in it. The lot and yard fences around homesteads are of cedar, hand-hewed and set upright so close together that a cottontail rabbit must hunt for a hole and then pinch himself a little to get through. This cutting, hewing, fitting, driving, and binding palings to form a verminproof fence, while not involving the backbreaking labor of stone-fencing, was still an enormous undertaking. Many of these pales, built by first settlers, remain hard and sound, close-knit and verminproof. They were fashioned from mountain cedar which lasts like bone.

When I look over one of these pioneer farmsteads, with its fields and pastures, lots, corrals, orchard or garden spaces, and yards, fenced with stone and hand-hewed cedar, I wonder how the people who left them to us found time to do anything else.[1]

Encyclopedias, generally, do not do fences justice. One of the best and most popular of these compendiums devotes nine of its huge columns to fencing, the sport, and only one column to the fencing which has to do with gardens, yards, fields, pastures, enclosures of any kind, or drift fences of the western cowman. Being an English encyclopedia, the article is listed under "Hedges and Fences," not "Fences and Hedges," an indication of that uncompromising regionalism which makes the English great. Under "barbed wire" we get two and a half columns dealing mainly with the manufacture of this particular type of fence.

This work treats with deference and at great length fenc-

[1]When Odysseus visits Eumaeus, he finds that his old swineherd has built not only "fences of loose stone," but "had fenced the whole length on either side with a closely set stockade made of split oak which he had taken from the dark heart of logs." These two types of fence, loose stone and upright posts "closely set," thus recorded on Ithaca *circa* 1000 B.C., are identical with the types used on the Edwards Plateau by Texas pioneers three thousand years later.

ing as a sport of aristocracy, while passing over with scant attention the ditch-and-bank, the hedge, the wall, pales, rails, stone, barbed-wire and meshed fencing. I think there would be wide interest and great educational value in encyclopedic articles by competent anthropologists on "fences of early man," or articles from classical scholars or antiquarians on "fences of the Greeks and Romans," or from the medieval historian on "fences and feudalism," or from W. P. Webb on "fences and the plains civilizations of the world."

The same catering to the quality is seen in the barely five columns given to "Ploughs and Ploughing" compared with ten columns on the sword. The editors lose interest in the sword after it has been beaten into a plowshare. Weapons have naturally been the main interest of the predatory, time out of mind; while tools have been the concern of people who produce and conserve the things which their masters appropriate to have and to hold until a stronger predator comes along. Machines of all kinds are adequately treated, and this is in part due to the fact that the ownership of machines forms the basis for a new exploitation.

But the common man is coming gradually into prominence. Even the most ponderous encyclopedia will eventually discover him and acknowledge his existence by giving the draft horse an even break with the racing breeds, and by devoting as much space and as sound a scholarship to "poultry and poultry-farming" as to "falcons and falconry."

That the word "fence" is a contraction of "defence" suggests that enclosures in the beginning were constructed for the purpose of keeping things out rather than for keeping them in. The vineyards of sacred literature, as well as the cultivated fields of the American frontiers, were fenced against stock which roamed at large; but now in all civilized countries stock is fenced in instead of out. This makes fences a concern of no small importance to the naturalist, as the construction and disposition of these artificial barriers change radically the flora and fauna native to the region.

2. Fences:
Right-of-Ways

How many species of plants have been lost entirely in the free-grazing areas of the world, no one will ever know; nor shall we ever know exactly what has happened to native vegetation in ancient cultivated areas such as those of Europe and China. Luckily in America, since fence we must, we discovered cheap fencing while much of the country was still virgin, and right-of-ways for rail and for automobile traffic were securely fenced with the natural growths still intact. This accident in our history has given us in effect a kind of wild-life preserve in elongated "relic areas," cutting across all vegetational regions from every angle of approach, crisscrossing them so thoroughly that a listing of all plants now flourishing in these enclosures would perhaps include all or nearly all of the species present when the white man first occupied the country.

This is a culture resource of significance. Unconsciously, and certainly with no such purpose in anybody's mind, the fencing-in of automobile and railroad right-of-ways has created far-stretching arboretums without which many species of plants would have been lost, at least to certain localities and even to certain regions, as well as the animal life depending upon them for survival.

The lanes of pioneer times did not serve this purpose to any great extent, since lanes and commons were ordinarily grazed more closely than contiguous pastures. But from the very first, railroads had to fence their right-of-ways to avoid paying one hundred dollars for damages for killing a ten-dollar calf. With the coming of paved roads and high-powered traffic, highways had to be protected for the same reason, especially those traversing grazing sections. So, up and down, far and wide, are strips of land varying in width from fifty to a hundred or more feet, in which native vegetation has been preserved.[1]

Perhaps the late President Roosevelt, nature-lover that he was, had the arboretum value of the highway in mind when he insisted that if super-highways are built across the country from coast to coast at federal expense, as was proposed, a strip of land a mile wide on each side must be held under strict government control. The possibilities, under this reservation, of parks, arboretums, wild-life preserves, natural scenery, sanctuaries, and so on, rushes out to greet the minds of the nature-conscious.

The fenced highway has been more effective in this matter mile for mile than the railroad right-of-way, as little care was ever taken in railway excavations to keep the topsoil on top. Long stretches along railroad tracks may now be seen with surface blasted and supporting little life, since the original topsoil lies buried under clay, gravel, or other sterile deposits. Moreover few railroad maintenance divisions have ever learned the art of vegetative drainage control. But we may be thankful that our own railroads did not imitate those of some European countries in parking the right-of-way, which means substituting lawn for native grasses, as well as clipping, removing, substituting, smoothing up, and other-

[1]Fencing off native vegetation is now practiced extensively by the Forest Service for experimental purposes, concerning which A. A. Simpson, Assistant Regional Forester, Albuquerque, New Mexico, writes me as follows:

"There are two types of projects . . . the purposes of which are to preserve small range areas under fence for ecological observation. The first type, the Administrative Study Plot, is most often fenced on strategic areas . . . for rough comparison with outside range in the same immediate locality. The second type, namely Research Plots, are fenced for studies which involve line transects, sampling by quadrats and various other techniques." These studies have furnished basis for many scientific publications issued by the Southwest Forest and Range Experiment Station at Tucson, Arizona.

wise eradicating the plant life which a given strip of land originally supported. This process usually masquerades under the alias of "beautification." In this country carelessness and lack of regard for appearances have proved to be a blessing.

From these strips of land strung endlessly across the country, wind, birds, and animals carry seed of native vegetation to fields and pastures. They flow with drainage into streams and are distributed far and wide. This amounts to a seasonal seeding of natives over great spaces. While in some farming sections the automobile highways are no longer fenced and land is often cultivated right up to the edges of the pavement, the railroad right-of-way still serves.

Should one want an object lesson in just how sensitive plants are to the construction of fences, let him wander down a laned highway through grazing country, in the springtime when plants in flower proclaim their identity. To test out this matter, apparent even from an automobile, I walked a mile stretch of highway on a May afternoon, listing every flower I could find. At the mile's end I found that I had listed sixty-eight species. Then I climbed through the fence into a cow pasture and walked back, covering a strip of pasture about as wide as the highway. I found only twenty-four species, roughly a third as many as were blooming on an equal surface of the adjoining right-of-way. The next day I made the same experiment on a mile length of highway bordering a goat pasture. In the highway I found forty-six species blooming; across the fence in the goat pasture, searching with equal diligence over an equal area, I found only eight.

The day following I moved my experiment to a highway running alongside a closely grazed sheep pasture. In the mile of right-of-way I found fifty-four species; in an equal area over the fence, I found only one blooming species, a solitary rain lily. This flower pops up and out as if it were set on a spring or explosive. It is one of the few species agile enough to elude the goat or even the sheep and get in its blooming while they are not looking.

So I would say cattle in their grazing reduce the number of native species considerably; goats are much more severe on them, especially on shrubs; while sheep obliterate everything except shrubs and grass. Fencing stock in permits a concentration of grazing animals greater than nature would tolerate, and sacrifices many species to a few.

Some flowers under heavy grazing bloom low and by stealth as if they knew the doom of those who hold their heads up and go about the business of blooming and seeding as normal vegetables do. They learn to hug the ground, or sneak through the grass and play hide-and-go-seek with the grazing beast. One of our natives most successful at this is the common stinging nettle (*Tragia nepetaefolia* Cav.). Although of a reclining nature, this plant undisturbed will lift its yellow flowers several inches aboveground, but among goats or sheep it will be found blooming right down against the bosom of Mother Earth. The common roadside aster is quite adept also: in soil of ordinary richness and with sufficient moisture this aster blooms on branches two or three feet high, but on mowed lawns or on an overstocked range it spreads its petals barely above the soil and there seeds successfully.

Some natives with tough, perennial roots last a number of years without blooming, but even they, after continuous exposure over long periods, must finally succumb. A few constant bloomers, such as the common verbena and the introduced horsemint, manage to survive the most rigorous grazing, since grow and bloom they will almost from frost to frost, rain or shine, in drought or deluge, on rich soil or poor, in sunny or shady places. Some seed delay germination for years awaiting a favorable opportunity. The Texas bluebonnet, or buffalo clover, is one of these. Seed of buffalo grass has been found in sod houses to be still viable after fifty years or more.

Traffic on railways and highways has been the chief

agency for spreading introduced plants.[2] The march of the sow thistle, the creeping from coast to coast of two species of caltrop, the interminable spread of the dandelion are due to seed mounting the wings of traffic. Those species which can survive in incult areas enrich our vegetable life, but in farming sections they sometimes become the worst of pests.

The airplane has not as yet made any notable contributions to our flora. It is safe to predict, however, that as cargo freight increases, we shall find strange plants from far-off corners of the world arriving in increasing numbers; and, using the same facilities, our own plants will appear along airways throughout the world wherever hospitable conditions happen to prevail.

The free range in the Southwest was threatening practically all wild life with extinction. It was a disastrous competition which in the end defeated every competitor. The careful grazier, who knew what the range could stand and with enlightened self-interest did not overstock, was soon swamped by hungry hordes of those who had no such knowledge or no such scruples, so that finally anyone, to hold a range, was compelled to overstock it.

The manufacture on a vast scale of cheap, prefabricated fence relieved this situation considerably—although use of it was violently opposed by the very individuals who finally profited most—by permitting the intelligent and conscientious to practice some primitive measures of conservation. Nevertheless, native vegetation, the soil itself, and consequently all wild life continued to suffer. Among extensive ranches there were few lanes; roads were unfenced and entered and emerged from pastures through gates or cattle guards. In the small ranching country there were lanes, but they also were grazed closely since horse-drawn traffic presented no hazard to loose stock.

[2]"Many highways parallel railroads and here [Missouri] we find many species of wild flowers which are not common to the section. It is supposed that the seed is distributed by railroad cars. Kansas gay-feather and sunflower have been scattered along such roads." Letter from Fred A. Bruto, Turf Engineer, State Highway Department, Kansas City, Missouri.

Two great inventions in the field of transportation intervened. The era of extensive railroad building, roughly from 1870 to 1900, left fenced strips of land stretching across the continent in every direction. Following immediately came the highway-building period, laying down an intricate and even more extensive network of fence-protected right-of-ways. In these two systems, continental in extent, is preserved a rich variety of life which is slowly coming to be appreciated and will finally be considered one of our richest legacies.

State highway commissions are becoming more and more conscious of the arboretum value of the right-of-way and are taking pains to extend the range of natives, especially of the ornamental ones.[3] Care is taken in construction to avoid burying topsoil under sterile deposits. Intersections are parked and decorated for the most part with natives, as are bridge ends and culvert abutments. In Texas many tons of wild-flower seed are sowed yearly along the highways, extending the range of the most beautiful and popular species. The Texas Commission has also undertaken educational campaigns to increase public appreciation of the native vegetation. For a number of years preceding World War II, each division of the highway system held annual flower shows in which were assembled and properly exhibited wild flowers growing over an extensive territory. The State Motorcycle Police co-operated, scouring the highways for specimens, while botanists busied themselves classifying and labeling the fresh and blooming plants for public inspection. I have attended a number of these shows

[3]The Public Roads Administration of the Federal Government, T. H. McDonald, Commissioner, in 1932 set up a Landscape Department for the purpose of promoting better roadside development in state projects where the Federal Government participated by matching the state funds. In 1933 approximately half of the states had set up Landscape Departments, and at the present time a Landscape Architect is employed in each of forty states. The Public Roads Administration still furnishes suggestions for roadside practices.

in which there were from one hundred to three hundred different species attractively displayed and properly labeled. With the support of the Commission, laws have been passed providing proper penalties for plundering wild flowers on the right-of-ways. It would be interesting as a sociological study to determine why highway managements became almost immediately nature-conscious while railway managements never did, and also why the respective managements of utilities and highways are so often feuding over items which affect natural beauty. In one state where the species is rather rare, a particularly handsome specimen of hackberry in the way of utility construction became a bone of contention. The highway management after a bitter controversy finally won out and the tree was preserved. Ordinarily, formal regulations are drawn up "governing clearing for construction or maintenance of utility lines along state highways," giving the highway commission complete supervision of all cutting, trimming, disposal of debris, and restraining utility construction and maintenance divisions from touching any native growths except by special permission.

Municipalities would do well to take a leaf from the highway commission's notebook and exercise immediate supervision over utilities, which sometimes become possessed of a rage for cutting and trimming, apparently imagining a menace in every branch of any tree waving innocently in the wind. I have within view from my own front porch a line of handsome post oaks unnecessarily mutilated by workmen of a utility a few years ago. I noted that the workmen returned after working hours in trucks and hauled off cords of good post-oak wood from the trimmings of the afternoon. Seeing that the market price of these trimmings was at that time $12 per cord, it naturally occurred to me to question whether cupidity had not in this case whetted the solicitude of these workmen for the interests of their employer.

Each year there is an increasing volume of literature on highway beautification, and the office of landscape engineer is gaining greater authority. The use of native growths in erosion control is the practical side: the choice of growths and the disposition of them are problems in aesthetics. Consideration of nursery importations is at once eliminated, except in special situations, for the good and sufficient reason that such importations cannot be maintained. In the interest of economy, natives must be used because natives maintain themselves. Then it becomes a question of which indigenous plants shall be chosen for a given situation. The criteria for selections are well-established: Safety, Beauty, Utility, Economy.

In the literature of highway landscaping valid distinction is drawn between parking and roadside improvement, and this distinction is vital to the nature lover. The park is one thing, the roadside another. You see the park as a "still" close up; the roadside is seen generally at a distance and from a moving automobile, often at fifty miles per hour or at greater speed. The striking, the outstanding, the exotic is therefore to be avoided in roadside beautification. The canvas is large. The eye travels over miles instead of inches. The literature on the subject insists that the highway is merely the frame, while the landscape is the picture. The function of the frame is not to distract the attention from, but rather to emphasize, the picture. Flowering dogwood in East Texas against the gloomy green of a bank of pines a quarter of a mile away delights the eye, while a row of this same glorious shrub set within twenty feet of the pavement's edge is out of perspective, draws attention from the picture to the frame, arouses the curiosity and becomes a driving hazard. In certain sections of the Old South staghorn sumac, with its vivid splashes of color visible for miles in the fall, is preferable to crepe myrtle as covering for an ugly cut or slope. Sumac forms a part of this particular landscape, is volunteer, rugged, and maintains itself. These are the important matters with which highway landscape engineers busy themselves. Their writings are strewn with phrases such as these:

"Shrubs that tend to emphasize the presence of intersections";

"indicator species";

"preservation of native vegetation";

"slope plantings";

"colony-forming species";

"a naturalistic approach";

"restricted right-of-way clean-up";

"educating the public in values of native vegetation for landscaping";

"exotics only for sections of highway in front of intensively developed residential areas";

"co-operation of garden clubs";

"functional and non-functional planting";

"streamline the highway and blend it into the surrounding landscape";

"softening the harshness of highway grading";

"warning against making our highways into botanical gardens";

"supplement natural beauty rather than create artificial beauty";

"flower beds cannot be used on account of maintenance difficulty";

"regularity, repetitions in planting, are unsafe since they tend to produce hypnosis in the driver";

"highways must become a part of the over all landscape picture";

"drainage vegetatively controlled";

"all highway features blended and warped into the existing landscape."

All these phrases arouse enthusiastic response from nature-lover and naturalist.

Beauty, Safety, Utility, Economy: these guides in selection are establishing indigenous growths throughout the country's highways and vastly extending the conservation for which protective fencing laid the groundwork. It is the most conscious work in conservation of natural beauty on a grand scale that is being done at all, overshadowing in extent, as it certainly does in influence on the public mind, even park systems, state and national.

The rivalry for passenger traffic between highways and railways is no longer a phony war. Luxury trains, smiling service, travel conveniences are offered on the one hand and not much more than landscape on the other. The high visibility offered by the automobile is its greatest asset in this developing competition. Perhaps this is one reason why highways have become nature-conscious while railways have not.

The two great commercial interests, oil and autos, profiting directly from automobile travel should be deeply touched by the work of the highway landscape engineer.

In another chapter I have touched more specifically upon the benefits of fenced-in right-of-ways to bird life. The northward trend of the Mexican cliff swallow is due largely to favorable nesting sites provided by concrete bridges. Traffic on automobile highways, particularly at night, leaves a mangled litter of small animals—rabbits, skunks, opossums, armadillos, snakes, dogs, cats, and so on—which must have increased our vulture population many fold over what it was before the days of railroads and automobiles. Carrion-eating hawks, such as the redtail and the caracara, also greatly benefit from this miscellaneous slaughter. Grain leaking from trucks and boxcars is gleaned by finches and seedeaters of every variety. Insects are attracted by the undisturbed vegetation of the right-of-ways as well as by traffic waste. Many of them are knocked down and crippled by traffic for the convenience of the lazier insectivorous birds. The planting of trees along highways in treeless regions is extending the range of tree-nesting species. The readily adaptable English sparrow, deprived of the horse dung once enjoyed, now haunts filling stations and gleans from radiators of freshly arrived automobiles its harvest of insects, quite as well pleased and certainly as healthy and fecund as it was on a diet of partially digested grain left in the streets by draft animals. This hardy interloper has moved his headquarters from the livery stable to filling station and effected the transition from horsepower to gasoline power with as little injury to the nervous system as any other creature I know.

But by far the greatest boon to bird life from protected right-of-ways occurs in wooded sections of the country. Here the right-of-way opens a space to sunlight in fertile bottoms, offering an opportunity for grass and weeds to grow and seed, thus creating a feeding ground for seed eaters alongside protective cover.

Now it is being freely prophesied that we are soon to have little use for right-of-ways of any kind, particularly railroad right-of-ways. We are being told that transportation is leaving the earth: passenger, freight, express, and everything else that it is of advantage to move about from one location to another, near or far, helicopter hop or distance flights— it will be all the same. We have become loosened from the earth, and the agelong tyranny of gravitation over man is at an end. Man, with all man's impedimenta, has taken wings, and no form of life except the erratic penguin has ever attained aerial status and later returned to the sorry business of plodding, paddling, rolling, or sliding.

Making due allowance for the ardent and imaginative zeal of the air-minded, the hard fact remains that in some parts of the country railroads are succumbing to the competition of other forms of transportation, discontinuing service, and abandoning right-of-ways. Fifteen hundred miles of track were abandoned in Texas during the thirteen years from 1932 to 1945.

A great automobile highway runs through a community where I spent my childhood. I stop sometimes long enough to visit the graveyard where my father and grandfather are buried. I have to cross a railroad right-of-way to get to the enclosure, which was originally a corner cut off a sheep pasture. In the ill-kept paths of this burial ground and in the right-of-way I see the sage grass (*Andropogan saccharoides*) growing. One might explore a dozen farms in the vicinity without finding a single tuft of that hardy native. But here, protected in the cemetery and in the adjoining right-of-way, are plots and patches of it, as lusty as it was when it covered the surrounding prairies for hundreds of miles as it had covered them for ages and eons. I never see these patches of sage grass without thinking of the vast extent of those grass-covered prairie plains. I think of them fenceless and abounding in wild life. On a gusty day the eye might trace sudden currents of air for miles, as they swept over gentle slopes, bending the tall grass, wave succeeding wave as on an ocean, driven along under the impulsion of the wind, and, like as not, a prairie schooner laboring up a distant hillside "far out at sea." Cloud shadows often mottled the green landscape, and I remember hearing a cowboy, hot and weary, encourage his sweating pony, as a cool shadow enveloped them, "Let's go, Pinto, there's a scab on the sun."

Parched but not barren in the droughts of July and August, this land was usually freshened up a bit by September showers before winter set in. No matter how tortured in the blazing days of summer, these lonesome and limitless prairies recovered their composure in the cool of the afternoon, as the "sundown shadows lengthened."

As I look upon tufts of this historic grass which the right-of-way and the cemetery have preserved, I think of the wild life which in its heyday it supported, but principally of its everlastingness under primitive conditions, of how it held the soil in place and deposited a mold that insured next season's growth in unimpaired vitality.

I never see a stretch of abandoned right-of-way, highway or railroad, thrown back into a pasture or a field, without feeling that a cultural resource of great value is being thrown away, a resource that can never be reclaimed.

Wherever these strips of land are advantageously located and rich in undisturbed natural life, they should be taken over by the public as arboretums, wild-life preserves, bird sanctuaries and the like. Schools, wild-life clubs, nature organizations, Boy Scouts, Girl Scouts, and Campfire Girls could have bridle paths and a hiking area of trails leading through swamps, forests, over the hills and far away. Hostels and camping places could be conveniently spaced. I might get down to such a detail as pointing out what an abundant supply of high-quality campfire wood the old ties would provide.

A few years ago there was talk of abandoning the Austin & Northwestern right-of-way running from Austin to Llano, a distance of about ninety miles. There is foundation for more nature study in that strip of ground than can now be found in all the formally parked areas of Texas put together. From the outcroppings of granite in the Llano area, through a good section of the Edwards Plateau, across the Jollyville Plateau, skirting the blackland prairies and finally easing down into the Colorado River bottom—in these ninety miles are samples of vegetational regions which in their extension include at least a fourth of the whole state. Numerous railroad cuts exhibit surfaces for the geologist to study. In the Liberty Hill and Cedar Park areas are to be found extensive Indian kitchen middens rich in archaeological lore. The Colorado River is followed in the hills and again after it has emerged into the open country. A tree-and-shrub census of this right-of-way will show at least a third of the species of trees and shrubs found throughout the state in the regions typified. Not less than four hundred species of wild flowers can be listed without crossing a fence; and from year's end to year's end two hundred and fifty species of birds may be found. Most attractive feature of all, this is an old right-of-way, hence vegetation is largely virgin. The communities located along it could well co-operate to preserve this cultural resource.

If and when the Soaring Age succeeds the Rolling Age, man will hunger still more for Mother Earth than he does at present. He may rediscover his legs, and perhaps win back the savage nose and learn that discriminating odors is one of the important sensuous delights of life. Perhaps pedestrianism will become a cult so popular that one's position in society will depend largely upon how much he walks and to what purpose, even as horsemanship, now outmoded as transportation, has taken on an aura of social distinction and prestige.[4]

Airplane travel obliterates intimate views of the planetary scene and spreads out before the downward-looking eye an unrealistic surface from which everything except the huger features of nature are eliminated. London from a great height on a clear day looks like insect mold of some sort strung along the valley of the Thames. Nature becomes impersonal. Automobile and train travel feed the hunger we have for natural sights and sounds, woodsy odors, landscapes and seascapes. So when we come to travel exclusively by airplane, the old urge for nature contacts will set in stronger than ever. We have so far merely dabbled in the great public business of providing recreational space—parks, sanctuaries, preserves, and the like: a vaster vision is required.

[4]Hemmed between coast and mountains for nearly eight hundred miles, California is perhaps the most nature-conscious and certainly the most tourist-conscious state in the Union. While Air Age enthusiasts are moon-gazing, the public mind of California turns to riding and hiking trails. The Master State Loop Trail, with thousands of miles of county trails feeding into it, is already blueprinted. The State Legislature (1946) appropriated $300,000 to begin construction. From the Mexican border to Oregon, and back by way of the Sierra foothills and the shores of the Pacific, with stop-over shelters every eighteen miles, the Master Trail alone will cost in the neighborhood of $3,000,000.

3. Still Water

Joy shall be in the bird-lover's heart over one new bird more than over ninety and nine already listed. If the newcomer is found to be nesting in territory well outside his usual breeding range, the event stirs the amateur still more deeply.

I say amateur, since the professional ornithologist through overindulgence tends to become insensible to this pleasure, or, in the manner now fashionable, conceals emotional reactions as bad form or as indicating untrustworthy observation. I sometimes think that we have become dominated by a cult of unemotionalism. We speak of "cold" scientific fact as if temperature had something to do with verity. We assume that strong feeling and sound judgment are incompatible, and regard with suspicion all facts which really excite us.

But surely only the phlegmatic person, professional or amateur, can see the vermilion flycatcher for the first time without a gasp of surprise and pleasure. When, on March 20, I found this vivid bit of color flown here from the Tropics on its own power, it came like an unexpected gift from one of those inspired givers who determine by divination, before you yourself do, just what you want.

Only within the past few years has the vermilion flycatcher been found nesting in central Texas as far north as Austin. Now I hear on good authority that this most striking member of the family of Tyrant flycatchers has been seen lately as far north as Glenrose. The species is evidently northward bound.

On that March morning the male was showing off, displaying himself advantageously, he hoped, before the eyes of the female of his choice. I found him soaring on wings that "beat the gladsome air," poising, shivering with anticipation, breast feathers all puffed out with pride and confidence.

Although in my eyes he made a creditable exhibition and finished in approved manner, looping gracefully earthward with a final flourish, the female viewed the performance with a more critical eye. He was not immediately accepted. She moved away upon his approach. I spent some time following these lively visitors about and was rewarded by seeing them engage in a flight and pursuit as mad and furious as any of nature's hurdle races with goal set to ravish or devour.

Beautiful in her own quiet way, especially in contrast with her suitor so gorgeously arrayed, I thought of her as modesty itself wooed by an aggressive egotism. Fast and furious was the race amid the tangled vines and branches. Too quick for the eye, first here, then there, dodging with movements indescribably swift, she fled like a gray leaf pursued by a darting tongue of flame. During my observation of them he remained a rejected suitor. Finally they rested quietly within twenty feet of where I was standing.

In a proper light, the female's back appears a dullish gray dusted over with iron rust. Her breast is slightly streaked with brown, the flanks yellowish shading into gray, the throat gray with deeper gray about the cheeks.

It is the male, however, which inspires the naturalist to raptures and to do his best at descriptive writing, seeking until he finds phrases and similitudes with which to set this bird apart from all others as a kind of special creation. He is a brilliant flaming gem, an outburst of gleaming color, and outshines the most brilliant scarlet flowers. To the imaginative Mexicans, he is *brasita de fuego*, a little coal of fire; and his scientific name, *Pyrocephalus*, signifies firehead. Poised high in the crystal-clear air that morning, he seemed to me to be a star of first magnitude which the vanishing darkness had failed to take with it from the daylight sky. All who know tanagers should be advised that after seeing this tropical newcomer, the summer tanager appears faded and even the scarlet tanager seems a bit tame. The gray-tailed cardinal is dull in comparison.

The courting flight of the vermilion flycatcher—tiniest of the tribe except those of the genus Epidonax—this soaring and poising high in air, would seem to be in deliberate scorn of the whole tribe of hawks, always on the lookout for a small bird to stoop at. But I have never seen a hawk show any interest in him. The flycatchers with their bulldoggish jaws have what is known in the athletic world as the fighting heart, and perhaps this ostentatious flight of the most colorful of the family may be considered as a red flag of defiance hoisted by Tyrannidae to assert its fearlessness, its challenge to all comers to do battle, if they choose, to the last extremity with no holds barred. Even the surly mockingbird shows great respect for flycatchers. The little ball of fire has the flycatcher fight in him. I should think that an observation of the display with which the male endeavors to win the favor of the female would give pause to those literal folk who attempt to reduce the mating of birds to the slot-machine reactions of an automat.

I wish I might report that this pair nested here, but they were only on an exploratory mission. Conditions did not suit them, and after May 2 I saw them no more, although I continued my search for a nest well into June. During their stay on Bear Creek, they occupied a feeding stratum midway between the phoebe and the scissortail. Along the creek and river courses of the Edwards Plateau, the phoebe's favorite feeding perch is a low limb preferably over water; the vermilion feeds from treetops down in the valley, while the scissortail stays on treetops of the more elevated terraces, occasionally taking advantage of a power line as it tops the hill.

The tails of these aerial acrobats are highly mobile, each one, however, with its own distinctive type of mobility. Much has been written of tail shape as an aid in maneuvering, but tail strength and tail mobility also are important. The family is noted for bursts of speed and lightning wheelabouts rather than for swiftness in sustained flight. The scissortail, for instance, darts like an arrow, but covers a hundred yards at less than twenty miles an hour. Perching, the tail of the vermilion moves fanwise, opening and closing, to maintain balance. The phoebe, on the other hand, raises and lowers its tail as a pipit does, but much more slowly and, so far as I can see, not merely to balance himself but simply because he thinks it becoming to move his tail slowly up and down. He often sits for a long time with no movement of the tail at all and then begins again with great deliberation. It seems more of a mannerism than movement with a purpose. The only other bird I know which, while perching, moves its tail in the same plane and through about the same arc as the phoebe, but with still greater deliberation, is the hermit thrush. The scissortail perching in the wind uses his ten-inch tail as a balance, but in still weather often lets it droop down completely relaxed. It is in flight, turning and twisting in pursuit of prey, or in threatening forays toward intruders coming too near his nest, that his tail takes on the scissoring motion which gives him his name.

There is no doubt that the vermilion flycatcher is extending his range northward, especially in central Texas. Chapman (1912) gives his breeding range as Central America and Mexico, north to southern Texas. Simmons (1925) records only a straggler, a single male, taken March 16, 1914. He predicts, but without giving reasons, that this bird "will probably appear more often and eventually become a rare summer resident." Bent (1942) gives the northern limit of *Pyrocephalus* in Texas as San Antonio. In March 1942 I found a pair on the shore of the new Marshall Ford Lake about six miles above the dam. They spent the whole season there but I did not succeed in finding a nest. The next season I did find a nest in that location and another nesting pair on the Shields Ranch ten miles away. These birds like people: both the nests were near dwellings, one of them within fifty feet of the back door of a ranch house.

The only good thing I ever heard about a South American dictatorship is that the South American form of the vermilion flycatcher is protected in Argentina by presidential decree.

The reason for the shift in breeding range of a given species is usually obvious. Dry up a marsh and as a matter of course the marsh birds move away. Make a marsh and they naturally flow in. The breaking up of the great, grassy ranches of the Panhandle of Texas has made the upland plover a rather rare bird there except in special locations. On the other hand, we sometimes find in the breeding range of a particular species shifts difficult to explain. I have as yet found no explanation of the European stork's extension of his breeding range during the past fifty years from northern Germany for hundreds of miles into Russia. I have found comments concerning the movement of the Carolina wren into New England, but no explanations.

To find a straggler five hundred or a thousand miles off his usual beat is an exciting incident. On Hearst Creek, ten miles above the Marshall Ford Dam, in 1942, I found the black-throated gray warbler and have bored my more tolerant friends with accounts of this discovery ever since. Such an incident is not worth a headline; but to find year after year a bird changing his breeding range in a given direction, a species overflowing into new territory, is of historical importance and first-page ornithological news. And if the bird moving in on you happens to be the vermilion flycatcher, there should be a celebration, and plaques of permanent character should be installed to commemorate and mark for all time his first nesting sites. We make greater to-do than this about occurrences of far less importance.

For a really scientific and comprehensive treatment of

such movements in this area we shall have to wait until map-series covering many years, showing breeding ranges of various species, have been prepared from accumulated data and made available, basis for which, of course, will be Dr. Harry C. Oberholser's great work on Texas birds, now in manuscript. In the meantime, there is no harm in indulging in speculations concerning specific cases.

The vermilion flycatcher seems to love two physiographic features not often found in conjunction, viz., a desert, or semiarid terrain, contiguous to a body of still water. This condition has been artificially created in many locations during recent years, especially in the Southwest.

In the San Antonio area this flycatcher hugs the shores of Medina Lake. He immediately occupied the semiarid slopes bordering the great lake formed by the completion of the Elephant Butte Dam a short distance north of El Paso. The bird is common on the Gila near Silver City, and on the Mimbres while that deceptive stream still flows aboveground through rather barren mountains. A mile or two back in the pasture from Santa Gertrudis, headquarters of the King Ranch, near Kingsville, Texas, is an artificial lake lying in the midst of semiarid growths of cactus and mesquite. Here are vermilion flycatchers in greater abundance than I have found anywhere else in Texas.

The enormous increase within the past few years of earthen tanks of considerable size and permanent nature is expanding and enriching natural life on the Edwards Plateau. Such artificial reservoirs are no new thing in this semiarid region, but the art of building one that will endure is new. The early settlers simply dammed up small streams and arroyos in the hope of holding over a supply of water from the wet winter season. Comparatively few of these attempts were successful. Floods, if they did not sweep away the dams, soon filled the reservoirs with mud. It has taken federal subsidy, government specifications, and a system of government inspection to teach the simple art of building a permanent earthen tank.

It has been found that the selection of a site is a matter of first importance. It must be in the way of enough drainage to fill, and yet not in the path of destructive floods. The excavation must be made in material that will hold water. The dam itself must be built to specifications which engineering experience has demonstrated as necessary to insure permanence. It would seem that a one-page itemization of simple directions would be sufficient to teach the public how to do it. But the public doesn't learn that way. To acquire the art of building an earthen reservoir right, it must have demonstrations and be paid handsomely to accept something for its own benefit. The AAA plan of subsidization in return for the privilege of governmental planning and inspection has been enormously expensive, but it works.

These small ponds, built to specifications, supervised and rigidly inspected before being approved for subsidy payment, present an impressive accumulation, distinguishing the enterprise as a successful governmental experiment in the field of geotechnics.

Within the past five years there have been constructed in Hays County 400 approved reservoirs; in Caldwell County, 550; in Guadalupe County, 650; in Travis County, 700; and so on. In these four counties alone, 2,300 permanent earthen tanks have been built following proper specifications with an average excavation for each tank of about eighteen hundred cubic yards. This development has been duplicated in counties all over the semiarid Edwards Plateau, with what immense implications for increases in wild life it is impossible even to estimate. In the four counties listed, there exist now around 4,000,000 cubic yards of water with aggregate surface area of nearly 800 acres where none existed five years ago. Moreover, these ponds are dotted in strategically for bird life. They are somewhat evenly spaced throughout the area.

I have just observed the filling by pump of one of these reservoirs having a water surface of about a quarter of an acre, and twelve feet deep in the center. The site chosen for it was a gentle depression in an old field which had been worn out and rendered worthless by fifty years of unscientific cultivation. The spot was barren and baked to a crisp in the blazing heat of the July sun. It took about three weeks to fill this reservoir; and from the time when there began to be a sizable puddle of water, life gravitated to it. Minnows were the first manifestation to appear—their eggs must have been sucked through the intake screen; next came water moccasins to devour them; soon numerous dragonflies were zooming back and forth over the surface, evidencing the presence of still smaller insects; certain water skaters came next. When the thing was about half-full, frogs began hopping out of nowhere along the borders, and the doleful kill-deer searched the dampened soil at nightfall in advance of the rising water.

Most vocal of all life here assembled, especially in the twilight periods, is the frog. I am tempted to say the most altruistic also, for he seems to make it his business in life to provide other species with succulent tidbits to be gobbled up or squeezed past the narrows of a throat in a leisurely, hours-long process of successive gulpings, depending upon whether it is a heron or a snake which accepts his invitation. There is hardly another form of life which is eaten so freely and with such relish by so many different species. It seems that the frog does not eat to live so much as he lives to be eaten.

Tied by his amphibious nature to a water's-edge habitat —happy hunting ground for both land and water predators —he has been equipped with only a hop-and-hide defense: and his "hop" is not far nor does his "hide" show any genius for concealment. A telltale toe may be left sticking out, or a propped-up leaf or a cloud of rising sediment may advertise his whereabouts. From the approach of a marsh bird, he plunges into the water with a resounding splash which attracts his water enemies to an underwater chase. Becoming short of breath or being routed out by some voracious enemy, he returns to land. Thus he is battered from watery pillow to earthen post, back and forth, hopping, hiding, diving, throughout a precarious existence which usually ends in catastrophe.

One afternoon a distress-croak attracted my attention and, looking about a bit, I found in a patch of weeds near the pond a young frog struggling to free himself from a snake—a dark, olive-green snake with a yellowish stripe down each side and speckled with yellowish dots along the back. His head was small and slender, and the largest diameter of his body was not much greater than that of an ordinary lead pencil. The head and neck were even smaller.

I judged the frog was at least an inch across the shoulders, while the spread of his forelegs added another inch. The hind legs were already swallowed when I arrived, and the upper lip of the snake was feeling along the rump of his victim. The lower jaw was forced back so that the angle made at the juncture of the jaws was about one hundred and fifty degrees.

The frog clawed frantically with his forefeet in the sand, and the snake took advantage of this struggle by backing gradually to increase resistance while the throat worked urgently with a swallowing motion. The reptile braced himself against the small weeds, and the tip of his tail showed a tendency to coil about a weed every now and then for a securer hold, as he exerted a steady backward pull against the forward struggling of his prey. This aided the swallowing process. If the frog had simply relaxed and allowed himself to be pulled and hauled about at will, the snake could not possibly have swallowed him.

With mouth now distended to the absolute limit and the comparatively huge expanse of the frog's body still in front, it seemed to me that the reptile had attempted an impossible task and was in danger of choking himself to death. But he continued to work steadily and with confidence. Gradually the serpent's upper lip edged on up the frog's back and, in the course of half an hour, reached the shoulders. At that point the effort seemed hopeless, since the forelegs were spread and the frog's throat was palpitating violently, showing that he was still alive in spite of the tremendous pressure on the lower part of his body.

Then the snake began stretching his upper lip to one side with strong, lithe action. It was clear that he was attempting to pick up the right foreleg and stuff it down. This required considerable time and a second attempt. He finally tucked the right leg deftly down his throat, but when he shifted the lip to the other side and attempted to get hold of the left leg in the same way, the right leg got free again. He patiently attended to that, his throat all the time alternately bulging and contracting with great vigor. Finally the right leg was again captured, and with less trouble he quickly disposed of the left leg.

This was the crisis of the operation. Slowly the tip of the snake's upper lip came flush with the tip of the frog's nose. Suddenly, after a short gulp and wriggle, the greatly distended mouth came back to normal, and the neck also thinned down to lead-pencil size. As the enormous mouthful passed down, a squeezing process set in which distributed the bulk evenly along about four inches of the central portion of the snake's body. At the moment I was bending closely over him. He pointed his head toward me, lifting about one third of his length upward in a graceful curve, darted his tongue out half a dozen times in quick succession, turned and made off.

Not only do birds, reptiles, and fish feed upon the frog, but one mammal, the coon, is the frog-eating epicure par excellence. The cunning creature will spend the best part of a night lying in wait or probing patiently in watery trash. When the almost human hand of this sly night-prowler finally closes on its prey down in the submerged leaves and sediment, he first kills it delicately with firm and continuous pressure of the "fingers." Then, with the happy flourish of an artist putting the finishing touches to a picture, he washes the lovely morsel in clear surface water and, figuratively pushing back his cuffs and smoothing out his napkin, consumes it in a fashion with which no censor of table manners could find fault.

The frog has little or no brains. The small boy captures a canful for fish bait while you wait. The fable of the frog and the bull has a sound basis in the former's often disastrous overestimate of his own swallowing ability. He is noted the world over for attempting to ingest objects much too large. A sizable frog can make away with a hummingbird or a duckling, but he is not always content with small fry. My friend, Professor Milton R. Gutsch, reports seeing a duck disappear mysteriously from the surface of his pond. Upon fishing him out, he found the duck's head lodged in the belly of a bullfrog. He pulled the frog off, as he would a glove, and released the bird still alive and little the worse for the experience.

Considering the frog's wide popularity as an article of diet, his own poor judgment in attacking his prey, his lack of defensive weapons, his ill-advised vocalism, and his general stupidity, it is a marvel that he survives at all. But, as is the case with so many defenseless and dull-witted forms of life, an enormous fecundity coupled with considerable protective coloration comes to the rescue of this tailless amphibian which, with its one hundred and fifty American species alone, occupies a secure position.

As night closes in about this new pond the frogs croak out a call that may be heard a good mile away. How many mouths water at the sound, and how many forms edge nearer in the gathering darkness, stealthily swimming, crawling, or treading noiselessly the oozy margins—all converging upon the hospitable chorus in a rivalry silent but intense, for the favor or the flavor of the croakers! Thus, offering himself as an award, the frog attracts a new and various night life to the pond.

Meantime, as these accommodating creatures call in night rovers, whose eyes gather strange luster from the gathering darkness, and while the faintest glow is still visible in the western sky, day-flying insects give place to those which night now teases out of hiding. Feeding upon them a solitary bat circles round and round over the pond. Awkwardly pumping, seeking his prey in nervous, erratic darts and dashes, what a travesty this mammal makes of flight! Thus the great business of eating and of being eaten goes on, night and day, underwater, on the surface, and in the upper air, twenty-four hours, right around the clock.

Morning brings two phoebes and a prospecting martin to find out whether the day-flying insects have yet arrived; a dozen doves come in for water; lark sparrows flutter down for a drink and a bath; a spotted sandpiper makes a complete circuit, teetering along, gathering a rich harvest; and an American egret courses in, flying majestically from the direction of the rising sun, takes two turns over the pond, high in the air, and returns eastward.

So, by the time the water had risen to the spillway, a cluster of living forms had already begun to gather, smoothly functioning and ready to receive constant accessions until every nook and cranny, hole, channel, or minute interstice of this many-chambered mansion would be crowded with life flowing in with the water.

Much of this life is new, an accretion, in the sense that it is life which would not have existed at all except for the opportunity thus created. What an ecological revolution has been set in motion by the introduction of water into this spot of desert soil! Plant life is yet to come, and its coming will effect a still profounder revolution and present a further extension of the opportunity for life in one form or another. Numerous species will find each its nook or niche in this artificial structure. And one niche, I think, is reserved for the bird I have been talking about, the vermilion flycatcher, especially around ponds which, like this one, happen to be in open spaces located on the more elevated terraces.

Thus I come to the conclusion that the New Deal has brought to the Edwards Plateau, among other things good and bad, the vermilion flycatcher by providing the two conditions which this bird seems to demand: one, a rather open, semiarid country; and, two, spaces of still water.

The first condition was created by subsidizing cedar-cutting. Under the stimulus of this subsidy, great spaces have been opened in the thickest cedar brakes, leaving growths of cactus, mesquite, scrub oak, and various shrubs intact. But this alone is not enough.

Then came the dam-building enterprises by which the Colorado River has now a string of lakes beginning at Austin and extending for two hundred miles up its course. As these lakes filled, water encroached on semiarid hillsides cleared of cedar, thus offering a hospitable habitat for the Mexican migrant.

Finally, the earthen tanks are now spaced somewhat evenly over hundreds of square miles, some serving as way stations and others as seasonable abodes. This gorgeous southern flycatcher will follow up the lake shores in the semi-arid country as far as the lakes extend, and at the same time he will find pond sites here and there which exactly suit him. There seems to be no reason why he will not penetrate farther north to similar lakes on the Brazos River, certainly to the shores of the one made in semiarid hills by the 'Possum Kingdom Dam.

4. The Wing
of the Swallow

South-central Texas entertains, during their nesting season, the purple martin and the lesser Mexican cliff swallow,[1] both members of the globe-encircling swallow family. The former is the largest and certainly the most civilized swallow in America, while the latter is the tiniest and latest member of the family to venture into close association with human beings. The indications are that this bird is now extending his range into central Texas and on northward. Scouting here and there, ever on the alert, traveling far and foraging as he goes, the swallow has been aptly called "the light cavalry of the army of birds."

Martins haunt the homes of men; the little cliff swallow prefers man's public buildings, a preference which makes him more of a city bird than his close northern relative, the eaves swallow, which keeps company with rural folk, nesting in the great barns and other outbuildings of prosperous farmsteads, especially in the North and East.

The books say that the original nesting range of the lesser Mexican cliff swallow extended no farther north than the rough country along the Rio Grande. However, as the country settled up, colonies found their way into the limestone

[1]I shall make no attempt to distinguish this bird from the Mexican cliff swallow, as I cannot tell the two races apart in the field. Since they interbreed and nest in the same colonies along the Mexican border, I leave the few subspecific differences to the museum naturalist. I use the name "lesser Mexican cliff swallow" because the species in the breeding range I am discussing is so designated in the books.

area of south-central Texas and were in all probability nesting in bluffs west of Austin when that city was founded in the valley of the Colorado in 1839.

Here, as soon as buildings of any considerable size became available, their eaves and arches were occupied by colonies which forsook all but the most favorable nesting sites in the wilds, as swallows all over the world have always done, liking artificial structures better those with which nature provides them.

Frank Brown, in his unpublished *Annals of Travis County and of the City of Austin,* noted the appearance of the lesser Mexican cliff swallow in 1865. He says:

> The swallows appeared at Austin for the first time in June of this year. They commenced building their nests upon the walls of the capitol. Old settlers asserted, at the time, that these birds had not previously appeared in this part of the country. The bats had theretofore been in possession of the old limestone building, but the swallows put them to flight.[2]

The capitol referred to by Mr. Brown is the First Capitol. This is the first definite reference I can find to the bird's nesting in Austin or even in the Austin area. However, bird observations were few, and the country west of Austin was thinly populated at that time and still subject to Indian raids. The bird may have been in the vicinity at that time without being recorded. Chapman[3] gives the range of this subspecies, after it was separated from the Mexican cliff swallow by Oberholser, as "Texas and Mexico. Breeds in western Texas, the Rio Grande Valley, and through eastern Mexico to Vera Cruz."

The First Capitol burned in 1881. The great granite statehouse was completed in 1888. Even before the state departments were well-settled in their new quarters, a colony of lesser Mexican cliff swallows occupied the high arch over the south entrance. At this time Congress Avenue, leading

[2]Mr. Ralph Bickler, Clerk of the Texas Supreme Court, gave me this reference.

[3]*Color Key to North American Birds,* 1912.

from the river to the capitol, was an unpaved expanse of soft limestone, yielding, under the pounding and grinding of horse-drawn traffic, an immense amount of floury dust which the south winds swept in stifling clouds up the main thoroughfare of the city. Thereupon a sprinkler system was established, which soon converted the powdered limestone into a pasty mulch which the swallows found very much to their liking. They swarmed down into the street, traffic or no traffic, oblivious of crowds which stared curiously at them.

While thus gathering mud for pellets, this dainty bird barely touches feet to the ground, supporting most of the weight of his body by fluttering his wings high above his back. Craning his short neck forward, he excavates the raw material with his bill and takes off, working the mouthful into pellet form as he flies. Arrived at the nesting site, he presses the little brick into its place in a jiffy and is off again on another hod-carrier flight. Hundreds of the birds covered Congress Avenue, each intent on getting a supply of the gummy mixture of dust and water which the traffic had providentially churned into just the right consistency. Many observers thought the birds were eating mud.

They soon proved to be careless masons, dropping this whitish, adhesive material upon people entering the building; and the acceleration of a four-story descent gave the pellet, as it reached the shoulders of its victims, considerable spattering and daubing power. The fire department came to the rescue with high-pressure hose, and the birds were driven from the city streets back into the hills.

Similarly, in 1920, when the main building of the Sul Ross State Teachers' College, at Alpine, was erected on a slope some miles from the rugged canyons of the Davis Mountains, a colony began building nests in the high arch over the front entrance. The President of the College, Dr. R. L. Marquis, a zoologist and bird lover, proposed to protect the colony; but here, too, it soon became obvious that the enthusiastic little creatures had chosen an impossible site.

No matter how charming the bird may be, coming in from the wilds and putting his trust in welcome from man; no matter how expert he is in destroying mosquitoes and other noxious insects; no matter if he fills the evening sky with "poems of motion"—no matter: he has habits which make him impossible as a guest lodged above the entrance to a public building. President Marquis regretfully summoned the fire department, and it washed down the nests each season until the birds finally gave up and returned to their granitic cliffs, cave entrances, and rock shelters in the mountains.

After two unsuccessful attempts to invade Austin, once in the temporary capitol in 1865, and again in the new capitol in 1883, these swallows waited another third of a century before appearing in force under the new Congress Avenue bridge when that structure, with its spacious arches across the Colorado River, offered an apparently ideal site. In one season as many as six hundred pairs nested under the new bridge. During the swallows' occupancy of this site, I have seen the mud-flats along the water's edge alive with these ocher-marked birds, tilting their bodies forward to obtain nest-building material and fluttering their wings high above their backs to keep their belly feathers above the slime. It was amusing to stand on the bridge at evening and see them snap insects out of the air, often so near that one might hear their bills click as they closed on their prey.

The swallow is no singer, but his twitterings are always pleasant; and the martin's voice is, I think, one of the cheerfulest sounds in nature. I put up with the pigeon nuisance in my yard only because the early-morning bass of these clumsy, half-domesticated creatures blends pleasingly with the high and joyous halloos issuing from the nearby martin house.

Regardless, however, of this vocal deficiency, there is a silent music in the swallow's flight. While the swift is certainly a greater master of the air, staying aloft longer and always moving with greater speed, his exertion is apparent. With the swift, flying is a business; with the swallow, on the other hand, it seems rather the carefree indulgence of a sportive fancy. He soars in still air or rides a vast commotion in front of an approaching storm with equal ease, grace, and enjoyment. He can hover, soar, dash, plunge, and play with air currents, as much a master of his element as a trout in the churning water of a mountain stream. If, as anatomists estimate, the goose has twelve thousand muscles whose sole function is to control the action of the feathers, how many similar muscles must this far superior flier have? Or if he has fewer, how much more efficient each of his muscles must be!

In late afternoon the swallow lingers even after sundown, as if loath to give up the fast-fading daylight for darkness in the tiny cavern where he must spend the night. It is in this farewell-to-day or twilight flight that he is at his best, rising now on an upward-moving current of air to higher and higher levels, swooping, pulling out of the dive with a flexing of the wings which lifts him on the momentum gained nearly to the level from which he plunged,—drifting, resting for a moment, and then repeating his routine, tracing time and again, but always with slight, spontaneous variations, those graceful lines against the sky. It is hardly ever a solo performance. Swallows associate in loose groups, as if enjoying their skyey sport together, each one spurred on to his best efforts under the stimulus of a friendly rivalry.

Finally night drives them in. The show is finished and the stage is cleared. You recall and try to trace out some element, at least, of the involved pattern, but you are soon lost in its intricacies. A musician who is also a bird-lover tells me that in his memory a flight of swallows in the twilight sky tends to become something heard, not seen, more musical than graphic.

For several seasons the lesser Mexican cliff swallow was the chief diversion of those happy loungers one always finds on a city bridge late on quiet afternoons of spring.

But the bottle-shaped nests make ideal marks for the small boy's favorite weapon. They crack and shatter like clay pigeons, and small boys delight in creating a scatteration. A continuous barrage was set up which, coupled with the fact that occasional floods in the river washed down some of the lower nests and threatened others, rendered the location untenable, and the birds again retreated to the wilds.

Large-scale highway construction began in Texas in 1916. Concrete bridges supported by sweeping arches spanned every considerable stream and canyon which cuts across the routes of the highway system, crisscrossing the state.

Soon there were made-to-order building sites strung along at convenient intervals from Devil's River to El Paso, a distance of four hundred miles, skirting the original nesting range of the species. Again we find them leaving their native cliffs for artificial structures; and there is now scarcely a bridge of any considerable size along the entire route that does not have its colony. Not only are they occupying bridges contiguous to their original breeding range, but they are now taking up highways running north and south, even penetrating the blackland prairies and appearing as far north as Waco along the San Antonio-Dallas highway.

When a swallow starts to change his breeding range, there is no telling just where he will stop. He is not tied down to some specific nesting material of limited occurrence, as in the case of our caracara, which seems bound to the broomweed. Neither is he parasitical on some other species for nesting site, as the burrowing owl on the vanishing prairie dog or the wood duck on the ivory-billed woodpecker. He has established and maintains with man a mutual toleration except under certain specific and unusual conditions. He can live wherever insects fly, building wherever a structure exists, natural or artificial, that will hold his nest a few feet above the ground and give protection against the weather. Distance from his winter home means nothing to this marathon flyer, and his manner of leisurely migration, feeding by day and resting at night, precludes the possibility of his outrunning his base of supplies, as far-flying night migrants sometimes do.

Moreover, he has few, if any, effective enemies. He is such a master of aerial maneuver that there seems to be no predatory bird able to catch him in the air. He sometimes locates his nest right in the shadow of the nests of hawks which prey on weaker species. As evidence of contempt for predators, perhaps, a pair of barn swallows plastered their nest to the carcass of an owl hanging from a rafter. Even the ferocious peregrine seems to realize the futility of trying to take a swallow in the air. Snakes cannot scale the precipices upon which they paste their nests, and the owl taking hold of the fragile entrance thereto with intent to plunder finds it crumbly and unsafe. Besides, there is strength in numbers and the colony organization is somewhat communistic.

The swallow has no rigidly set pattern for building his nest. He doesn't have to have a limb with a certain slant, or a crotch of a certain angle, or a hole of specified diameter. The materials he uses are the most widely distributed of any in the world, dirt and water. Instead of beginning from scratch every year, a colony uses the foundations of its old nests and repairs those not too badly damaged. There are cases on record of a swallow's doming over an old robin or phoebe nest. In one case, nestlings falling out were restored in a strawberry box, which the parent birds immediately covered over with mud. Not only that, but they repaired this box for use the following year. When nestlings were restored in a tin can, the parent birds built the neck of a nest over the opening of the can.[4] In Balboa Park, San Diego, a few years ago, I found cliff swallows nesting in the grottoes of bear, unperturbed by throngs of visitors which that popular animal attracts especially at feeding time. It is this adaptability in using available means to accomplish his purpose that gives the swallow a great advantage over his less adaptable or less intelligent rivals.

Adaptability, flight strength—by which I mean to include

[4]Correspondence published by Bent, Bulletin 179, pp. 470–71.

distance-flying, swiftness, and maneuverability—taken together with the wide distribution of natural nesting sites and nesting materials, the acceptance of artificial sites, the high percentage of insect food upon which it subsists, and the protective advantages of communistic organization are factors which give the swallow his world-wide range. Our barn swallow, including the European swallow which differs only subspecifically, has the widest range of any bird in the world.

Wherever insects fly, the swallow may live; and wherever moisture makes mud or a friable bank of earth exists, one species or another of this family can rear its young. Although originally a cliff-dweller or tree-dweller, he follows man out on the prairies and the plains of the world. The martin was on friendly terms with Indians when America was discovered. Early explorers record finding holed and hollowed-out gourds with these birds nesting in them, hanging in front of wigwams. The fact that the cliff swallow now occupies the very ruins which human cliff-dwellers left suggests that possibly here was a still more ancient intimacy. The barn swallow's breeding range follows roughly the migration route of the first immigrants from Asia to America, as traced out in bone and flint by Hrdlica, from deep in Siberia across Behring Strait to Alaska, Canada, the United States, and on south. It is pleasing, but unscientific, to think of early man and the barn swallow coming along together to a fresh, new continent some twenty thousand years ago.

"Ever since the human race has had a history," writes F. E. L. Beal in a fine bit of research completed just before his death and concerned with the food of seven American species, " 'the swallow twittering from the straw-built shed' has roused the peasant at break of day to resume his labors, and he has returned to his cabin to rest 'when the swallows homeward fly.' "[5]

[5]United States Department of Agriculture Bulletin No. 619, p. 1, March 8, 1918.

If we wish to distinguish the European swallow as a separate species, we may say that it divides the habitable portion of the northern hemisphere about half-and-half with the American barn swallow. The Old World bird breeds throughout Europe and far into Asia, where our barn swallow picks up around Lake Baikal and comes on clear across North America.

The fluidity of the swallow's nesting range is well illustrated by the case of the northern cliff swallow. Originally, of course, they nested in natural sites. But in the agricultural sections of the North and East this bird immediately forsook its wild haunts and flocked to the farmsteads, as the country was settled up and farmers erected barns and other outbuildings. It soon became as much of a home bird as the barn swallow or the martin. Since acceptable sites were thus multiplied in a comparatively short period, the numbers of the northern cliff swallow in that area vastly increased.

With the spread of the English sparrow, however, farmers began systematically chinking up the holes and protecting the eaves against the litter-making and otherwise obnoxious intruder. This handicapped the swallow. Paint also altered the great barns unfavorably as nesting sites. Thus we have had a rise and subsidence of the northern cliff swallow take place right under our eyes. So low had the swallow population of New Jersey become in the 1920s that the New Jersey Audubon Society "proposed a campaign . . . for increasing the summer resident cliff swallows" in that state.

I have often wondered why the lesser Mexican cliff swallow is always so ready to forsake his native cliffs for the arch of a building or a concrete bridge the moment the artificial structure becomes available. Of course, pressure of population has something to do with it. Granting that the swallow population is increasing, there must always be a search for new sites, *lebensraum*. There are at least four advantages, in my opinion, which ordinarily incline the bird to the man-built structure: 1, better protection; 2, the right inclination; 3, regular surface; 4, uniformly stable and adhesive base.

Exposure to wind and rain is fatal to the fragile and dissolvable nest. Moreover, any moisture at the base of the nest loosens it and lets it fall. In the limestone area, certainly most of the cliffs, although ordinarily dry, develop wet-weather seeps. This bird is known to have an uncanny knowledge of cliff areas in which wet spots may develop. It has been a matter of much speculation how the cliff swallow in the driest weather demarks on the face of a given cliff spaces for nests not subject to trickles of water or any dampness during extended wet spells. I have seen colonies set in most curious patterns to avoid this threat from the rear. The concrete structures of man, especially the under surface of the arches of bridges and buildings, if extensive, usually have areas in them well-protected from wind and rain, and they rarely develop any show of moisture.

The arch bends gradually from perpendicular to horizontal and thus includes every degree of inclination, from which the bird may make his choice. This is particularly true of the long and spacious arches supporting bridges over streams or canyons of considerable extent.

The proper inclination permits the installation of the nest at just the right angle without compelling the bird to give too much attention to the conformation of the neck of the nest, which must be the most troublesome portion to build.

This feature has also, I suspect, something to do with that dramatic period when the young are being impelled to leave the nest and try themselves in a new medium. The largest colony of the lesser cliff swallows I have ever seen—some two thousand nests, as nearly as I could estimate—was established on a cliff gently inclined from the perpendicular, fairly smooth, and leaning over water backed up into one of the tributary canyons of Devil's River by the Lake Walk Dam near Del Rio, Texas. The nests were densely massed, and the young were just beginning to fly at the time I visited the colony. As I saw the young go out from the cliff on their maiden flights, I could see another reason why the angle of inclination might be important. The young bird as he leaves his hole descends a short distance before finding his wings. If flight were made from the face of a perpendicular cliff, he would lose sight of his own nest and find himself in alien territory more quickly than he does going out at approximately a right angle from the leaning cliff. If the inclination were too great, I judge the unpracticed flyer would find difficulty in looking and flying straight up, and would thus sooner lose touch with the parent birds. He certainly has a more difficult problem than the young martin in similar case, since the lighting board of a martin box is a comparatively large mark to fly at, whereas the hole which the young cliff swallow has just left is a bull's-eye.

I tried to imagine what the world looked like to the nestling sticking his head from the hole and gazing about just before taking his first plunge. Close about him are the nests of other birds, each hole usually framing a protruding head. He cannot see along the cliff for any great distance on either side, but the view above and below is better. Finally the impulse comes and out he goes. As he turns to confront the cliff, he sees hundreds of holes all massed together, indistinguishable one from another. I was unable to tell whether or not a young bird returning from its maiden flight is hospitably received in other than his own nest, but during the whole time I spent there, while hundreds of young were trying out their wings, I didn't see a one fall into the water. A few days later, I saw what seemed to be indiscriminate feeding of young after they had secured perches along the cliff some distance from the colony.

The regular surface of a concrete arch must also appeal to the cliff swallow as a decided advantage, permitting, as it does, the massing of nests over large surfaces, a condition rarely found in nature. A massed colony is a more efficient protective unit than one scattered about, with a dab of nests here and another group there. The larger the number of nests and the closer they are packed together, the simpler the problem of policing becomes. Colony-nesters always find strength in numbers. It has been noted that even semi-domesticated pigeons do not attain colony stability until there is a sufficient number in one dovecote to provide adequate protection.

Natural cliffs, especially those of limestone, have a disconcerting habit of sloughing off now and then, shedding a little; while a crumbly surface, such as is often found in limestone rock shelters, provides insecure footing for any kind of masonry. Concrete, on the other hand, does not slough off or crumble but provides a smooth, stable, and adhesive base.

Using the many concrete bridges along the highways as nesting sites, there seems no reason now why the lesser Mexican cliff swallow may not fill in the gap which has heretofore existed between him and the northern race of the same species. Says Bent: "The typical form, the northern cliff swallow, is the race breeding in Canada, on the west coast of Mexico, and in the United States south to Arizona, New Mexico, and Texas; the lesser cliff swallow breeds in southern Texas and eastern Mexico."[6]

[6] Life Histories, etc., Bulletin 179, p. 483.

5. Killers

When the armadillo started his northward trek, forty years ago, and began arriving in central and even in north-central Texas in considerable numbers, this curious little beast was slaughtered mercilessly. It was confidently predicted, especially by sportsmen, that he would exterminate the wild turkey since he fed, it was claimed, principally on birds' eggs. But the calamity never materialized. With more armadillos[1] there are more turkeys; and quail also are just as plentiful.

Judging from my own observations of the feeding habits of this animal and the information gathered by other observers, I doubt if any ground-nesting species has been much disturbed by him. He roots like a pig for his food and takes with relish whatever his busy little snoot uncovers. He sees

[1]It has been suggested by Mr. F. Wallace Taber, of the Department of Wild Game, Agricultural and Mechanical College of Texas, that the killing of carnivores by southwestern stockmen has allowed the armadillo to build up to such a degree that the "resulting pressure caused an expansion into new territory." Also the partial clearing of woodlands, the same authority surmises, has created a more favorable environment for this animal. Vernon Bailey, as early as 1905, set the northern limit of the armadillo's expansion as 33 degrees north latitude, and this limit appears to hold true to this day. One thing sure, an extended spell of freezing weather is known to wipe out a whole armadillo population.—*Journal of Mammalogy*, Vol. 20, No. 4, November 14, 1939.

Mr. E. R. Kalmbach, Biologist, Division of Wildlife Research, Fish and Wildlife Service, United States Department of Interior, disproves the contention that armadillos constitute much of a menace to ground-nesting game birds, in pages 44 to 51 of a pamphlet entitled *The Armadillo: Its Relation to Agriculture and Game,* published by the Game, Fish and Oyster Commission, Austin, Texas, 1944.

so poorly that he will sometimes bump against you in his meandering course if you remain stock-still as he approaches from windward. Occasionally he will root into a nest and devour the eggs, but the chances of his finding one are almost infinitesimal.

Hunters often jump the gun, declare war on slight pretext, and find later to their regret that they have charged into the ranks of their own friends. I have noticed that sportsmen generally—there are exceptions, of course—take false alarm over the occasional interferences by any species, bird or beast, with game of any kind or character, and make it an excuse for extending their killing range. If a redtail hawk is seen to dive into a covey of half-grown quail, immediately every redtail must be killed. If the paisano is caught eating the eggs of the bobwhite, a holy war is proclaimed upon this interesting species. I once had to exert all the puny political influence I could command to stop a sportsman's drive against the hawks in my home county. Schools had been organized and valuable prizes offered to children for every dead hawk produced, it mattered not what species. Even the sparrow hawk, greatest enemy we have of grasshoppers, tiniest of the falcons and the only representative of the genus *falco* in central Texas, and certainly the most colorful hawk here, was proscribed and a bounty placed upon his head. Thus hawks, good, bad and indifferent, were all to be destroyed. Happily the County Superintendent of Public Instruction proved to be a civilized person who, when the situation was explained, put a stop to the campaign in so far as the schools were concerned.

A game warden on the Aransas Game Refuge near Austwell, Texas, killed a paisano in my presence in order to protect, he said, nesting quail. I insisted on an autopsy, and we discovered that the bird's crop was packed with the remains of grasshoppers, and with nothing else. There was just then a pest of these insects destroying grass and weeds, which normally produce food for quail. It was clear, therefore—in this instance, at least—that a friend of quail, not an enemy, had been shot down.

These birds do get into bad habits. Sometimes one will raid hen's nests and eat his fill. I have known dogs that were guilty of the same violation of farmyard etiquette; but it is as unreasonable to kill all paisanos for the sin of one as it would be to kill all dogs in order to get an occasional egg sucker.

Scientists have established beyond peradventure that the brown pelican's food consists chiefly (above 90 per cent) of non-game fish, but these birds are persecuted shamefully on the Texas coast, killed in flight for practice, and their nesting places destroyed. On Bird Island near Flower Bluff in 1932, I found nests broken up and pelican eggs scattered about so thickly that one could hardly walk along the beaches without stepping on them.

But the reduction to absurdity in the hunter-naturalist feud was reached some years ago in England where sportsmen demanded the extermination of martins and other swallows, because they ate mayflies, mosquitoes, and other insects and thus starved the trout to death!

I believe that some sportsmen develop a lust to kill, and that if this lust cannot be satisfied on game, it attacks other forms of life. It is well-established by psychologists that we do not act so much from reason as from desire. We do what we want to do and then, if our action is questioned on moral or other grounds, we use our reason to justify ourselves. Act first, inform yourself and reason later in defense of the action: that seems to be the pattern. In the present instance, the sportsman who kills a pelican has probably not studied available scientific data concerning the feeding habits of this charming, if grotesque, creature which always reminds me of a flying baby, but shoots him from the simple impulse to kill. Then he justifies himself by furnishing you with fisherman's folklore which classes this bird among the worst enemies of game fish.

I have rarely known a genuine sportsman into whose

head you can drive the idea that there are people in the world, and a considerable number of them, who would rather look at wild life than kill it. To this simple-minded individual such an attitude on the part of anyone is either feigned or foolish. The sportsman interests—by which I mean to include industrial concerns which manufacture and sell game equipment from fishhooks to high-powered guns and ammunition, as well as the persons to whom this material is sold—naïvely assume that all wild life belongs to them, that their rights in it are paramount, that they always have first call, and that thereafter other interests may take the leavings. The great blue heron, moving by majestically on steady wings that beat in solemn rhythm; the gull soaring with grace no artist ever captured; the vermilion flycatcher, a red bull's-eye in a field of blue, are all targets upon which to test the marksman's skill or the choke of the marksman's gun.

But if they often do damage with a casual disregard of any interest in nature except the killing interest, they sometimes, in ministering to game, inadvertently load benefactions upon other species. Consider the vast and successful enterprise of the united sportsmen of this country and Canada, undertaken to restore water and swampy conditions to the desiccated breeding grounds of geese and ducks, the so-called "Ducks Unlimited." What an amazing conception, and what really big-business genius it took in the execution and administration of it! What gains my enthusiastic approval in this enterprise, however, is not so much the boon to geese and ducks, as the godsend given many other marsh-breeding birds which edge in unasked and take advantage of the anserine paradise.

Really, the most deadly hunter from the naturalist's standpoint is not the game hunter. Sports are highly organized and well-financed, and they have a tender regard for all game birds whose population curve begins to show a downward trend.

They throw around them very quickly the protecting arms of the law and see that it is adequately enforced. It is the scientist turned hunter, with his passion for mere collecting, who is most to be feared. His scent is especially keen for those species which are on their way out. A nest, a clutch of eggs, a specimen or series of specimens of a bird which in a few years will probably be extinct is the prize he seeks. Be it in the field of jewels or painting, books or bird's eggs, the zest of the collector for possession of a unique has inspired a thousand crimes. The scientific collector, if given a free field with no restrictions, can exterminate a species in less time than one would suppose.

The scientific killers remind me, in a way, of sheepherding dogs that revert to the old wolfish lust for blood and begin taking toll of the flock they have been set to guard. These animals are more dangerous than wolves, not only because they are trusted, but because they are so familiar with the exact range and habits of their prey.

A ranchman friend of mine trains a fierce breed of dogs to mind his goats by taking the day-old puppies away from the mother bitch and putting them out to be wet-nursed by nanny goats. Thus they inhale the odor of the goat and come to love it along with what they consider their mother's milk. As soon as they are able to travel about a bit, they follow the flock afield in care of a capable Mexican herder, who sees to it that at nursing time some nanny goat is made available. They know nothing but goat life, goat milk, and goat odor from puppyhood until they are grown, when their guarding instinct asserts itself. Not only do these dogs protect their fostering flock from wolves, but also from goat-killing dogs which are often a greater threat than the wild predators.

But I do not forget the advice my friend gave a neighbor who wanted to raise dogs in the same way, "Never let them taste the blood of a goat." When the scientific collector, reared though he has been in the tradition of wild-life protection, permits collecting itself to become a passion, he is in the way of becoming a mere hunter, and his ready formula, in the interest of science, tends to disarm criticism.

There is a happy hunting ground for rare species stretching from Brownsville, Texas, along the Mexican border clear to the Pacific Ocean. The United States can lay claim to dozens of species which barely cross the border from Mexico, and they are all rare in so far as this country is concerned. Some of them are rare not only relatively, but absolutely, and their population trend is as yet undetermined. There are records of expeditions which have taken numerous specimens—numbers, it would seem, out of proportion to the requirements for scientific purposes. In all such cases I suspect the collector of having tasted "the blood of the goat."

Not only does indiscriminate collecting threaten to exterminate, now and then, a tottering species of animal life, but it may become a similar menace to rare forms of vegetable life as well. Nearly a hundred and fifty years ago, the gentle Wordsworth protested against indiscriminate collecting of wild flowers. "Botanists will not, I hope," he says in his suavest manner, "take it ill, if I caution them against carrying off, inconsiderately, rare and beautiful plants. This has often been done, particularly from Ingleborough and other mountains in Yorkshire, till the species have totally disappeared, to the great regret of lovers of nature living near the places where they grew."[2]

About ninety years later, Sir Patrick Geddes, in less conciliatory mood, attacked the same abuse. "The inventory done," he declared, speaking of a collection prepared for an herbarium, "the interest of the consignment . . . was exhausted, or thereafter oscillated between the petty pride of priority and possession and the exercising of the surviving commercial passions in incessant barter."[3]

[2]Note to "Elegiac Verses, in Memory of My Brother, John Wordsworth," etc., in allusion to the Moss Campion. *The Complete Poetical Works of William Wordsworth,* p. 799. The Macmillan Company. New York, 1898.

[3]Article on "Botany" in Chambers Encyclopedia. Ed. 1898.

6. A Bird and
a Flower

There were many flowers, that afternoon, on hills which a month ago were bleak as indigence. Recent rains followed by warm weather had coaxed out the tardiest buds, bringing to a climax a varicolored harvest of vast extent.

Flowers were everywhere.

A few stood up bravely on exposed ledges; some sought the protection of rugged boulders which were pausing for a few centuries or more on their way down the hill; others luxuriated in seepy depressions which detained sediment washed down from emaciated ridges.

Out in the open on shelflike formations I found scattered specimens growing freely and, it seemed, miraculously out of a natural pavement, surely an audacious invasion of enemy territory. Here, blooming cheerily among the toughest and most presumptuous, was the blue gilia, well named golden-eye, delicate and coquettish.

It does seem to be a miracle that from the bones of tiny organisms deposited millions of years ago on the floor of an ancient sea there should now arise to greet the sun a little flower marked by such ingenious and beautiful workmanship. The lily comes unstained from the muckheap, but this proverbial alchemy does not daze the beholder like the blue gilia lifting its golden-centered cup on a stalk apparently rooted in solid limestone. I know that a hand glass will reveal the tiny fissures into which soil and moisture find a way.

I know that a seed happening to lodge in them swells, bursts, and puts out a web of lacy rootlets, but for all the factual explanations I prefer still to regard this particular germination, growth, and florescence as magic, pure magic, and nothing else.

In the more open glades, star-scattered on the grass, bloomed phlox, most widely distributed of the more spectacular flowers of Texas, and therefore a better choice than the blue-bonnet for state flower, if you are careful to exclude from consideration the species of phlox which now returns to us after its one-hundred-year cruise around the world, tamed and subdued, an expatriate, nurseryman's pet, hothouse darling—in short, a degenerate. Near by nodded drowsily the long-stalked yellow daisies, hundreds of them, tough and tufted, seeking out soil pockets in unbelievable places. Blooming close to the ground, as always in early season, I found the yellow Texas star—one of five Texas stars, quintuplets born of a perfervid patriotism; also the common verbena, one wild flower which everybody knows, along with the vervain, its cousin, but not the slender, skinny one; also the tiny lesquerella with petals stretching themselves horizontally to the utmost as if to take in a final deep breath of sunlight before coiling up for the night; and I know not how many others.

The table was pleasantly decorated. As a final triumph of the afternoon, down in the bed of a gully in a washed-out place among the roots, I found a solitary Mexican evening primrose. I say solitary, for this pink-veined flower is sociable and usually blooms in patches. For me it was the first of the season, and, though hiding is not its habit, I found this specimen secreted in a cubbyhole, barricaded by rotten wood and moist, decaying leaves, but with petals perfectly cupped and its long anthers loaded with golden pollen.

I never see this flower without being reminded of a certain bird which has no striking features, as the flower has, to remember it by; no vivid colors, no song, no spectacular flight—in fact, no anything which centers the attention except its pleasing habit of not getting out of your way. The

Inca dove is about half the size of the mourning dove, and longer but not so chunky as its cousin, the Mexican ground dove. It rarely goes farther north than Waco, and always stays in town in preference to the open country. On the ground it has a pacing or waddling movement, if one doesn't mind applying to this dainty creature a word suggestive of ducks or geese or of certain human beings too hefty for their ankles. The Inca appears to have scales instead of feathers, like the scaled partridge, or cotton-top, of western Texas. In flight it shows an ocherish area under the wings and white-margined tail; otherwise, simply a dove-color with tendency to buffness on the belly.

George Finlay Simmons[1] gives a circumstantial account of the Inca's invasion of the Austin region:

> The bird is said by Ridgway to range into "south-ern Texas, casual or occasionally at . . . Austin." Formerly it was little known in southern Texas, but has gradually moved northward until it is rather common over the southern and central parts of the state. On October 23, 1889, one was shot from a flock of three at Austin: this was the first record for the Region. Then in the winter of 1891–92 it was seen by other observers, who thought it the young of the Western Mourning Dove. [Little boys with "nigger" shooters still do.] In 1894 another was shot; and in the winter of 1896 a flock of thirty was noted on the top of a low shed in town, protected from the cold by a wall on one side and a hackberry tree on another. Year after year they kept appear-ing in late fall and winter, but none were seen in summer until 1900. The first nests were found in 1905 in the southwestern and southern parts of the city, where the first birds had appeared. In 1909 they became common and were found nesting in numbers but, as before, they were restricted to the semiarid southwestern parts of the city. In 1910 they began spreading over the entire city, and since that time have become rather evenly distributed.

[1]*Birds of the Austin Region,* University of Texas Press, 1925, p. 91.

Many curious shifts in bird populations occur which science records but does not always explain. Before 1925 the chimney swift was of rare occurrence in the Austin region. Now it is one of our commonest birds; and the Inca dove has moved northward in Texas until there are recent records as far north as Decatur.

While making the northward thrust into Texas, this gentle species has slighted both Louisiana to the right and New Mexico to the left. Oberholser[2] remarks, "The Inca dove is of entirely accidental occurrence in Louisiana," and Florence Merriam Bailey[3] finds only two records of the bird in New Mexico, one at Silver City and the other eighteen miles northwest of Lordsburg. She calls attention also to its urban bias, and tells her readers not to waste time trying to find it in the wilds, for "it is strictly a bird of the towns." According to Grinnell, Bryand & Storer,[4] there is no record of the Inca's ever occurring in California.

The docility of this dove disposes one to speculate concerning its history and how, probably, it got that way. It is small but certainly edible, and if, in the land of its origin, it had been a game bird, it would now show more fear of man. Individual birds of any kind may be gentled in a little while, but this whole species came to us almost in a state of domestication, confiding as chickens. Anthropologists may dig up the fact that aborigines in its prehistoric range held the Inca to be sacred, or harbored some other taboo which established its confidence in man. When a wild bird from a wild country invades your home and begins at once eating out of your hand, there must be a reason.[5]

[2]*The Birds of Louisiana.* Department of Conservation. New Orleans, 1931.
[3]*Birds of New Mexico,* 1928.
[4]*Game Birds of California,* 1918.
[5]The custom of eating small birds of any kind is widespread. Little distinction is made between "game" and other birds in many parts of the world. My daughter, Mrs. Alan C. Pipkin, writes me from Lebanon commenting on sale of songbirds hawked by peddlers about the streets, and adds: "The saddest, however, are the dead ones hanging in bunches of ten or more in the market. They are stripped of feathers except for a few around the head—*all* the tail feathers are removed. I saw a whole bunch of thrushes so hanging. I remarked on this

This town-haunting, people-loving characteristic has endeared the Inca to many who have only a casual interest in nature, and it would have endeared it to many more if it were not mistaken for the young of the mourning dove.

There are quaint stories of this bird's attractions.

In 1915, watch was kept over a nest which a pair of Incas had built on the intersection of guy wires with the trolley wire at the corner of Duval and Twenty-third Streets in Austin. On their fifteen-minute schedule, cars lifted the network of wires, nest and all, at least two feet. The brooding birds took these regular push-ups from 6 A.M. when the first car passed, until the midnight car gave them a farewell up-heaving on its way to the shed.

The intersection happened to be near the entrance to old Clark Field where athletic events were then held. On baseball afternoons the street car schedule was whipped up to five-minute intervals, and cars stopped on this turn to discharge passengers always noisy and sometimes uproarious. Thus the birds got what might be called a delayed lift; that is, they were raised and held up until the noisy throng was unloaded, then dropped again as the car moved on. Baseball or no baseball, they brought off a couple of fledglings on schedule around the first of June. I know of no other bird which would have persisted amid such violent interruptions, such noise and commotion. Even the man-loving, pertinacious wren, I believe, would have given it up.

The Inca has a curious call, monotonously repeated, especially in morning hours, all through the spring months. Nothing quite like it comes from the throat of any other bird or beast. I had occasion a few years ago to identify this call for an old man, a stranger from another state, and an invalid in a home for convalescents.

The keeper of the home telephoned one night to ask if I were the man who knew the names of birds. I admitted some knowledge of local birds, whereupon she told me that

slaughter of songbirds to my Arabic teacher. She replied that we [Americans] kill cows and chickens to eat. I am told that the natives eat the fledglings in toto except for skull, just as we eat oysters."

one of her patients needed my help. "He can't sleep at night," she said, "for worrying about that bird." She asked me to come around at my convenience.

The next afternoon she introduced me to a palsied, bedridden gentleman, whose speech was rendered almost unintelligible by his ailment.

Although his words and phrases were badly scrambled, I did, by listening carefully, get the drift of what he was trying to say. It was about a bird and mainly about the bird's curious call, which he made attempts to imitate. I found this rather trying: it was as if he were trying to shuffle his weak and uncertain legs around in imitation of a dance step. Finally he resorted to writing with his violently trembling fingers, and I made out from the scrawl that every morning around nine or ten o'clock he heard a strange bird. "I have traveled all over the world," he wrote, "but I know I have never heard that call before." He then endeavored to indicate the sound by means of written syllables, but I could make nothing of it.

I saw that he was overexerting himself, so I left him, promising to return next morning and try to identify the call. He scrawled on a piece of paper, "if sunny and still," which indicated to me that he was enough of a naturalist to have noted that the call was associated with the weather, as is the case with so many birdcalls.

It was sunny and bright next morning, quite warm for the twenty-second of February. I had been sitting by his bed only a little while, when he held up a hand shaking like a leaf in the wind and said with evident excitement, "There it is!" I listened but heard nothing. His hand went up again, but still I heard nothing. Then with great effort he pointed toward a south window, and I leaned out, listening, and sure enough, there it was, faint and far away, but distinct enough to be identified.

"Inca dove."

His whole body relaxed, as I pronounced the words, and a look of quiet satisfaction overspread his face.

"Thanks," he muttered, and soon fell asleep.

Next morning I returned with several books containing descriptions of the Inca; and, curiously enough, a specimen came and perched near the window, giving forth his crowing call right in our ears, but unfortunately not in a position to be seen from the room. My patient smiled in recognition of the visitation. Then we talked a long time about birds.

For the first time I noticed some dried botanical specimens in his room, and I found that he was curator of botany in a nationally famous museum.

Soon, with the warming up of the Texas spring, he was able with some assistance to take little trips into the country, and I had great pleasure and profit from his conversation. He was a botanist who felt deeply the living presence in nature. He was interested not only in mechanism, but also in the mysterious force that uses mechanism for its occult purposes.

One dewy morning we passed a shanty on a river-bottom plantation where a man was cutting weeds. He had just attacked a patch of Mexican evening primroses, and my companion turned to me in great concern:

"It's a pity," he said, "to slash them down like that. They're such friendly flowers—they creep right up to your door." So does the Inca dove: like this primrose, it creeps right up to your door.

Since then I never see a patch of these flowers and never hear an Inca dove without a memory of this fine old character, trembling with a palsy on the brink of the grave but still, like a youth, in love with sun and flowers and birds and generally with the out-of-doors.

7. Co-operatives

In a 1937 notebook of mine I find a page headed, "Lufkin Club—14,000 acres—Good God—dead sweet gum in cut-over pasture." The 14,000-acre tract begins about ten miles west of Lufkin at the Neches, third largest river in Texas. Along the highway it is protected by a high fence on which Game Preserve signs are prominently displayed.

This forest is an island of life in the midst of a weary land devastated by unscientific cultivation which followed in the wake of the insatiable sawmills. Although protection of the wild life here is meant only for the few species which furnish meat for the table and sports afield, thousands of other forms of life profit by it. Things are so arranged in nature that you cannot support one form of life without maintaining others which in turn support it; and, by the same token, one form cannot be destroyed without pulling down the structure upon which it rests, and the superstructure it upholds. Thus the naturalist and the sportsman should be allies and stop their feuding.

There is no profanity in the excerpt from my notebook. I happened to be getting directions from a native when suddenly a pair of pileated woodpeckers near by began their unearthly clamor.

"What bird is that?" I asked.

"A *good* God."

"A what!"

"A *good* God," he replied with more emphasis on the "good," and forthwith explained, "You see, people ain't usta seein' a woodpecker as big as a crow; so when they do see one, they jes' natchally say, 'Good God'!"

Indian hen is another name for this magnificent woodpecker with his brilliant red cap and striking facial pattern —another instance of the folk tendency to attach Indian to any form of life showing striking colors.[1]

But the dead sweet gum is still another matter. Wandering about, that morning, I finally got out of the forest and walked a long time in pastures of cut-over lands where scrawny cattle, principally cows and calves, were managing to stay alive at a bare subsistence level. The big lumber interests had moved out years before and were succeeded here by small ranchers who were mere gleaners, picking up crumbs after the rich and ancient life of the country had been ravished.

The monster sweet gum lay almost prostrate. It had crashed years before and now reclined partially supported by a few of the larger limbs that failed to crumble completely in the shock of its fall. Many of its branches and even twigs remained intact. Not counting its great bole, the top alone covered a space, oval in shape, approximately one hundred feet long and fifty feet wide at the center.

I had found few flowers and fewer birds after getting away from the immediate influence of the forest. There were numbers of rotting stumps here and there, ragged clumps of sprouts, rank frostweed in some of the ravines, scattering trees, and many erosion gullies leading up the gently sloped hillsides.

Presently I heard a humming of rubythroats and I knew that somewhere in this waste they must be enjoying a feast of nectar. I moved in the direction from which the sound was coming, and when the dead sweet gum first came into view I thought it was a mound of flowers, so thickly were blooms massed among its branches. Sure enough, buzzing over it were dozens of hummers. As I got nearer I saw

[1] I discuss this more at length in Chapter 15.

around the edges of the mound—tucked in just out of reach of the grazing animal—masses of deep purple tradescantia mingled with red mallow in full bloom. A skinny vine clambered about in the interior dotting in small, white, purple-centered blooms. A mass of sunflowers occupied the central section, while across the top of the fallen tree a morning-glory vine had effectually suppressed all competition. There was also here and there a bell-shaped flower, pale blue with yellow center which I did not identify, and finally, on long, naked stalks, a coneflower called locally queen of the meadow.

The deep bass of the rubythroats, almost too low at times to hear at all, was accompanied by humming in a higher pitch, heard only on nearer approach, coming from numerous honeybees which had also discovered this bonanza. A few highly-colored butterflies associating with many drab ones were about also—some perched on exposed twigs, slowly opening and closing their gorgeous wings, some feeding, some flitting about.

The massive corpse of this tree was disintegrating amid a display of life's most lively and colorful expressions: bees, butterflies, hummingbirds, and flowers. Of course, less conspicuous life was thriving therein, but I can't find that I made any note of it. I rarely notice an insect until it is in the bill of a bird, and then I want to know all about it.

I found that morning, brush piles, which were performing the same protective service for blooming plants but on not so large a scale. One learns to look around the brush piles in fall and winter for finches. It is not only as a protection from hawks that small birds like brush piles as a winter harborage. Under a brush-pile protectorate, flowering plants flourish and come to seed to be harvested by the seedeaters who pay for their winter keep by distributing the seed far and wide against the time when the rains come and the fructifying warmth of spring is again upon the land. The ends meet, and the circle is complete—all as if it had been thought out and planned in advance.

Even the botanists, whose business it is to know the ways and wiles of vegetable life, were amazed to find growing in the bomb-blasted blocks of London one hundred twenty-six species of wild flowers never before recorded on or near those plots of soil. How did this rich assortment of native plants filter in and begin thriving immediately in the wake of Hitler's devastating explosions? What magic! For centuries, solid masses of brick and mortar had fenced out and sealed over those areas lying in the fertile valley of the Thames occupied by the older sections of the city. In a moment the covering is violently removed. Rains wash and the sun again warms the soil after its five centuries or so of moldy chill. Winds visit it and birds hop gaily about amid the rubble. Spring brings the ancient flowers to life: the creeping buttercup, yellow corydalis, three mallows, scarlet pimpernel, and a hundred others bloom as they did in identical locations long ago, as if nothing had happened in the meantime.

In nooks and crannies here and there these plants somehow found shelter even in this most densely populated and artificially built-up area of the world, seeding secretly in sequestered hide-outs, season after season, cribbed and confined for centuries. And now at long last when the opportunity for colonization opens, they travel by one means or another, spreading themselves amid the rubble.

Much the same kind of thing is happening under my eyes in this overstocked goat range where I am staying at present. Plants are clubbing together for protective purposes. When the goat, most expert of browsers, enters a virgin range there must be consternation among shrubs and among the young trees which have not yet lifted their leafy parts well above reach of the rearing animal.

The goat's day is, on the average, 12.8 hours, forty-eight

per cent of which is spent in feeding. In daily travel under similar range conditions, he moves approximately twice as far as a sheep or a cow. He is not only a tireless traveler but, as the author of Proverbs puts it, "comely in going." The scientist who provides me with these statistics failed to compute the number of goat nibbles per minute and set them against the more leisurely croppings of the cow.

The lip of the goat is tough, excellently muscled, adaptable, and of extreme mobility. It is while he is gathering his provender from a thorny shrub that his upper lip shows to best advantage. It elongates, retreats, flattens, stretches itself this way and that to meet effectually the defensive tactics of the plant which is undergoing the attack. It pushes up, down, or sidewise, nosing undesirable material out of the way, while occasionally exercising in conjunction with the lower lip the power to grasp, pull at, and even nip off promising morsels. But chiefly the upper lip of the goat simply opens the way for the keen-cutting front teeth, and then skins itself back while they do their work.

Nearly any tree or shrub is grist for the goat mill. Even the young mesquite, toughest of Texas natives and thorned to boot, is often browsed to death, when the range is short and the going gets really rough.[2]

The goat is not only an industrious but a clever browser. He gets every palatable leaf or shoot within reach on all fours and then rears on his hind legs, bracing himself against the trunk, or even balancing precariously upright with fore hoofs on the uncertain support of a limber and swaying branch. In this position his long, supple neck gives him an increased vertical browsing range of at least two feet. His vaulting ambition, however, occasionally overleaps itself, and he hangs by the neck until dead in crotch of tree or

---

[2]In sections where the mesquite attains size and carries its foliage out of reach of the goat, it attracts another animal. Bulls horn down the lower limbs to make cropping available for themselves and for the dehorned cows. I have been told by ranchmen that a bull surrounded by his dehorned flock, will often horn down mesquite limbs long after he has supplied himself with all he can eat.

shrub unless rescued. Goatherds have to be constantly on the
lookout for such mishaps.

On this particular goat range there are provided safety
zones where the appetizing shrub, even if thornless and lacking other defense, may find a refuge. Certain plants defy the
hungriest goat. In this pasture two species stand out as
mothering plants, that is, shrubs which shelter other species:
the agarita[3] and the spring herald. But for these two, a
number of others would be quickly exterminated.

Most conspicuous, because most widely distributed, is the
agarita which goes armed literally cap-a-pie. It presents
to the browser not the long, daggerlike points of the yucca
family, nor the porcupine aspect of a thousand-thorned
cactus, but the cambric-needle points of tiny spines protrud-

---

[3] "Agarita" is one of the many corruptions of "agrito." It is a spell-
ing, however, so fixed that it is doubtful if even the weight of Webster's
New International Dictionary can overturn it. "Agarita" is the only
spelling found in the following publications:
    The Vegetation of Texas, by Benjamin Carroll Tharp. The Anson
Jones Press, Houston, 1939. (Dr. Tharp is Professor of Botany in the
University of Texas.)
    The Seed Plants, Ferns and Fern Allies of the Austin Region, by
Marie Sophie Young, Ph. D. The University of Texas Bulletin No.
2065, 1920.
    500 Wild Flowers of San Antonio and Vicinity, by Ellen D. Schulz,
M.S., Head, Department of Biology, Main Avenue High School, San
Antonio, Texas. San Antonio, 1922.
    Valuable Plants Native to Texas, by H. B. Parks, Chief, Division of
Agriculture, Texas Agricultural Experiment Station, Bulletin No. 551,
1937.
    The Practical Encyclopedia of Gardening, edited by Norman Taylor,
Garden City Publishing Company, Inc., 1941–42.
    Ellen D. Schulz uses the spelling "agrito," but puts it in quotation
marks, which is the symbol she uses throughout her book to indicate
a Mexican form.
    H. B. Parks and V. L. Cory use "agrito" in their *Catalogue of the
Flora of Texas*, Texas Agricultural Experiment Station Bulletin No.
550, 1917.
    The shrub has become a commercial product and is listed by all the
nurserymen's catalogues which I have examined as "agarita." A street
in San Antonio, Texas, uses the same spelling. H. B. Parks, author of
one of the works above listed, and co-author of another, at present
Curator, Museum Botanist in Charge, Tracy Herbarium, writes me
July 16, 1946, as follows: "My idea of a common name for this shrub

ing from every lobe of its multitudinous three-to-seven lobed leaflets, each leaf oriented to offer a dozen punctures to the nibbling lip, no matter how tough the lip may be, and no matter from what angle it seeks to intrude itself. The agarita has rather skinny foliage, hence doesn't cast so dense a shade as to deprive its refugees of the sunlight which is necessary for their growth. Indeed, this shrub casts fewer units of shade per hundred spines than any other in this section of the country.

Snugly set up in a clump of one or the other of these mothering shrubs is the cedar elm, not defenseless, but ready enough to get all the help it can. The goats like this elm next to the oak and, if it is exposed, gnaw it to the bone. Left to its own devices it has a way of putting out near its base stiff, short arms which, unless the plant is completely overwhelmed before it gets a good start, become stiffer, straighter, sharper, and tougher the more they are browsed, until a cordon is thrown around the main stem so that it may pursue its upward way. After many delays, discouragements, fatalities, and the expenditure of a vast amount of energy in defense, the central shoot may finally lift itself out of harm's way and spread its top in the sun. As this expansion occurs, the lower protective arms, being shaded, wither away.

The soapberry, the ashes, and many others, however, have no such resources to fall back upon. They are true dependents. The yaupon, like the elm, can also, if it has to, take care of itself, but even this hardy native prefers to defy

---

is 'agarita,' as this plant is becoming more and more common as a cultivated shrub in Southwest Texas, and the name under which it is sold is 'agarita.' I at one time compiled twenty different spellings of this same word from newspapers, nursery catalogues, and books, and I am still undecided just what the final outcome of the spelling evolution will be."

Mr. Parks also informs me that "agrito" is the Mexican's name for the berry and not for the bush. In Zacetacas another shrub, *Lippia ligustrina* (Lag.) Britt. is called "agrito."

It seems to me that general use, and the spelling given in authoritative books touching Southwestern botany for the past thirty years, will eventually compel the acceptance of "agarita." It is an interesting case of the rebellion of the lazy southern palate against a grinding "g" followed by a burring "r."

the goat from the center of a mothering clump; and the oaks do, too.

The yellow buckeye has a defense of another character, a skunklike defense, I should call it. Either its odor or its taste is so obnoxious to browsing animals that they avoid it. I have found only two animate creatures feeding on this buckeye: a webworm and the hummingbird. I have heard mating hummers buzzing over patches of buckeye with a drone which sounded like a fleet of approaching airplanes. They love it for the nectar that it offers deep down in the bottom of its slender, tubular flowers. It is often the first woodland blossom to greet the midget migrants when they arrive in the spring. City parks and private lawns of this section should cultivate the yellow buckeye not only on its own account, but to encourage the rubythroat and the black-chinned hummers. It is attacked by a webworm. In midspring I have seen bush after bush of it, with their great, deep-green, palmately compound leaves all tied together into roughly globular clusters as large as big grapefruit, in which later you find hundreds of little wigglers on their way, I suppose, to becoming flying creatures of some sort. Except for these two, all the rest of animal creation hereabouts leave it severely alone.

Shrubs that can neither fight, flee, nor make themselves personally obnoxious are eventually exterminated on a well-stocked range. The evergreen sumac, for instance, although not so pleasing to the goat as other species of the same genus, cannot stand up against him: it survives the deer but succumbs to the goat. In some localities it is called deer laurel from the fondness which that browser shows for it. It grows to no great height except under special conditions, tends in early life to assume an umbrella shape corresponding very nearly to that of the agarita, carries its leafage exposed on the tips of its branches, and therefore cannot very well be "mothered."

If and when the cow or the horse or some other grazing animal more lenient than the goat succeeds this terrific browser, species of shrubs thus preserved are ready to spread out again and occupy their original range; for, whether in the heart of London, in the blasted, cut-over lands of East Texas or in a West Texas goat pasture, life throws up its defenses against internecine strife, or scales the barriers set up against it by the rude and clumsy accidents of the material world.

This mutual dependence, solidarity, or community of interest is after all and generally nature's most distinctive characteristic. The sin of non-co-operation is severly penalized. "Nature red in tooth and claw" is only a partial view, and expresses incident rather than plot or principle. Those unaccustomed to considering the world in the amplitude of time fail to see this. The hawk rends his prey and the more powerful hawk hovering near robs the killer of his prize; but this is a mere detail or byplay. The whole must be seen not as a still but as a motion picture—as plot, counterplot, and drama of the limitless fecundity of nature, unbelievably clever stratagems and devices, infinite mutations, protean adaptability, all unfolding amid the "dance of materials" in an endless flow of time.

Now it turns out that man lends a helping hand to the shrubs that have survived the goat, as an examination of any southwestern nurseryman's catalogue will show. These plants are advertised, sold, and shipped to the utmost limits of their natural range, and are grown experimentally far beyond. It is the ability of a shrub to protect itself against browsing animals which marks the possible hedge plant, for what are the teeth of the browser but a pair of nature's hedge clippers? The evergreen yaupon has learned this trick in the wilds, hence has to be taught nothing when it is domiciled on a city lawn. It reacts perfectly to the shears, putting forth two rich, green, leafy twigs for every one that is clipped off. It becomes dense, stays green, stands drought, resents coddling, and throws in, as a *pilon* to its domesticator, decorative red berries in the fall and winter.

Moreover the yaupon is plastic to the hand of the topiarist and may be trimmed into fantastic shapes to represent lions rearing and roaring, strutting peacocks, chairs, tables, divans —a bastard art which the English gardeners of the Victorian era affected. We do well, in my opinion, not to imitate the English in this.

The mystery of the survival of the Ligustrum and other species of privet in the land of the yaupon and the agarita can be explained only by the power of advertising and the salesmanship of nurserymen. Mr. H. B. Parks has done a fine thing in preparing and publishing a pamphlet describing many native plants in Texas which richly repay domestication, giving hints on their culture and indicating the regions in which respective species thrive. Better still, Jac Gubbels, Landscapist for the Texas Highway Commission, has scattered demonstrations along every automobile highway in Texas. Bridge approaches, culverts, borders, roadside parks, highway intersections, wide places in the road, and unsightly corners are landscaped and ornamented for the most part with trees, shrubs, and flowers native to the area so adorned.

It is true that some tourists seem to pay little attention to these exhibits, taking in only the larger view: that is, they see a mountain, may even observe a hill or butte which happens to be conspicuous. They admire big trees, exclaim over the trailing moss of our coastal bottoms, gaze long at wide-sweeping valleys, and—oh, yes—vistas; they are strong on vistas. Big things that are distant too often take precedence over important things right under the nose. Anyhow, here are seeds of culture sown broadcast, not all of which fall "upon stony places where they had not much earth."

I once came across a small rural school stuck away in the brush of a semiarid section, the grounds of which were surprisingly fresh and attractive. On closer inspection I saw that only native flowers and shrubs were used. The rich yellow borders were of Engelmann's daisy, a determined bloomer, and zexmenia which, water or no water, manages throughout spring and summer to hold up to the sun on long, naked stems a daisy which is almost the color of old gold. In the background was a row of twisted-leaved yucca six feet high with immense, creamy clusters of bell-shaped flowers, each individual flower as large as a hen's egg. Slender bear grass hanging from the brow of a low ledge in a far corner of the schoolyard was trimmed squarely across, reminding one of a sturdy little girl with her back hair rather touseled but her front hair down over her forehead, combed, straight, and trimmed as bangs. As it happened, rockbrush was having one of its brief blooming periods and perfumed the whole campus with an odor not sweeter, but more delicate, than that of plum blossoms.

The teacher who was responsible for this told me she had got the idea from a piece she had read somewhere. She said that the main advantage was that the plants stayed in good condition during the vacation period without anyone to look after them. This young lady didn't even know the common names of all the plants she was using. She said she wished she did, for the children were always asking her for them. I happened to notice a grassy plot in one corner of the schoolyard and inquired if she were transplanting native grasses also. She said no, that that little plot was there when the school was built. It occurred to me that a local collection of this sort should have some space devoted to grass. There are ordinarily a dozen different species in any community. Altogether, growing within the borders of Texas, there are about 550 different grasses, which is more than half of all the species of Poaceae to be found within continental United States.

I have on my place a conglomerate hedge consisting of a dozen or more different natives, which hasn't been watered except by rainfall in ten years, and yet it stays in much better health than a privet hedge near by which in that period has drunk up oceans of water.

There used to be a filling station, on the highway leading out of Junction, Texas, toward Sonora, whose proprietor deserved a medal for making his station into a home for native birds and plants. He had bird boxes and bird shelter stuck around in every likely nook and corner; and, being something of an artisan, if not an artist, he gave to each one an attractive as well as distinctive appearance. He had a small cactus garden showing some twenty different species; a number of the yuccas; also the leucophylum or, as the Mexicans call it, *cenizo,* gray ghost of the desert, which dreams purple dreams after every summer shower; and he had even caught the wild and wickedly thorned ocotillo which, when I was last there, was flaunting its red blooms.

This is good business. I will stretch my gasoline to get to fill up in such a little island of natural history, and many other motorists will, too. It sometimes happens that even the person quite indifferent at home becomes suddenly alive to the animate world as soon as he gets out on the road. With more leisure than he ordinarily commands, deprived of associating with people interested in local gossip, he wants to talk. Here, too, custom has not staled the normal, and he begins investigating with fresh interest flowers, trees, animals, exhibits of local geological specimens, and any other natural-history objects he can find. It is a wonder to me that service people along the big transcontinental highways do not more generally avail themselves of this easy, pleasant and inexpensive means of attracting the wandering tourist.

8. "Co-operatives"
(Continued)

Plants associate, and we might well say co-operate. Animal groups also are fitted into interdependencies, of which some are quite intricate. Folk tales of world-wide distribution bolster belief in universal kinship making each living form a part of one great whole. Thus fiction supplements authentic examples to satisfy the human craving for reducing all animate nature to the mutual-aid pattern; while every instance of animal behavior which seems to show a spark of sympathy crossing the species line is cherished as if it were a special revelation. The cat which nurses the puppies, the hen's adoption of the ducklings, horse-and-rooster friendships, and a thousand and one other freak features in natural history all have sure-fire popular appeal.

Here nature-faking flourishes and here debunkers are bristling and busy every minute. They chop off one head only to be confronted with two growing out from the stub of the same old neck. The wren which picks the alligator's teeth is immortal; and, although the dragon turned out to be a mythical beast, he nevertheless bequeathed to his legitimate heir, the snake, a device for swallowing his young whenever threatened by an enemy.[1]

Fable-making of the ancients embodied an actual belief

[1]Without taking sides, J. Frank Dobie presents affirmative evidence from a surprising number of eye-witnesses, for which see Publications No. XXI of the Texas Folklore Society, Austin, Texas, 1946.

in the human motives, emotions, and intellectual processes of animals. A complete sympathy was established. Science has destroyed the basis for much of this by gradually depriving lower animals of human traits and powers; but this has not put an end to nature-faking except of the crudest kind. The root is perennial and flowers in a vast profusion of sympathy stories. Man holds on to a belief in a sympathetic nature for the dear life of his soul. The readiness of the popular mind to accept spurious stories of how one animal helps another, and its childlike faith in long-discredited myths of similar import, indicate an unconscious rebellion against science which we suspect of taking away from us something we must not lose. The point is, we want to believe; we *want* to endow the animal world with our own feelings, and we do it willy-nilly.

Farm machinery is pushing farm animals out of the picture. Restrictive codes in urban communities are breaking age-old animal ties. Since we have become largely a nation of apartment dwellers and housing has become scarcer and scarcer, the landlord can enforce more stringently his edict, "no children, no pets." This deprivation has come on so gradually that we fail to realize the deeper tragedy of it. Not only are we brought into unhealthy propinquity with our own species, but at the same time we are divorced from other species with which we have enjoyed intimacy for ages.

When I was a boy living on a small acreage near a rural village, the safety bicycle was just appearing, but there were no smooth roads, much less anything that resembled a pavement. I was brought, therefore, into daily contact with a sentient being as a means of transportation. It had moods, just as I had. It responded to caresses, and to scoldings or ill-treatment. This animal knew my voice and reflected its intonations by quick changes in behavior. In short, my pony was my pal. At the same time I associated on terms of a flea-exchanging familiarity with anywhere from one to half-a-dozen dogs. I got my milk from a cow the hard way—not out of a bottle.

Well do I remember the sense of companionship with which, in the deeper darkness just before dawn, a Texas norther howling about the barn, I settled down in a comfortable stall, my forehead pressed firmly into the flank of the great beast, to do the milking, talking soothingly to her as every good milkman does.

While in this intimate contact with the cow, I heard around me the soft, guttural complaints of the hogs; also the protesting sniffs of the tied-off calf. Presently the rooster quit crowing, and began gently clucking to the sluggish hens, which communication I faithfully translated as, "Come on, come on, come on now—time to get up—cluck, cluck, cluck"; and, of course, my translation was shortly verified, for the hens did follow their lord and master off the roost.

This cluster of animals, or biotic colony, as the biologist calls it, was then and still is a big part of the rural child's life on the small, unmechanized farm. There are fewer rural children, however, every year, and fewer animals for them to associate with.

Another thing that the rural child experiences every day of his life is maternal love as exhibited in domestic animals —that is, the care, solicitude, tenderness, and the infinite pains as well as the evident satisfactions, of sow with brood, bitch with litter, hen with chicks, ewe with lamb, goat with kid, mare with foal, and cow with calf. The concept of maternity, thus daily enriched, sinks in and becomes a part of the developing child and affects his thoughts and emotions deeply and for all time. Bergson comments with a striking figure of speech on the significance of maternal love. He conceives of all life as motion which possesses the consciousness most convincingly as the operation of maternal love is observed in nature. "It shows each generation," he says, "leaning over the generation that shall follow. It allows us a glimpse of the fact that the living being is above all a thoroughfare, and that the essence of life is in the movement by which life is transmitted."

Our contacts with the animal world in pioneer periods were even more intimate and more extensive since many wild animals were included. It was not the sympathy of the animal for man, but certainly man's belief in that sympathy, which was largely responsible for domestication. How many ages and how firm a faith it took for the human being to coax into life a genuine interspecies affection between himself and the jackal, one of the most disgusting of beasts, we shall never know. But faith and infinite patience finally accomplished the miracle. The transformed beast now licks man's hand or face, while man on his part accepts these lingual caresses with evident satisfaction.

The caves of prehistoric man are decorated with drawings, ninety per cent of which are animal representations. The human community of towns and cities and the isolated family group as well, rich or poor, have always associated with them a cluster of animals: the sacred geese of Rome, doves of Venice, sparrows of London, vultures of Calcutta; parrots and magpies in the mansions of the nobility; cats, dogs, and other commensals in the hovels of the poor. These, and their like, affection alone detains, to say nothing of that vast horde of parasites, dependents, sneak thieves, and so on, which have, time out of mind, invaded or hovered about in the vicinity of human habitations. Refuse heaps of Romano-British London "have yielded bones of oxen, pigs, sheep, horses, goats and dogs among the domestic; red and roe deer, hares and birds among the wild animals." The bones of the raven, a favored scavenger, are second in quantity only to those of domestic fowl in kitchen middens of ancient Silchester.[2] An excavation of a stone wall in Crete (1500 B.C.) shows a mass of sculptured leaves in the

[2]*London's Natural History*, by R. S. R. Fitter. Collins. London, 1945, p. 31.

center of which a cat is crouched to pounce upon a bird which is joyfully unaware of the danger.

Our kinship with animate nature is so deep and our sympathetic ties are so strong and of such long standing that a sudden break with them is more serious than is generally supposed. Indeed, it requires some such historical conception of the relationship to account for the irrational fondness for lower animals and for our determination, whether or no, to have them constantly around us. I wonder why even the most scientifically trained and unsentimental of parents permit Junior to sacrifice the peace and cleanliness of the whole apartment in order to gratify a passion for pups! Is it not astonishing that we, a scientific generation, ignore studies proving the dangers of psittacosis, and still keep parrots; and not only keep, but kiss them! Despite the warnings by competent epidemiologists against the dangers of pneumonitis and other dreadful consequences, pigeon lofts abound in residential sections of all our cities. We hold the gratifications of contact with animals above considerations of health and convenience. This is not irrational: quite the contrary. We have come to our present state as a part of nature, and we have an instinctive fear of the isolation which now threatens. Emotional ties of long standing bind us to the animal world, and we would rather risk germ diseases and other physical ills and inconveniences, in maintaining animal associations, than the nervous disorders of isolationism. The cat which carries dangerous germs may bring much-needed psychological repose to the household; and if she has kittens, all the better.

Natural history subjects have a fascination for old and young, wise and foolish. Theodore Roosevelt and Viscount Grey, during their only personal contact, spent the daylight hours of the twenty allotted to them near the little village of Tichborne in Hampshire, and in New Forest, listening to the songs of birds and discussing them with the enthusiasm of a couple of schoolboys.

A large percentage of Mother Goose rhymes and other kindergarten verses have to do with the antics of imaginary animals or with the behavior, appearance, or characteristics of real ones. Aesop's Fables after 2,500 years are still read with relish and quoted almost as frequently as the Bible. A spontaneous cheer bursts from the youngsters in the theater as the animal cartoon is announced.

The swift advance of technology redistributing our population into huge clots, called cities, and the rapid mechanization of the farm, have broken the rhythm of life. We have been dissociated too suddenly from the placidity of rural or village life. We have been expelled from an environment in which we were part and parcel of the other life about us.

> Though inland far we be
> Our souls have sight of that immortal sea
> Which brought us hither.

That startling novelist, Aldous Huxley, follows out this break with nature in his extravaganza, "This Brave New World," caricaturing the specialization and regimentation toward which we are tending under the monitorship of "pure intellect."

The attraction of beast for beast within a given species is still another matter, and one which more readily commands human understanding and sympathy. Being gregarious ourselves, we actually experience the same gravitational tug that holds the individual within the flock, herd, or other group of his kind.

Shortly after taking up my residence here, the owner of the pasture gave temporary refuge to a cow pony belonging to a friend of his. There were no other horses about at that time. Spike was restless. I ran across him first in one corner of the pasture and then in another, always on the move. After a rain his tracks were everywhere. They showed that he had crossed and recrossed Bear Creek dozens of times, night and day. He became noticeably leaner, although grass was plentiful.

But within two weeks he changed his habits, settled down, and began acting as a normal pony should. I missed him for a day or two, and, after some looking about, I found him grazing contentedly in a glade bordering a division fence which separates this place from a pasture just to the south of it. I concluded that the buffalo grass in that part of the pasture was maybe a little more flavorsome, and thought nothing more of it.

One morning, however, I heard a sharp whinnying and went to investigate. With breast leaning hard against the barbed-wire fence, Spike was launching his calls with great vigor. Presently, from far down in the woods of the other pasture, I heard an answer. Soon two disreputable-looking ponies, both geldings, came in sight. Then over the fence was much nosing, and playful nibblings, neighings, ecstatic little squeals, greetings, and felicitations.

Thus by spying upon him, I discovered his secret. His long search had been for company, just the company of his kind, and nothing else. His gregariousness was completely satisfied with the knowledge that by uttering a call he could soon have two of his own species feeding just across the fence from him. It would be as unscientific to say that Spike was lonesome as it would be to refer to my own desire for company as a frustrated gregariousness, but the two terms are interchangeable. They mean exactly the same thing and either one may be applied with equal relevance to this particular variety of hungry-heartedness, whether it occurs in me or in Spike.

So it was with a snowy egret which spent the night in a tree among the white leghorn chickens of a coastal farm not so long ago. It was just after sundown when the farmer happened to notice a white bird sailing far above in the clear sky. He came lower in downward spirals until he was circling the tree in which the white leghorns were just going to roost. Alighting on one of the topmost branches he carefully folded his wings, adjusted his plumes, and stretched out his long neck, peering down suspiciously at the company he had chosen for the night. He shifted his position several times, but finally settled down on his stilts, heronwise, neck folded in sleeping posture.

"Next morning," said the big Norwegian farmer to me, apparently delighted to find someone interested in the occurrence, "the chickens flew down to the ground and the white bird flew up again into the sky."

This incident has stayed in my memory for months. I sometimes resort to it in bed when I can't go to sleep. The vision of that bird, the beauty of whose plumes fifty years ago spread a fierce rivalry among all the best-dressed women of the world—the picture of this, the most delicate and lovely of all the egrets, sailing down out of the blue sky to spend the night in a tree with dung-scratching fowls of the farmyard, and, come dawn, taking off again—really, the details of this evidence of a yearning for his kind are so quieting, the folding of the egret's wings is so suggestive, and the whole idyl is so clothed in sedative colors, white and blue, that I usually lose consciousness just as the bird disappears into the depths of the clear morning sky. I recommend it to others troubled with insomnia.

The bird was lonesome.

What means this roaming with a hungry heart? Spike searching ceaselessly until he calls up two disreputable ponies to provide himself across a barbed-wire barrier with a sense of companionship; an egret descending to consort for the night with earth-bound creatures because they happened to remind him of his own kind—mere white spots in a tree, they must first have appeared, but suggestive of the rookery for which he was longing, as he saw from his great altitude the fast-approaching shadows of the night.

What does it mean? Simply that Spike and the egret were both lonesome.

Many observers record touching instances of sacrifices made or offered by one animal for another. The squeal of a pig caught in a crack will bring to the rescue every member of the herd within hearing. Waterfowl often linger near a wounded member of the flock at their own peril. It was this instinct, also, which was largely responsible for the extermination by man in the last century of the Carolina parakeet, the only species of the genus *Conurus* which ever extended its range far into the United States. "This fatal habit of hovering over their fallen companions," says Bent,[3] "has helped, more than any one thing, to bring about their extermination. Their social disposition has been their undoing." He then quotes C. J. Maynard: "This is not a mere liking for company, as they are actually fond of one another, for, if one out of the flock be wounded, the survivors attracted by its screams, will return to hover over it and even if constantly shot at, will not leave it as long as their distressed friends calls for assistance."

This is the power which gives the decoy its effectiveness. Here is a deadly device literally baited with love. When, deep in some woodland by a quiet stretch of water, alert and expectant, hoping to surprise some wild thing in its secret maneuvers, I come suddenly upon a bunch of decoy ducks bobbing and leering like manikins, I am filled with resentment. There is something especially hateful to me about these painted dummies, representing, as they do, a malignant cunning whereby man ranges against another species its own altruistic impulses and puts devotion itself to perfidious use. A trap set with food catches the unwary animal in his effort to satisfy an egoistic appetite; so also with the wolf trap baited with the rutting odor of the female, although the method often used to secure this lure is too ghastly to describe in print; but the decoy derives its attraction from the gregarious instinct, parent of those moral motives which induce in man a regard for the interests of others—"spark of the divine," and placed by general consent on a pedestal above every other human virtue.

In cases of mutual advantage, or of even one-way benefits, association and amicability between or among entirely different species are easily explained. Along Bear Creek

[3]*Life Histories,* etc., Smithsonian Institution, Bulletin 176, p. 4ff.

this spring I have found small sandpipers in association with killdeer. They fly when the killdeer flies and settle down with him, because the killdeer act as sentinels for the smaller birds who keep their bills plunged down into mud and water up to their eyes, so busy feeding in this posture that they have no time to look around for possible enemies, and trust to their associate with his high-pitched voice to give any necessary alarm. There are many instances of one animal's standing guard—unintentionally, of course—for another species. There are two vegetarian ducks of different species in constant association in our southern waters, one an underwater feeder and another a surface feeder, because the underwater feeder grabbles aquatic plants, pieces of which float to the surface to be snapped up in the greedy bills of the species that doesn't like to dive for his dinner.

Down in the pasture I see at this moment cowbirds at the nose of a grazing cow, feeding along on insects which the beast is flushing from their hide-outs in the grass. I once found myself in association with hundreds of swallows on this same unilateral basis. The birds swarmed about me, darting uncomfortably close to my head in their ambition to be on really intimate terms with an animal of another species. When I stopped, they stopped; when I moved on, they played along with me. I was flattered by this attention, but a prosaic explanation of it arose when I noticed that my feet moving in the high grass started thousands of small and, to my eyes, almost invisible insects flying over the bluff. Since the swallow is not equipped to go after his insects in the grass, he welcomes assistance from any lumbering, big-footed land animal that happens to come along, man included.

Outside my window at the present moment, a solitary mockingbird sits on the topmost branch of a huge live oak and charges furiously down at any intruder, bird or other animal, that dares approach this particular tree. The browsing goat shuns his wrath, robins dodge, jays fly screaming away, while the ill-tempered isolationist returns from each foray to his perch, his spleen purged, apparently quieted in the consciousness of successful self-assertion.

This solitary outlaw has never surrendered his will to man, beast, or even a group of his own kind. Being now undisturbed for a little while, having for a moment or two experienced the feeling of mastery and of unchallenged lordship, this mocker has broken into song.

On the lawn fifty yards away is a "charm of goldfinch," as the English say, feeding amicably together. Occasionally, as one starts for a nearby tree, all rise, as at a given signal, and group themselves in an elm to feed upon the tender buds. These tiny birds, still in winter plumage, move together, feed together, rest together. They live in cohesion, in an atmosphere of complete sociability. They diffuse goodwill and mutual toleration. In sustained flight, however, the goldfinch becomes less cohesive. Flocks have a tendency to divide, and individual members move in an erratic manner inside the flock, darting here and there about the edges, as if the individual birds were resisting but unable to overcome the will of the flock. Starlings and waxwings, on the other hand, surrender themselves completely, fly as a unit, apparently subservient to a single will.

A few weeks from now hundreds of chipping sparrows will occupy this same lawn. They, too, feed on the tender grass shoots but not so close together—they space themselves fully twice as far apart as the goldfinch do. When the chippies rise, startled by something, they, too, seem to move at a given signal, but not all together. A group takes off here, a moment later another, and another, until they have all left the lawn. They will go to the same trees, but in this short flight the course of one individual will cross that of another. You do not get the impression here, as you do with goldfinch making this short flight, of automata pulled by one string.

Again, the chippies do not cluster themselves so compactly in the trees as goldfinch do, but spread their perching order. In short, the flock will has a looser hold upon the individual. There's a trifle, but not much of a trifle, less freedom of enterprise.

From the ragged formations of grackles stringing across the country—hardly to be called a flock at all—ready to fall to pieces any time, anywhere, to the regimented, mathematical designs of migrating geese, there is every gradation of flock form, from pure anarchy yielding itself little at a time to this mysterious will of the group until something resembling a flock appears, and on by easy gradations until the individual will fades out completely, and the group, so far as the act of flying is concerned, becomes an organism.

Last fall, all one morning, I watched white-fronted geese, thousands and thousands of them, coming into the bay near Austwell, Texas. There was a perfect discipline, not a feather out of line, until a flock descended to within about two hundred feet of a stretch of open water upon which it intended to alight. Then a curious thing occurs. The formation suddenly dissolves, and they all begin rolling over and over sideways until within a few feet of the water, where they straighten out and glide to rest as one expects normal geese to do.

It would seem to me that this tumbling, rolling, and cavorting in midair is an expression of the joy the individual feels in becoming once more a free agent. It may well be an expression of exhilaration in the recapture of his will from a domination to which he surrendered it in order to accomplish the long flight from the oncoming winter in his northern habitat to the safety of southern waters. It was like nothing else so much as a bunch of boys breaking out of school in late afternoon, freed from the day-long discipline, out in the open air at last for fun and frolic and the anarchy of individualistic expression.

Across the pasture I hear the raucous and continual cawing of crows. There is method in this apparently senseless cawing. It is not done just to irritate every man and beast within hearing distance, but for the purpose of maintaining contact among individuals widely separated. A crow becomes restive unless he can hear now and then the caw of another. Isolated and out of hearing, he soon seeks a perch within the sound of another's voice. If one crow finds food, he calls others to him, as jays do, participating share and share alike, until all appetites are satisfied or all the food is gone. They are just as sociable as the goldfinches, but their feeding habits compel, and the carrying power of their voices permit, dispersion over a wide area.

There is another bird on the Mexican border, the chachalaca, whose call permits an even wider dispersion. I have been told by credible observers that one of these birds will pick up another's call just as it ceases, carrying the same note on until another far away chimes in, thus making of the succession one continuous call stretching, so to speak, for miles and miles across the subtropical undergrowth in which the birds are hidden. It is thus co-operative, in a sense, and introduces between and among many individuals, secluded and lonesome, the fellowship of a game, like a party line relieving the tedium of the rural housewife's daily duties.

This is all a way of life worked out as a part of nature's plan. As, in an individual life, there is a principle of unity and symmetry always active, always harmonizing and constraining anarchic forces, bringing them into due subordination, so in the whole of nature, as diverse and contradictory as it may appear in any partial view, there is a "dark, inscrutable workmanship that reconciles discordant elements."

"Praise Allah," says the Arab proverb, "for the infinite diversity of his handiwork"—and also, we may add, for multitudinous evidences of design. We understand associations such as I have been describing only because we experience them. Alliances, mutual dependencies, parasitisms, preyer and preyed-on, linkages joining into one chain a dozen widely differentiated forms, and other relationships amazingly intricate weave all life, animal and vegetable, into the unity of one vast organism. It is exciting, especially

when we of more mystical inclinations fancy we feel a pulse of sympathy beating through it all. "I could not," says Spinoza, "separate God from Nature."

An English professor whom I much admired in college days used to be fond of reading to his classes Browning's "An Epistle, Containing the Strange Medical Experience of Karshish, the Arab Physician." It was many years before I understood why his voice invariably broke and tears filled his eyes as he read the closing lines:

> "So, the All-Great were the All-Loving too—
> So, through the thunder comes a human voice
> Saying, 'O heart I made a heart beats here!' "

9. Denatured Chickens

More than anything else, I miss from the barnyard of the farmstead where I am at present staying the hen and chickens of my boyhood's home. Although hundreds of chickens are raised to broilers, fryers, and adulthood, there is no hen clucking around with her cluster of animated puffballs. Visiting the mechanized farm of the present, I cannot "behold the parent hen amid her brood."

I miss the industrious scratching, the rapid-fire cluck which calls the scattered chicks to come at once and get a piece of the newly uncovered worm. I miss seeing the soothing alternation of exercise and rest—the hen in hovering posture with the little ones nudging in among her feathers for a nap, a head protruding here and there, sleepy-eyed. There were always two or three adventurous chicks who climbed atop, warming their dew-chilled feet against the mother's skin as they nestled down amid the feathers. This particular staging lingers in my memory as one of the more appealing of all barnyard idyls. The spring barnyard without hen and chickens has lost no little of its ancient charm.

My mother had among her many brooding hens a large, stately Plymouth Rock, nicknamed the "old forty-eight hen," because one spring this creature was given a brood of forty-eight which she reared without losing a one. Nearly every hen on our place had her points which were discussed with interest and great partiality by respective members of the household.

Hens, as well as other farm animals, were individualized, and even though it involved some nature-faking, still it established and maintained a bond of sympathy which unified the cluster of animals round about into a kind of family, with human beings—not so much set apart—crowning the consociation. The discovery of traits and the personalizing of farmyard fowl, giving certain outstanding individuals a more or less appropriate name, is a pleasure which mechanized chicken-raising has destroyed.

Our whole family was greatly concerned during the brooding period. There was the anxious watching of the calendar for the twenty-one-day interval to be up, the occasional inspection to see if the hen was covering all the eggs and whether or not she had broken any. Some hens break many, some break few, some break none. I spied on the nest to catch the brooding hen in the act of solemnly turning over each egg, an observation which was my introduction to instinct, as such. How, I asked myself, could the hen know that the eggs needed turning? More remarkable still, how could the pullet on her first setting know that the eggs must be turned and how often they should be turned? I didn't know then; I don't know now. But my wonder was excited.

Wonders never cease, but the capacity of the average person for wondering declines. How could the setting hen know that there was no time to lose, as she foraged for food, rushing here and there, flustered, hurried, gobbling up whatever scattered grain was available, and racing back to her nest? The sense of wonder in certain individuals becomes, on the other hand, more and more sensitive and excitable, as their eyes continue to dwell upon the works of nature, and they persist throughout life in asking questions which some people choose to term childish. Outstanding among such wonderers and questioners is William Blake. His "Tiger, Tiger, Burning Bright" is a series of questions which any intelligent child might ask and which, like intelligent children's questions, have a deceptive superficiality. These queries are as valid today as they were in Blake's time which antedated "the wonderful century" of science. Science explains little, or comparatively little. It concerns itself merely with a few steps in a process, backward or forward or both, in no case joining up more than a few links in the infinite chain of causation.

And now come the thrills of the hatching period! On the morning of the twenty-first day, I followed my mother to the nest and saw her lift the clucking and gently protesting creature, catching sight of two, three, or half a dozen little fellows still damp from the moisture of the shell. Gathered into an apron, the new life was put into a safe, warm place to await the tardy ones, upon whose arrival the whole brood was given back to the mother hen. This coming to life was another never-ceasing wonder of my boyhood, a cycle which is rudely broken in the farmsteads to which I have access at present.

I got into an exchange of views about chicken-raising with a little boy from a neighboring farm, the other day, and found out to my surprise that he had never seen a hen and chickens. His mama took her eggs to Petmecky's, and there they put 'em in a big box—he had seen it himself—and hatched 'em out for her. I tried to tell him how the normal, unmechanized hen acted with her brood, but he objected that his mama's didn't do that way. He was like the sailor lad who, having never before seen a horse and buggy, couldn't for the life of him understand how they could guide the thing without a rudder. The interchange soon got down to the his-mama-did-and-my-mama-didn't stage and ended thus futilely.

From this clicking of gadgets, lights on, lights off, filling this trough with mash and another with water, emptying and scraping dung trays—from all this deadly, mechanical routine of chicken-raising on the mechanized farm, especially in suburban areas, I miss the motherly concern of the hen as you approach her brood or as any possible enemy approaches them. What a laugh I got, as a boy, when an incautious and good-natured pup of mine, meaning no harm but out of mere idle curiosity, sniffed a little too near the sacred brood, and the hen flew raging into his face, driving him, tail between legs, under the house! The hen with chicks presents the very incarnation of solicitude, moving about here and there among the farm animals, now and then flustering up her feathers belligerently, and now making a strategic retreat with sharp, warning clucks to the little ones to get right out of here, and quickly.

As the chicks grew older, more athletic and enterprising, I remember the exciting chase after the fleeing insect, the capture, the dispute, and tug of war between two or more over the corpus.

I remember, as many others do, the approach of the storm, lowering clouds and threatening thunder, and the anxious precautions of the mother hen herding her chicks into the coop. The storm over, you see the tentative exit, the fearful glances at the sky to be sure the danger had passed, the exuberance of the little ones rushing here and there, when the temporary confinement was over, but still restrained by the incessant warnings of the mother hen clucking constantly in their ears, "Children, do this, don't do that, come here, go there," on tenterhooks for fear the dampness will give her charges their death of cold. At least, this is the interpretation you, as a child, placed on all this fussing and to-do.

In modern suburban poultry-raising, so far as I have observed it, these spiritual values have been allowed to escape along with much of the mineral and vitamin content of poultry considered solely as produce.

As a matter of fact, man has made a cuckoo of the hen on a scale far vaster than any cuckoldry as yet known in nature, unless there is something comparable to it among insects whose world is still largely an undiscovered one. The hen has become parasitical upon a mechanical gadget. The sum of animal enjoyment destroyed by our interference in the course of nature in this instance alone is incalculable, constituting debits which never appear in the cost-accounting of scientific poultry-raising.

It is fashionable in the modern literature of agriculture to refer to the farm as a "manufacturing plant," and to a large extent it is becoming one. In this transformation one of the most ancient, delightful, and effective educational institutions that civilized man has ever known is warped away from an understanding sympathy with the animal world and into an education in the utilization of mechanical forces. There may be an educational gain in so far as the pure intellect is concerned, but there is a loss on the emotional side which tends to dehumanize those involved in the work. Of course, there cannot be any going back, but there should be a compensation introduced into the education of the young in the way of natural history studies in order to preserve some sparks of that emotional sympathy which was developed between man and the animals about the farm in the agelong processes of domestication—an emotional sympathy, not only with the domesticated animals themselves, but through them, a tenderer regard for the whole of the animate world. The "loves" in the human heart brought to flower by the domestication are a precious link joining us to the lower animals which we can ill afford to lose.

Lately I passed by a negro cabin in the Colorado River bottom, and happened to notice a lot of fine Rhode Island Red hens feeding out in the pasture. It occurred to me that here would be a good place to buy some vitaminized and mineralized eggs from naturally fed and contented hens, so I stopped and engaged an aged Negro in talk about eggs.

I asked him if his hens, running out, ate bugs and grasshoppers.

"Naw, suh," replied the wily old fellow, thinking that I,

a city man in a shiny automobile, objected to eggs produced with such food, "dey skasely evah touches a wum or anything like dat. Mos' time I keeps 'em up and feeds 'em sto'-bought food."

"I was in hope," said I with an appearance of disappointment, "that I could get some eggs from those fine, healthy hens with the flavor of real country eggs, like the ones I was raised on. At home, when I was a boy, our hens used to get plenty of bugs and grasshoppers and worms, and they laid the best-flavored eggs I ever ate."

"Jes' zactly what I allus say," he agreed, ignoring without embarrassment his sales talk of a moment ago. "Jes zactly what I allus say," he repeated. "Dem deep-yellow-yolked eggs comes from hens dat run out, and dem pale-yellow-yolked eggs comes from sto'-bought food. I seen it a thousand times. And you oughta see dese hens o' mine ketchin' dem bugs an' grasshoppers in de early mawnin' when dey fust gits out. Dey's got 'em pretty well ketched up by dis time o' day, an' dey's jes' grass-grazin' now."

His reversed sales talk was more convincing. I bought three dozen, all he had, and they were really "dem deep-yellow-yolked eggs" and certainly worth more than I paid.

The laboratory-vitamin expert will lift an eyebrow at the rough-and-ready technique with which the old darky and I disposed of the vitamin-and-mineral-content matter. But, whether or not scientific chicken-farming sacrifices vitamin and mineral content, I know that it sacrifices much of the poetry of poultry.

Your poultry expert will generally warn you against the flavors of flesh grown on the knockabout poultry of the farmyard. I remember all about chickens fattened on army worms, as does every other person who grew up near a cotton patch. But a few weeks' finishing-off of these chickens on grain reduces the army-worm flavor to something delightfully "wild," just as garlic, although impossible taken straight, will, if rubbed around the edges of the mixing bowl, impart a not unpleasant savor to the salad; or as the odor of musk, duly attenuated, gives a special deliciousness to the more expensive perfumes.

The element of surprise is as essential to a really enjoyable meal as it is to a successful dramatic performance. It is a mistake to reduce the savor of all chicken to the dead level of the simply tolerable. The palate should be seized by an unexpected attack. This is what gives game its appeal. The diet of the mallard is unsupervised: he feedeth as he listeth upon dead salmon, beechnuts, acorns, slugs, snails, frogs, lizards, usually topping off in the stubble of grain fields— wheat, barley, corn, and rice. Think of trying to eat penned-up and mash-fed mallards! Investigations of the United States Biological Survey have shown that at times sixty to seventy per cent of the food of the canvasback, as well as that of other diving ducks, consists of wild celery and varieties of pondweed, which, in the opinion of Dr. Thomas S. Roberts, accounts for the fine flavor of the flesh of these ducks. Dr. Roberts reports also that the flesh of pintails feeding on bulbs and roots of pondweeds in a rank-smelling slough acquired such a strong, marshy odor and taste as to be hardly edible at all.

Wild turkey, most delicious of meats, has one flavor if the mast of oak and pecans is plentiful, and another when forced to grains, berries, plant tops and grasshoppers. Of course, an accidental superfluity of some food may render the taste of game unpleasant, but that is a natural hazard one must take if he wants to humor his palate with the delights of the unpredictable.

But savor is not all; the consistency of meat is just as important. "Tenderize" has become a word to conjure with in chicken-shack advertising, as if all the teeth of the world had suddenly started abscessing, and as if all the jaw muscles in the world had become paralyzed. Either this, or we are mollycoddling our organs of mastication by giving them nothing whatever to do. One sips soup, mouths mush, *chews* meat. There is hope for a nation that still prefers its corn on the cob. The jaws do a noble work.

Chickens are now battery-raised.[1]

A battery is an enormous cage of many divisions, each compartment with a water trough down one side and a feeding trough down the other, with holes above the troughs just large enough to permit the incarcerated victim to stick his head through and thus gain access to food and drink. Into these cells, wards, or compartments chicks are received from the brooder—literally stuffed in almost too thick to stir with a stick. As they grow, they are thinned out by transferring some of them to other compartments, giving more space per chicken, merely to prevent their actually squeezing each other to death. Transfer after transfer is made until the chicks become broilers and fryers, never in all their lives having had quite enough room in which to turn around comfortably.

The object of this lifelong squeezing process is to prevent exercise which might interfere with the production of fat. So the modern, scientifically reared chicken is born of an incubator, is immediately transferred to a brooder, kept there until he is too tight a fit, moved on to a compartment in a battery, and then from one crowded ward to another only a fraction less jammed, until the employee in a city produce house mercifully slits his throat.

I have looked attentively at chickens raised in this fashion, and to me they seem to be unhappy and in poor health. Their combs are dull and lifeless except for glaring and unnatural patches of color that appear occasionally. I have seen the face and combs an ashy gray with subtended wattles a brilliant vermilion. Their faces thus splotched with aberrant coloring are all the more ghastly on account of the absence of face feathers which have been rubbed off from sticking their heads through too small holes in order to get at the mash and water.

The movements of these birds are generally sluggish.

[1]Conceived originally as a backyard industry on a city lot, the battery has been spread by skilful advertising to farm and ranch. On farmsteads where a reasonable number of chickens could be reared on grass, weeds, worms, bugs, and waste from kitchen and cow lot, the battery is installed, and the farmer reduced to dependence upon a feed store.

Sometimes one gets down and can't get up: the bones in his legs are too limber. Throughout their lives they are soft and fat: you rarely see one in the naked gangling stage so familiar to anyone accustomed to normally grown chickens. They get a prepared food—a growing mash, it is called— whose sole end and aim must be to produce weight, for the chicken is sold by the pound, not per unit of mineral, per unit of vitamin, or per unit of flavorsomeness, if it were possible to apply unit measurement to the fragrance of a rose or the taste of proper chicken. How weary, stale, flat, and unprofitable in comparison do all the uses of pampered poultry appear to me! How mushy, how lacking in savor of the yellow-legged roamer of Sunday-dinner-for-the-parson fame!

The battery chickens I have observed seem to lose their minds about the time they would normally be weaned by their mothers and off in the weeds chasing grasshoppers on their own account. Yes, literally, actually, the battery becomes a gallinaceous madhouse. The eyes of these chickens through the bars gleam like those of maniacs. Let your hand get within reach and it receives a dozen vicious pecks—not the love peck or the tentative peck of idle curiosity bestowed by the normal chicken, but a peck that means business, a peck for flesh and blood, for which in their madness they are thirsting. They eat feathers out of each other's backs or, rather, pull out each other's feathers and nibble voraciously at the roots of the same for tiny blobs of flesh and blood that may adhere thereto.

They have stampedes. With no apparent cause a wave of hysteria sweeps over the whole battery: wild, unnatural chirps, jumbled screams, and a fluttering as if every feather on every chicken had become possessed and frantic.

It is no wonder these chickens are driven crazy. Battery life is one frustration after another. Just out of the egg, moist, incubator-hatched, their first instinctive desire is for the breast of the mother and the feathered, drying warmth which it supplies. Instead, the newly hatched chick finds himself crowded into a cage with other chicks just his size, all chirping as plaintively and ineffectually as he does. Instead of the mellow, motherly cluck of the hen falling reassuringly upon his ears, he hears nothing but the complaints of a hundred of his fellows as uncomfortably quartered as he is, along with the steady, monotonous drone of the electric heating device.

The nervous and muscular mechanism which responds to the scratching instinct is immediately defeated. Chicks are not provided with solid ground or with solid anything else to stand on. For convenience in cleaning the battery, their feet must rest on net wire with mesh large enough for droppings to fall through to the dung pan immediately below.

The next instinct to awaken is the following instinct. Any normal chick wants to follow something. I have seen them, in the absence of the mother hen, follow a dog, a cat, or a human being. This instinct the battery nips in the bud. There cannot be even token following in a battery.

There is no way of knowing how keen a sense of smell a chicken has, or if he has a sense of smell corresponding in any way to our own. But if he does have this sense, it is constantly flouted and outraged by keeping his nose practically in his own dung. Constant droppings of the confined chickens in any one division of the battery is caught warm and steaming in the dung pan resting within an inch or two of the wire netting on which they stand. All day and every day and all night the temperature is kept at about 80 degrees, which gives the odor of the excreta a maximum intensity.

The nervous mechanism of the chick—and of every member of the family of birds to which he belongs, for that matter—is geared to successive frights followed by periods of security. The hen issues from her coop in the morning followed by her hungry brood, scratching, clucking. Presently you hear the here-is-a-worm cluck, and the whole brood forms a close circle around the mother's vigorously dissecting bill, and preserves this concentration until the morsel is distributed and consumed. Then the assembly is dispersed in search of another worm or other food, and so on. Suddenly, out of nowhere, the shadow of a hawk!—and the mother issues a warning note upon which every chick, in fright of its life, rushes to her for protection. The danger past, they go again awandering. This is repeated in a state of nature perhaps a dozen times a day. The scare-safety mechanism which nature has given them, a biological inheritance, is completely frustrated in the battery: no scare, no safety—just a dead level of tenacious and maddening discomfort, nothing more. It is the perversion of this instinct, I think, which accounts for the sudden and unmotivated panics already mentioned. As is the way with biologically determined habits denied expression and use, they exhibit themselves sooner or later in abnormal behavior.

It is much the same with the exercise-rest rhythm. After scratching about the farmyard for a little while, letting the brood run wild, the mother hen selects a safe place and utters her hovering call, and here the little ones come for their rest period, nestling under the maternal feathers. There is an alternation, a tiring and a rest, a dispersal for the one and a concentration for the other, a pulsation, a timed and regular beat throughout the daylight hours.

How rudely has man devised to tear apart this instinct, beautiful to think upon as are all the wise and noble—I had almost said *humane*—contrivances of nature! Since sleeping during the daylight hours is impossible in any madhouse, you would think the brooder-battery chick would be permitted the boon of insensibility during the night. If you think so, you have underestimated man's avidity for fat and poundage. Man has devised an infernal contraption which automatically flashes on a bright light at regular intervals, on and off throughout the night. This is to awaken the chicks and tempt them to eat. It is feared that they might sleep off some of their fat, and fat, pure fat, weight, pounds and ounces, that's what the machine is after and nothing else.

Thus every sound, natural, instinctive chick inclination

or impulse is thwarted, every normal motion is torn asunder, defeated or perverted by a fiendish ingenuity intent on marketable fat and on nothing else.

And let not the urban citizen gather any unction to himself at this exposé of rural indifference to humane considerations in the rearing of domesticated animals. The life of the apartment-reared poodle offers almost an exact parallel to that of the battery-raised chicken, in so far as stuffing and confinement and the thwarting of instinct are concerned. What city-dweller has not had the embarrassment, during his early-morning walk, of meeting the leash-led poodle, humbled and hangdog, sniffing from one side of the sidewalk to the other, tripping his attendant and forcing him to change hands with the leash, pursuing an eternal and never-satisfied search, sniffing with his clogged nostrils, impelled by an ancient instinct to try to exercise, even under the handicap of his apartment distemper, a nasal discrimination in a matter to which the whole dog world assigns the greatest importance! It is embarrassing to me, to the attendant, and to the dog. A philanthropist of London, touched to the bottom of his heart by this canine tragedy, set up an endowment a few years ago to plant and maintain a mile-long row of trees, each tree in a huge tub of soil, along the solidly paved streets of an apartment area which he frequented.

I read this section to a friend, a humanitarian, hoping to stir in him some of the indignation I feel, since indignation loves company, and thrives and multiplies upon it. I had hoped to see him exhibit fury, outrage. But nothing of the sort showed up. At the conclusion of my impassioned rendering, this friend of mine, who happens to be a professor of educational psychology, remarked quietly: "What's the use of getting all het up about the life of a battery chick or an apartment poodle? We city people serve our own children almost as badly. Our apartment houses are the human batteries we stuff our children in, landlords permitting, to experience a life fuller of thwartings than that of your battery-raised chickens, for the simple reason that the child has more impulses, instincts, emotions, more 'desires and dreams and powers,' than the chick has, and an infinitely greater ingenuity and tenacity in beating against the bars in an attempt to exercise them."

And again all this emotional upset which I personally experience may come from merely a nostalgic backward-looking. Incubators may be as cherishable by another generation as the brooding hen snugly nested is to mine. Recollections of brooder and battery will be as pleasing, perhaps, to the gray-haired of 1970 as memories of nest and coop are to me. But I believe I shall leave it to the poets of that generation to celebrate the beauties of mechanized poultry-raising, songs of the balanced mash, poems of the fat-producing regime.

Besides, authors are usually unusually squeamish people; and when they turn their eyes from the stars toward the preparation of foods, they are apt to see and magnify things ordinary people pass without notice. Even the greatest of them cannot seem to attain the emotional stability of a genuinely scientific outlook. Thoreau, although a native in "the land of the bean and the cod," was turned from the latter article by seeing workmen spitting tobacco saliva on the codfish as they forked them from huge piles into wheelbarrows. Tolstoy, visiting an abattoir, was horrified by workmen wading around ankle-deep in blood, and returned to his study to thunder forever afterward in behalf of vegetarianism. Upton Sinclair turned the stomach of the nation completely over by overrealistic reporting of what he saw in a Chicago packing house. Even ordinary people are sometimes affected. A housewife is often unable to eat the chicken she has dressed for dinner. A Korean proverb advises him who would enjoy his dinner to avoid peeping over the kitchen wall. An advertisement which pictured a fattened hog in his muddy sty in one corner of the page, contrasted with the delicate bloom of a cotton stalk in another corner, bearing the legend, "Pure Cottonseed Oil; Contains no Hog-fat,"—that advertisement, appearing for a few years in all the principal papers and magazines of the country, turned the whole nation from one shortening and cooking grease to another.

One item not always included in the expense of raising denatured chickens is the rather considerable one of medical treatment. There's a lotion for every bruise, a pill for every digestive disorder, and a hypo-shot for every disease-contingency. The medicine shelf of the battery is quite impressive and must yield no little profit to the drug trade. There is no old-time family doctor to visit the ailing lad with that prescription magical for the youngster but profitless for the prescriber, "Exercise in the sun and fresh air and let him have what he wants to eat," written out in English, not in Greek. So certainly the feed trade should be backed up by the drug trade in encouraging the chicken-raiser to become more and more dependent upon them, and in advertising to enlarge the consumer market.

And just what does the customer who buys these crazed, doped, stuffed, abnormally fat, soft chickens get out of all this? Well, science says he gets just as good food as if the chickens were grown in a state of nature. The food expert will say, "Oh, yes, the vitamin-mineral content of these fryers is just as high, perhaps higher, than in poultry produced in the premechanized era." Hotels and restaurants and the ubiquitous chicken-shack advertise such chicken as tenderized, as indeed it is.

Frankly, I don't believe what the experts tell us about this. The science which is principally concerned with commercial profit has an awful case of big-head and has become intolerant of any suggestion coming from the laity. If, with no array of statistics, no graphs, none of the parade or paraphernalia of research, you even suggest that this science might have overlooked something, you are set down as an ignoramus: and if you introduce any humanitarian consideration, you are catalogued not only as an ignoramus, but as a slushy sentimentalist, on a par with the circulation-hungry newspaper that raises a hue and cry against vivi-section.

This is true, of course, only of the science in whose results profit is at stake. There is another science, as everyone knows, of quite different character and outlook. The man who tries to make fun of Science is a fool. Science is sacro-sanct, but scientists are not; and especially not are those scientists who have been bitten by the commercial worm and tend sometimes to prostitute science by calling it "ap-plied." These may profess science in season and out, and may even be professors of science, but they are guilty of the same kind of desecration which gave English the word "pro-fane." A certain kind of science defends cigarette-smoking, whisky-drinking, patent-medicine fakes, adulterated foods, low valuations for tax-purposes of corporate assets, and the like. Indeed, lawyers as well as advertisers have found out that experts can be secured on either side of any case in-volving the so-called "facts of science" which happens to become tangled up in some way with profits. All that goes by the name of applied science is not so. Here's much bastardy claiming kin, as is usual in such cases, with re-spectability, but upon grounds which tend to melt away as the claims are examined with any care. Profit, or some form of self-interest, will be found to be the sire of most of these off-strains.

The science here involved in stuffing chickens has an eye too much, it seems to me, on production, sales, and profits. Hence let us take its conclusions with a grain of salt and remember that even laboratory demonstrations are not con-clusive when applied to the rough-and-ready procedures of the food processor and the farmstead.

I was observing a woman dressing one of her battery-raised fryers the other day. She held up the entrails and ex-claimed with satisfaction, "See what a wonderful lot of fat," and indeed there was a lot of it.

"But," she said doubtfully, "they haven't put on the weight they should. I haven't been able to get any grain."

"What!" said I, alert and scenting some meat for my argument. "I thought your mash had everything in it necessary for producing a perfect chicken."

"Well," she replied, "it should have, but lately this old mash we've been getting is poor quality. When you find ground-up cornstalks and binder twine in your mash, you know that doesn't help your chickens any."

Your fryer doesn't come to your kitchen tagged with the food elements he has received since leaving the shell signed and certified to by a food inspector responsible only to the United States Government. "Man is literally made from the dust of the earth," says Dr. Alexis Carrel. "For this reason his physiological and mental activities are profoundly influenced by the geological constitution of the country where he lives, by the nature of the animals and plants on which he generally feeds."

It is easy to say that the vitamin content or mineral content is just as high in the mash-fed as in the chicken that gets his natural food in a natural way, but the fact is that all the vitamins have not yet been isolated. Several others are suspected to exist. Until a complete vitamin list is available, how can one say, comparing two foods, that the vitamin content of one is just as high as that of the other? Moreover, research has not yet presented us with a complete survey of the results of every vitamin and the results of all permutations and combinations of vitamins. We are led to believe by some vitamin advertising that it's not necessary anyway to get your vitamins in food since you can get them much more easily, if more expensively, by taking pills.

Let us rear a monument here to the Unknown Vitamin and place a wreath reverently at its base. Perhaps it lies concealed in the body of a grasshopper or other insect, so securely imprisoned that only the digestive apparatus of the chicken can make it available for men. It may be that this vitamin is the one, and the only one, which awakens a glandular action inspiring sensitized souls to write great poetry and music or paint great pictures. A mockingbird turns today's bug into tomorrow's song almost while you wait. No mash-fed mocker could ever sing a decent song.

Food has a lot to do with art. Aubrey Beardsley used to eat a pound of raw meat before going to bed in order to get from nightmares ideas for drawing the following day. Quite

"Let us rear a monument here to the Unknown Vitamin" . . .

competent physiologists give the Carnivorous School considerable comfort by pointing out that dominant nations as well as dominant classes in society, euphemisms for "master-races," are most generally meat eaters. Vegetarians have their scientists also; but whichever one is right, it seems that both sides are agreed that it is at least not ridiculous to contend for spiritual values in food.

Cattle raisers, I am told, are experimenting with injections which by disturbing certain glands cause the injectee to become abnormally large in a comparatively short period. Human beings with this symptom are said to be afflicted with elephantiasis. Producing in an animal a disease which makes two pounds of meat grow where one grew before will become quite profitable, provided the injections which produce the disease cost less than the cost of the food it would require to deliver an equal poundage of marketable meat. Selective breeding is producing animals so heavy that they can't stand up.

But civilized man cannot take exclusive credit for discovering all the devices for outwitting the normal food bill, and tenderizing the flesh of animals into a delicacy for the epicure. Travelers report that certain savage tribes in the mountainous areas of the Philippines eat their dogs. A normally fed, exercised, and therefore muscular dog, however, doesn't appeal to the savage palate. So the dog-raiser has learned to pound him before killing, as the housewife pounds a cheap round steak with a rolling pin. The animal is mauled with a stick a few days before slaughtering, so that he comes to the butcher swelled up to nearly twice his normal size and tenderized. No tests have yet been made to determine the vitamin or mineral content of mauled as compared with unmauled dog.

The farm turkeys are in somewhat better case than the chickens en route to tenderization. Little more than their chickhood is spent in crowded confinement. Month-olders are put out in a pen where they have greater freedom of movement and, a month or so later, are permitted to roam and feed as normal turkeys would.

There is, however, another intervention by man in the modern breeding of turkeys which is an offense against good taste, aesthetically speaking. I refer to the saddling of the turkey hens. They sew pads of ten-ounce duck on the backs of turkey hens to keep the gobblers from treading the skin off their backs—"skinning 'em alive," so to speak.

I sense sex discrimination here. Every other season, at

least, I think this protection should come from sewing gloves on the feet of the gobblers.

Had Ben Franklin had his way, the turkey gobbler would have been named our national bird instead of the bald eagle which, Franklin complains, not only is a thief but eats carrion. Had he been successful in getting this suggestion adopted, the gobbler as a national bird would never, in my opinion, have survived the feminist movement in this country, for of all the birds and beasts known to man, none treats the female of his species with more disdain.

Under modern, high-pressure chicken-raising, the stock hens of the farmstead do not have a great deal to complain of. They are permitted to run out, secure natural food in the natural way, cackle upon laying an egg, and in some cases steal their nests off in the bushes. They are denied, however, the privilege of setting, and as the season progresses they become harder and harder to break. Placed in confinement, they proceed to "set" on the floor of the coop. Turn them out after a week, and they go right back to the nest, determined to have their way. One farm woman told me that the only way to break them is to duck them in a tub of cold water. Another said the floor of the coop should be slatted or, better still, made of hardware cloth, so that when the determined setter sets herself down to "set" it out in the coop, the cold air from underneath, penetrating her under feathers, cools the setting fever effectually.

I should think that the continual rearing of chicks from incubators for generation after generation, short-circuiting the setting instinct and destroying the survival-value of conscientious setting, would finally weaken or perhaps destroy this instinct altogether. The geneticist should be able to offer an opinion worth considering on this point. If my supposition is true, we should then have to go back to India and capture some wild chickens and begin the process of domestication all over again, in case a demand arose for brooding hens.

Sole among the domestic fowl of the suburban chicken farm which the evils of mechanization have not yet touched is the stock rooster. He still stalks with his ancient pride of mastership over the whole barnyard. With orgulous disdain of all other creatures as beneath and unworthy his notice, he carries himself with his accustomed deliberation and aplomb, as if incubator, brooder, and battery had never invaded and revolutionized the world over which he knows he was born to preside. He eats, crows, scratches, and clucks up his dependents, and performs his other functions gallantly unaware of, or sublimely ignoring, the frustrations of his hens and the degradation of his progeny. His strut is an expression of overweening pride which so far has failed to precede a fall. Armored with an obsession of his own importance, he is proof against any criticism or ridicule that might break the spell. He still treads the barnyard stage with unshaken confidence that the sun rises because he crows.

10. Davis Mountains[1] Holiday: En Route

Toward the end of each August I have an attack of Davis Mountain Fever. Nothing will do it any good except a visit there for a week or two weeks, or just as long as I feel that I can afford to stay.

The summer tourist with Davis Mountains as a destination is *forced* into an enjoyment of immediate and quite surprising contrasts, since every approach, except by air, is so guarded that he is fairly exhausted by the time he gets there. It is a long pilgrimage from any one of the more popu-

[1]"The Davis Mountains of southwestern Texas . . . are made up of a rugged and irregular mass of igneous rocks surrounded by a relatively level plain. The main mountain mass lies mostly above an altitude of 5000 feet and consists, for the most part, of rugged peaks and ridges alternating with broad smooth valleys. This area is about thirty-five miles wide from east to west and about forty-five miles long from north to south. The eastern part of the area is more sharply dissected than are the western and southern parts, where the broadest intermontane valleys exist. Several peaks are two thousand to three thousand feet above the surrounding country. The several intermittent streams in the region have cut narrow steep-walled canyons. There are varying outlying peaks and ridges, particularly east of the mountain mass." *A Contribution to the Ecology and Faunal Relationships of the Mammals of the Davis Mountain Region, Southwestern Texas.* Miscellaneous Publications, Museum of Zoology, University of Michigan, No. 46. University of Michigan Press, June 28, 1940.

I suppose that it is technically correct to say that the Davis Mountains are in "southwestern" Texas, since they lie just south of the thirty-first parallel which exactly bisects Texas. However, it is twenty-one times the distance from their eastern extremity due east to the Sabine River as it is from their western limit due west to the Rio Grande. Therefore, it throws the casual reader considerably off balance to speak of the Davis Mountains lying in *south*western rather than in *western* Texas. Courtesy Museum of Zoology, University of Michigan.

lous centers in Texas. I have tried every route. Coming in by the Del Rio-Devil's River way, you get to see the awful gash cut in the stone by the lower reaches of the Pecos; and you have hills chalky and for the most part barren and "not worth a damn," a cowboy told me, "except to hold the world together." These white hills are hot and monotonous, and the road weaves around and over them, and then along and across flat-bottomed arroyos channeled out by freshets on their way to the Rio Grande. Finally, somewhere between Sanderson and Marathon, the whitish soil turns red, gray hills turn green, and you have reached the tip of a cool finger of the Rockies. Now for fifty miles or so the hills become higher and greener, and the air is sweeter and cooler. The introduction by this route is more gradual, hence the contrast is slightly dulled.

From the west—that is, from El Paso—the road courses the Rio Grande for nearly a hundred miles, keeping to the edge of the desiccated foothills while yet in sight of river verdure which serves to underscore the desert and make the traveler more fully conscious of it. Finally this highway cuts through the breaks to Van Horn, and then follows another hundred miles, mostly desert, rather featureless. Of course, one might trickle down from New Mexico through the Guadalupe Mountains due south, but, once in the pleasant Guadalupes, the temptation is to let well enough alone and camp there for the duration. There remains Highway 290, due west from Austin, which runs across the Edwards Plateau to Sheffield, bad enough in August, and then for a hundred and fifty miles the country is typical Trans-Pecos.

I prefer the road of the most violent contrasts: the Bankhead Highway, U.S. No. 80 to Pecos, thence south to Balmorrhea and on up Limpia Canyon into the mountains.

I can assure the August tourist that, if he takes this route, he will arrive well-baked, so weary from looking over plains alternating with greasewood flats glazed with alkali, and peering into the mirage shimmering down long stretches of overheated pavement, that his eyes will welcome anything to lean upon. When, finally, the mountains are recognized—

first mistaken for a bank of cloud along the southwestern horizon—the spell begins to take hold.

This past summer I left Dallas and the Trinity Bottom one bright August morning and, driving conservatively, reached Sweetwater for lunch. I faced the sun that afternoon for another two hundred miles and still had enough energy left to make camp on my own power among the sand dunes near Monahans. I left the highway, following an old road which led me to the site of some wildcatter's dream and disillusionment, a cleared-out space among the dunes littered with oil-drilling debris.

I found myself in the midst of a miniature forest of oak and mesquite.[2] Each dune is crowned by an oak tree, ten to twenty-four inches tall, loaded with acorns. Interspersed among the oaks and towering above them is scrub mesquite,

[2]This area is sometimes, but incorrectly, referred to as *chaparral,* which suggests denser and higher growth. As I have heard this term used since childhood, it suggests to me a growth dense enough to offer some difficulty in traversing, about as tall as a man on horseback, and more often green than not. These oaks of the Monahans sands are not dense, not tall, not evergreen. Mesquite is the predominate growth here, and I have never heard mesquite referred to as chaparral. J. Frank Dobie gives me the following note on this widely and variously used term:

"The suffix *al* in Spanish means *pertaining to;* thence, *a place where,* or *place of. Encino* (oak); *encinal,* place of oaks, or collection (*motte*) of oaks. *Mesquite* is a tree; *mesquital,* an extense or thicket of mesquites. And so on.

"*Chaparro* is a bush, any bush, as used by the Mexicans. Mexican usage differs from Spanish usage as much as American usage differs from English as exampled by the English 'cowboy' who barefooted and afoot drove the lowing herd slowly o'er the lea and the wild Texas cowboy spurring the guts out of a Mexican bronx, roping wild bulls, and letting daylight into some Tonk's liver with his sixshooter.

"So chaparral means an extense of bushes, or, perhaps, place of bushes. The ranch people in the Brush Country of Texas use chaparral in two ways: (1) to designate what the Mexicans call *chaparro prieto,* or black brush, *Acacia amentacea;* (2) to designate thorny brush in general. However, no one to the manor born would call a mesquite thicket 'chaparral.' We speak of a 'white brush thicket,' a 'coma thicket,' 'granjeno thicket,' etc. and very often of a 'chaparral thicket,' meaning thicket of the *chaparro prieto* (black chaparral). In southern California chaparral means the manzanita. Nobody in the Southwest has any idea of *oak* when he hears or uses the word chaparral."

heavy with clusters of long, yellowish beans hanging nearly to the ground.

I venture the statement, without research, that in no other forested section, the Amazon Valley not excepted, is there to be found a higher proportion of fruit to wood than in this Lilliputian jungle in the northern portion of Ward County. Vegetatively considered, it is as much a natural curiosity as the Painted Desert or the wonder-areas of Yellowstone. This hummocky expanse of stunted growths, or an ample sample of it, should be reserved and protected as a state or national park.

Dr. B. C. Tharp informs me that the little oak (*Quercus havardii*) is confined to the sandy South Plains of Texas and of eastern New Mexico. Rarely reaching a height of thirty inches, its slender stems arise from a thick rootstock buried four to eight inches below the surface. It bears a fat acorn nearly an inch long and more than half an inch thick. Thus the old proverb, "Great oaks from little acorns grow," is reversed in this topsy-turvy land where only miniature oaks from giant acorns grow.

The transformations of the genus Quercus as one passes from East to West Texas is a demonstration in ecology that he who runs may read. Other genera doubtless present as conspicuous adaptations to the practiced eye of the botanist, but not to the casual observer, for oaks are spectacular, even dramatic.

Certainly the live oak (*Quercus virginiana*), noblest tree of Texas soil, appears in this trek from east to west in a greater variety of disguises than any other oak. Rows of live oaks adorn long stretches of Texas gulf shore, following its sinuosities, rooted in immense sand dunes, where they are beaten in the face, so to speak, by the salt spray whipped up by the violent gulf winds. This has the effect of stunting their gulfward exposure but permitting their landward growth to continue unimpeded. Thus after years of facing the salt spray they present as perfect a picture of streamlining as can be found anywhere in the vegetable world. In profile and particularly in twilight they look like regiments of maenads fronting the sea, with long tresses blown backward toward the land, sculptured by the prevailing winds.

A little way inland, the same species grows to enormous proportions. A specimen near Rockport is said to be the largest tree of any kind in the state. Still farther inland, reduced in size, they assume regular proportions, achieve an immense spread supporting graceful festoons of Spanish moss, and constitute the most prized lawn tree of a wide belt skirting the coastal prairie southwestward for a hundred miles, roughly from Houston to Victoria.

Still further reduced in height but not in spread, and therefore squattier in appearance, the live oak ranges across the southern half of the Edwards Plateau and remains an outstanding feature of the landscape. Here it emphasizes the habit of extending its limbs horizontally until the weight of the foliage tends to depress the tips to the ground fifty or more feet from the trunk. Wherefore Walt Whitman called it a "loving lounger in my winding path"; and indeed it does seem to lounge rather than stand. Locally, however, throughout the Plateau, this aged giant is often reduced to the status of a mere bush or shrub.

Again, a Texas white oak (*q. breviloba*) takes curious shapes as it leaves the river bottoms and struggles up tributary creeks, finally mounting slopes of shallow soil and insufficient moisture where the species is ill-suited to the competition it encounters. Once atop the limestone ridges, it becomes definitely dwarfed. But in shady creek bottoms where cedar elms, green ash, pecans, vines, and other shade-producers thrive, this white oak begins a hopeless search for a place in the sun. It twists and turns this way and that in pursuit of sunshine, frustrated and indecisive as one growth after another beats it to a promising position. It is headed off here and there, back and forth, until it becomes so deformed as to be scarcely recognizable as a tree at all. Its bole sometimes makes a right-angle turn and skews off in one direction or another, around and about, writhing like a wounded serpent, and offering a very good representation of arboreal agony after the manner of the Laocoön group.

Also, wherever the sturdy post oak and blackjack leave the congenial sandy soils and invade the limestone hills, they become scrub oak, not more than twenty feet tall.

And finally, as a last gasp of genus *Quercus* in its due westward extension in non-mountainous country, we come upon the most spectacular adaptation of all, a species weed-sized, perhaps the least oak in the world—Harvard's oak, sharing with the mesquite the apparently sterile sands and, in spite of terrific winds, holding these sands in comparatively stable dunes.

Here I found hogs of normal size browsing on acorns in the tiptops of this pigmy white oak. I followed for a short distance an immense sow with litter of eleven pigs, her nose barely skimming the sand, apparently searching for something. It turned out that she was water-witching and to good purpose, for presently she began rooting. Soon her long, vigorous snout unearthed a spring of crystal-clear water—a result quite as miraculous to me at the moment as the sight the thirsty wanderers in an ancient desert beheld when their leader "lifted up his hand and with his rod smote the rock twice." This water the sow and her well-mannered progeny *sipped,* after the manner of swine that are permitted a free range. Hoggishness, gulping, and filth are forced upon this naturally dainty beast by close confinement and competitive feeding in the most degrading animal slums. Instead of the folk simile for filth, dirty as a hog, we should say "dirty as the hog's keeper."

Having satisfied the family thirst in this leisurely manner, sipping and savoring the cool spring water, she lay down in it, cooling her belly and, turning first this way and then that, extended the grateful moisture as far up her immense sides as possible. Thus refreshed, and now slightly suspicious of my continued interest, she wandered on with a gurgle of soothing grunts to keep her brood closely huddled about her; for there is the strange carnivorous creature, man, and also the sly coyote abroad, either of whom has been known to snap up and make off with a straying and too adventurous suckling. So she disappeared among the dunes while loose and flowing sand crept in and covered up the spring to filter and keep it uncontaminated for the next patron. I was told that hogs get killing fat here, feeding on acorns and watering from their rooted-out springs in the sand.[3] The popularity in West Texas of the so-called "tall story" is often a mystery to me. There are so many incredible facts there lying around on the surface that the manufacture of the tall story is a futile exercise of the imagination. It's a matter not only of transporting coals to Newcastle, but of delivering a cheap grade of lignite.

Early anthropologists were mystified, it is said, by litters of Indian camps—flint slivers, chips, cores, scrapers, arrowheads and other artifacts—scattered about in this sandy

---

[3]J. Frank Dobie notes in his travels in desert portions of the state of Sonora, Mexico, that coyotes dig in the sand for water that is sometimes "two or three feet beneath the surface."

desert. "No water, no kitchen middens" is a maxim of anthropological explorations in Texas, and this apparently waterless waste gave the maxim the lie until the Indians' ancient water supply was discovered a foot or two beneath a surface of dry and blowing sands.

I turned from this sagacious sow to note a cactus wren relining its nest. Before I became acquainted with this species, I had always thought of the wren as quite a midget among birds. I had grown up with the Texas Bewick wren, small and dapper, gray like a mockingbird and marked like him, except for the mocker's wing-spots. I knew the Carolina wren, of course, a little larger than the Bewick, of rich coloring and of bolder song. Familiar, also, was the canyon wren as well as the rock wren, fuller of curiosity than is any other member of the tribe which is noted the world over for prying into affairs which are none of its business.

I had had fleeting glimpses of the marsh wrens; and from late fall to early spring, we have throughout central and eastern Texas the winter wren, tiniest of them all, which, stripped of its feathers, is no bigger than your thumb.

But here in the Monahans mesquite, among other marvels, is a huge wren, almost as big as a robin; and he scolds from afar in an unwrenlike voice that is often mistaken for the bark of an angry rodent. The little winter wren could be hovered under this bird's wing; indeed, the winter wren from tip to tip is but a trifle longer than the tail of this giant species.

There were three other nests in the same mesquite, clustered near the one my bird was relining, each with its side entrance, and each one bigger than a man's head. I thought I had the only case on record of a nesting colony of wrens until I was advised by Mrs. Merriam Bailey that other observers had formed the same erroneous conclusion. There is only one real nest in the shrub: the other are dummies to fool lizards, mice, and suchlike stupid, homeless ones, sleepy and seeking a lodging for the night. The male wren, it is said, sometimes sleeps in a dummy nest while his mate is brooding.

Cattle fare as well as hogs in this part of Ward County. Cow men have told me that there are times when not a fat range steer is to be found anywhere between Fort Worth and El Paso except in the Monahans sands. I am told also that the cattle grown on this soft terrain, which yields to the slightest pressure, cannot be driven afoot on hard ground for the reason that their hoofs grow to such lengths that the moment these members are put on a resistant surface, they break and bleed. In pretrucking days this was a serious marketing inconvenience.

Horses are not so happy here, or at least were not during my last visit. There had been barely two inches of rainfall in seven months and the range was short. Horses were lean and had turned to gorging themselves on mesquite beans, occasionally dying of a colic. A veterinarian told me that his chief income during droughty summers is derived from dosing horses for overdoses of beans.

Of course, *now* the Monahans country is thought of only as an oil field; but the old-timers still think of it in terms of fat hogs and tender-footed cattle.

Across Ward County westward from the sand dunes, north of the highway and still east of the Pecos River, high on a desert mesa, are marks, designs, and figures called petroglyphs, pecked into the surface of smooth, flat-topped rocks. The aborigines, who chose these rocks upon which to indite their letters to posterity, seem to have run more to geometry than to anatomy—that is to say, geometrical designs predominate over human and animal representations. However, rude caricatures of both man and beast occur, as well as lines suggestive of tools or weapons or obviously symbolic figures—all fascinating to look upon.

What a dismal place, this mesa, overlooking a far-stretching valley, scantily clad in ragged, semiarid growth! Winding through it runs a sudden little river, deceptively clear, tempting the thirsty, but bitter as gall. Here, where one would least expect it, is this indisputable evidence of an urge in the savage mind to communicate, to leave a record—faint echo from a distant past, hint of an imagination striving to make its vision manifest.

These and similar writings scattered pretty generally over parts of western Texas always bring before my mind the figure of a man—it's always a man, never a woman—sitting cross-legged on a stone, leaning forward with back bent like a bow, tangled hair dangling about his cheeks, eyes burning with an inward light and intent upon his strokes as, stone hammer firmly grasped, he pecks away with a terrific determination to set down the recollection of some dream, or remembered forms, or images seen through a glass darkly— or maybe simply a trail-marker.

In spite of all the learned speculations concerning what these and similar writings may mean, much is left to guess and surmise. Little wonder! Give Leonardo da Vinci or Praxiteles or Walt Disney a stone hammer without a handle, a flat rock on a wind-swept mesa for a canvas, and a steady diet of meat, cactus apples, and mesquite beans, and I doubt if any one of them could make himself more intelligible.

It may be that this primitive artist and thinker lacked only the writer's alphabet, brush and canvas, marble and chisel, or the cinema mechanisms and organization. Maybe modern progress has been only in tools, materials, and technique and not in mentality itself. Anthropologists, generally, believe there is no indication that the modern mind in and of itself is in any way superior to that of human beings who lived forty thousand years ago. They attribute present wonders to the flowering of a long accumulation of facilities, to the coral-like deposition of agelong successions of myriads of minds, cultural inheritances, and so on.

But this is not the place or the season for indulging the dreams that relics or records of a prehistoric past inspire. The rocks this August afternoon are too hot to sit down upon. The light falls with such intensity as to rob the landscape of its charm. A certain amount of physical comfort is necessary, anyway, to fruitful speculation. Spring is not the time, either: season of winds driving sharp dust across these exposed mesas with such abrasive violence as eventually to erase the record, some say, and wipe the ancient slate clean. But even so, all will not be lost after the winds of centuries have done their worst. Under the direction of the late Professor J. E. Pearce, Mr. A. T. Jackson and his many helpers have collected and published two volumes comprising more than nine hundred pages wherein with pen and camera thousands of Texas pictographs are preserved.[4] This Ward County location is officially designated as Site No. 50.

Volume II of this work contains a map showing the distribution by counties of Indian picture-writings, a glance at which suggests that prehistoric West Texas was much more literate than the East Texas of the same period. But sectional pride should not be stimulated by this circumstance, since the writing materials of the west are more durable and the climate more favorable than those of the east for the preservation of such records. Nature supplied the prehistoric literates of East Texas with fragile materials—inkberry juice and bleached pine logs in some instances—as well as with a moldy climate. Few evidences of picture-writings occur east of the Colorado River, and hardly a scratch east of the Trinity.

No, the philosopher should stop by Site No. 50 later, in the fall of the year, say, when the land is cooled down in a tempered sunlight and has become quiet as only the desert can become—calm without stir or motion and with a meditative haze resting upon the purplish horizon. Then, with sufficient leisure and toward sunset when the sheer vastness of the landscape seems designed as a mete and measure for eternity itself—just then, with physical conditions right, he might with feeling or intuition, not with thought, get a

---

[4] *Picture-Writings of Texas Indians,* The University of Texas Publications, No. 3809, March 1, 1938, Vol. II, Bureau of Research in the Social Sciences, Study No. 27.

glimpse of the significance of these curious messages, as of rappings coming to the faithful through a spiritualistic medium. Maybe it is in tiny rivulets such as this that the great river of human communication has its source; maybe we have found here a birth spring of artistic creation, hidden from the eye deep in the cavernous past, and inaudible except to the sympathetic ear alert in the desert stillness to catch its natal murmur.

Beasts have left us records from a million years ago: tracks, rubbings, wallows; aimless, idle pawings in the primeval mud; but how many worlds away in purport are these scratches and scrawls left by the human hand, for in them is perceived the mind of man responding to a creative impulse. In such rude markings we get intimations of a will to create, of the mind's budding ability and determination to impress itself upon materials, communicate its thoughts, visions, dreams, to demonstrate that, as the poet declares, the mind is "a thousand times more beautiful than the earth on which it dwells," and that truly and in fact, it is

"above this frame of things
In beauty exalted, as it is itself
Of quality and fabric more divine."

11. Davis Mountains Holiday: In Camp

That night I camped in a valley about ten miles west of Fort Davis in sight of the famous Bloys Camp-meeting Grounds at an elevation of about six thousand feet. The first animal acquaintance I made there was a squirrel, not the red fox squirrel of the central Texas creek and river bottoms, nor the rock squirrel of the Edwards Plateau, but the half-black and slightly smaller rock squirrel. It is curious that the same variation in color occurs in European species. "Thus, while squirrels of north and west Europe are of a bright red color those of the mountainous regions of southern Europe are of a deep blackish gray."

This animal approached my camp after very little reconnoitering and began digging a burrow within ten feet of my cot. If I lay perfectly still, he proceeded with confidence. But if I made the slightest motion, even to turn the page of a book, he scampered away, and returned only when the great beast, as he doubtless considered me, had gone back to sleep.

After he had excavated enough of a hole to hide his head and shoulders, he evidenced his suspicion by backing out every now and then to look me over and see that I had not changed position. Sometimes he would study me for two or three minutes before recovering sufficient assurance to resume his digging. It took him two days to complete the burrow, and from then on he improved each shining hour, storing in the deep-delved earth the tiny acorns of the gray and Emory oaks near by, which bore a heavy mast.

He came in from his excursions with cheeks puffed out, giving his whole physiognomy a blowsy, dissipated look. A few moments later he would emerge from his burrow with his face not lifted, but considerably let-down. On leaving the burrow, he made the same round many, many times: first, a short gallop to a small oak tree, up to its topmost branches to feed a while; then, without descending, across to a larger tree, sampling, sampling, sampling—finally gathering a supply of fruit proper for storing. Then down he came and by another route back to his burrow. At the entrance he would pause for a moment with his cheeks ridiculously inflated, take a long look at me out of his wild, lustrous eyes, and dive in. He must have repeated exactly this routine a dozen times in one morning.

I was told that often the squirrel is ousted from his painfully dug burrow by a skunk, a kind of squatter who prefers ousting others to digging a place for himself. My friend, Ross Graves, who has been a professional trapper in the Davis Mountains for many years, doubts this story, especially in so far as concerns the hog-nosed skunk, which is too large to enter the burrow of a rock squirrel. If any skunk does this, he says, it must be the small spotted skunk. In summer months the skunk avails himself of a variety of shelters, such as pack-rat dens, brush piles, or prickly-pear bunches. In extremely cold weather he occupies abandoned prairie-dog holes, an armadillo den, or a burrow of his own making. Mr. Graves is of the opinion that the skunk is able to take over a den from any small animal, provided it is large enough for him to enter. Apparently he sometimes makes the mistake of intruding upon coyotes or even red wolves.

Says the trapper, "I have seen a number of instances where a coyote or a red wolf had killed a skunk near his den." Whether the skunk was attempting an eviction, or just happened to come along, innocently inspecting the mouth of the burrow to see if anybody was home, the record does not make clear.

This rock squirrel I was watching seemed to prefer acorns from the topmost branches. He sampled those of the lower limbs but took those from the top for storing. The band-tailed pigeons in a nearby oak fed from the topmost branches also, but not so daintily as the squirrel nor with such discrimination. They gobbled up these small acorns voraciously, swallowing them cup and all. The Mexicans with reason call them *belloteros*—acorners.

The rock squirrel is nothing like as wasteful with his acorns as the central Texas fox squirrel is with his favorite nut, the pecan. I had lately been observing the ravages of the latter in a pecan orchard, so the contrast impressed me. The fox squirrel begins his operations in July while pecans are tightly sealed in the husk. Impatient for his favorite food, he gnaws the green outer covering down to the shell of the nut itself, where the bitter juice bites his thievish tongue, and then throws the nut down. Not only does he throw down the one he has tasted, but also the two or three others growing on the same twig, rejecting them after tasting only one of a whole cluster. About one in fifty of these green nuts the squirrel seems to find a little palatable, for he eats about a third of it. I sat under a tree in which two were feeding one afternoon in August, watch in hand, and counted the nuts they threw down in five minutes—forty-six!

When the pecans ripen, the fox squirrel grows provident. Then, turned thrifty, he husbands his resources, carefully burying a supply of good, sound nuts. No one, I think, begrudges the squirrel his hoard of ripe pecans, but I remember the vast crop the wastrels destroy before the nuts ripen, just for a tiny taste now and then of a pecan almost but not quite ripe.

"All the motions of the squirrel imply spectators as much as those of a dancing girl," says Thoreau. And we agree that his capers, his poses and posturings, the flirt and curve of his tail, and his quick, teasing behavior are entertaining. We are willing to toss him a few nuts as an admission fee, but the performance is not worth a whole crop when ordinary pecans are selling at forty cents a pound.

I doubt if there is any connection in the squirrel's mind between a green nut and a ripe one. Once the ripe nut arrives, however, he seems to associate it with a winter shortage. Or, say the scientists, squirrels have no such association

of ideas, no intentions, as such, of any kind. Hoarding is a blind instinct, a reaction automatic and irresistible.

I can agree that an instinct which fails to tell them that a green nut will ripen is certainly blind. I have noted that after pecans ripen, the squirrel inspects very carefully the nut he chooses for hoarding. In his preseason forays it may be that he is searching among green nuts for ones suitable to hoard and trying to beat the other hoarders to them. Maybe it is this sense of competition which moves him to ravage a pecan tree. If so, his instinct is certainly working against his own best interests.

Naturalists have noted many times the nut-burying activities of these rodents and ascribed to them the march of nut

trees across the forest. Each squirrel is a little Johnny Apple-
seed, and it may well be that their careful selection of pecans
for burying through the long centuries has bred up a nut
more and more nearly approaching the squirrel's nut ideal.
They say, also, that the squirrel buries his nut at just the
right depth for best planting results and that horticulturalists
learned this proper depth from him.

On top of a peak a couple of miles west of the Camp-
meeting Grounds I had my first encounter with the Mearns
quail. I had read descriptions of the weird antics of this
creature and should have known just what to expect, but
still she took me completely by surprise. There is no warning adequate to prepare one for the impersonation which
this miscalled "crazy quail" puts on when startled from her
hiding. I had reached the summit after a long climb, leg-
weary and winded, and was about to sit down on a boulder
when, from right under my feet, the bird flounced out of the
grass. She shattered the armor of my suspicion at a stroke
and made an open-mouthed, wide-eyed gull of me before
I knew it. I am glad there was no one looking on. Indeed,
for a moment I didn't even identify the bird. I saw only a
flapping ball of feathers, emitting a variety of nerve-shatter-
ing sounds as of excited guinea fowl mingled with squawks
and cackling of hens. She flounced around just out of reach
of my hand for several minutes, often lying on her side in the
grass and fluttering her upper wing as if mortally wounded.
Finally it dawned upon me that this was a Mearns quail.

I walked over to a boulder and sat down to see her finish
the comedy. She seemed puzzled for a moment, like an
actress hearing boos when she expects applause. Flying away
about twenty steps, she again began her hysterical chatter.
About three minutes of this and a young quail, perhaps half-
grown, appeared. It took its stand on a boulder ten feet from
me and began answering. Both birds were greatly disturbed
but showed no disposition to run.

I then had a good opportunity to study the markings of the old one and compare them item for item with my memory of the famous painting of the Mearns quail done by Fuertes in the Chisos Mountains. Here I saw the wallpaper pattern of the head, the dark front, the streaks, the dots and dapplings, all said to make up one of the most perfect pieces of camouflage in nature. Presently both birds quieted down and the youngling rejoined its mother who, pausing for a moment to mushroom her crest, led her darling quietly away into the tall grass.

Of course, this bird is not really crazy. "If this be madness yet there's method in it." Feigning is a standard device. Several other species of birds assume a fictitious disability to lure an enemy away from threatened young, or nest. The killdeer runs off trailing a wing and uttering a cry like that of a lost soul. The mourning dove's performance is less convincing, but the intent to deceive is just as obvious. The crazy quail, however, takes you by storm, startles and confounds you, finally excites your compassion, and then wanders away as if nothing whatever had happened. After the play is over, you feel rather silly to have been taken in by such a synthetic tantrum.

The next day I climbed the same peak again, hoping to find another crazy quail, but no such luck. I did get to see a couple of paisanos[1] posed on a granite boulder outlined against the sky: the male with his crest flushed up and tail

[1] The paisano is one of the "most-named" birds of the Southwest, as the flicker is in the North and East. From his fondness for low growths, he is called a chaparral cock or simply a chaparral; from his occasional lapses of memory, confusing his own nest with that of another, he is slandered as a ground cuckoo. One of the commonest English names for him is road runner, taken from the Mexican *"el Correo del Camino,"* in reference to his curious way of pacing the traveler along a highway. The Mexicans also give him a name in imitation of his call, *churea*. He eats snakes ravenously and is able to cope with even the largest rattlers, and is hence called snake-killer.

I prefer the name paisano because it is euphonious and because often in the lonely desert, where company is scarce, this large and lovely bird will travel along with you for miles, staying only a few yards ahead. The word *paisano* suggests congenial companionship, fraternization, fellow countryman, or fellow traveler without the evil connotation with which the spy literature of World War II has now tinctured that originally innocent term.

tilted at a festive angle, as he is usually drawn or photographed, but the female more alarmed, alert and stooped, making ready for a sneak.

I found also, on the high table-top, a pair of Townsend warblers, early migrants, cousin to the golden-cheeked warbler of the Edwards Plateau and rivaling him in striking patterns of yellow and black. Then, off a cliff, dashing by at lightning speed, I saw for the first time in these mountains the white-patched form of the white-throated swift.

Any swift is exciting. One species of this family is the fastest animal that wears wings.[2] It has been clocked by airplane at two hundred miles per hour in sustained flight. The swift, G. C. Aymar contends,[2a] flies with alternate wingbeats; it has a continual fever raging in his body (111° Fahrenheit); and whereas man's eye has only one area of acute vision, the swift's eye has three.

Swifts have always been mystery birds. The older ornithologists classified them as swallows. Now they are put into the same order with goatsuckers and hummingbirds. The disappearance in the fall of the common chimney swift is so sudden as to seem almost magical. Today you hear hundreds squeaking in your chimney; tomorrow there is not one to be found anywhere, high or low—gone they are until the insects fly again in the spring. This abrupt disappearance of the swift so puzzled the delightfully cautious Gilbert White that he flirted all his life with the theory, widely accepted at

[2]According to A. C. Bent, *Life Histories of North American Birds of Prey,* Part II, Bulletin 170, pp. 59–60, United States National Museum, the utmost speed of the duck hawk "has been estimated as ranging between 150 and 200 miles per hour; it may attain or even exceed such speed in its swift plunges, but no such speed could be maintained for any great distance. D. D. McLean timed with a stopwatch a hunting duck hawk and estimated its speed as between 165 and 180 miles per hour." The same authority reports a duck hawk passing an airplane which was in a nose dive at an estimated 175 miles per hour. The aviator reported that the hawk diving at a duck "passed me like I was standing still." But that was a "stoop" and hardly to be counted as flight proper. The stoop of the bearded eagle has been estimated, also, at 200 miles per hour.

[2a]*Bird Flight,* Garden City Publishing Co., Inc., New York, 1938, p. 140.

the time, that the English swifts simply crawled into the mud and hibernated for the winter.

With all the research of the past fifty years lavished on problems of migration, tracing the routes of birds to their destinations in minutest detail, the chimney swift until recently outwitted the researchers. Only lately has his winter residence been discovered on the upper reaches of a tributary of the Amazon in a far corner of northern Peru. Chapman guessed "Amazonia" in 1931, certainly wide of a bull's-eye, but at that, nearest the mark of any guess until, as a result of grand-scale banding, the winter resort was definitely determined.

I made a note on September 10, 1942, of seeing large numbers of swifts coning up hundreds of feet in the air at Seventh Street and East Avenue in Austin, Texas, with the City Market serving approximately as the base of the cone. A year later, seeing the same exhibition, I added, "Probably catching insects rising from the fruits and vegetables of the City Market."

Late one afternoon of spring I was sitting on a window balcony on the third floor of the Driskill Hotel in Austin, watching a nuptial flight of swifts. Suddenly two came together in mid-air and maintained contact throughout a fall of about three hundred feet straight down before separating. This may have been the consummation of the nuptial flight, or it may have been two rivals fighting for the favor of a female, or mere play.[3]

But the climax of my bird-watching on this trip occurred in the lowlands at a ground tank near the Fort Davis–Marfa road where a fork leads off to Valentine.

[3]The probability that the nuptial flight leads, at least sometimes, to sexual contact in the air is increased by Sutton's (1928) careful study of the swift. He says: "In this courtship flight, the pair of birds may fly rapidly about, twittering loudly; suddenly the upper bird will lift its wings very high above the back and coast through the air, sometimes for several seconds, while the bird beneath may soar with its wings held in a fixed position below the plane of the body. It may be that this graceful and interesting display is at the culmination of the courtship activity."—A. C. Bent, ibid., Bulletin 176, p. 273.

Although on several occasions I have hunted for him along the Mexican border in Texas and New Mexico, here I saw for the first time the famous phainopepla—and not only one, but a whole family. There is no mistaking the male, since his field markings are unique. He is velvet black with a greenish sheen about the shoulders; has a tall slender crest, curved forward, and a reddish iris. He is not quite so long as a mockingbird, carries himself with great pride, and in flight shows white spots on the wings. The female and young are of a dirty brownish color with little to attract the attention except the crest.

I returned to the pond the following morning and had the pleasure of seeing the whole family again. The morning following that was cold, cloudy, and drizzly. I waited two hours, but they didn't show up.

It is confusing to call the phainopepla a silky flycatcher, for the casual reader then assigns him to the family of Tyrant flycatchers common throughout the United States. The fact is, this bird belongs to a different family entirely, the *Ptilogonatidae*. He does take his prey on the wing, but there the resemblance to the Tyrant flycatchers ends. He is the only species of the family to breed within the borders of the United States. Indeed, there are only four species of *Ptilogonatidae* in the world, and they are peculiar to Mexico and Central America. The taxonomists group them with the waxwings. As far as external characters go, the phainopepla's forward-curving crest and his fondness for berries do suggest the waxwing even to one who knows little or no taxonomy.

Droughty conditions over the mountains generally had brought other species to the pond. Flycatchers had gathered in, hungry for insects. Western wood pewees were active, feeding at fifteen- to twenty-five-foot levels. The black phoebe took its food closer to the water, at five or, rarely, ten feet above the surface. This flycatcher accordingly occupied a lower perch, sometimes not more than two feet above the water level. Different species of flycatchers in the same locality always have a way of parceling out strata of the air in which they are feeding, never rising, however, into the exalted regions of swift or swallow.

The wood pewee is a peaceful flycatcher and picks no fusses, but when an Arkansas kingbird took over a perch on the pewee's level and began feeding, he protested sharply before being driven off by the more powerful kingbird. Until this intrusion the pewees had enjoyed a monopoly on their own particular levels. When one of the small flycatchers (genus Empidonax; I couldn't identify the species), invaded the pewee's domain and actually usurped a perch, the pewee chased the intruder out, but not before the little fellow during the chase had the impertinence to snap up an insect right at the surface of the water.[4]

In still weather the wood pewee sits on his perch almost bolt upright. In wind, however, he leans forward and balances himself with his tail, assuming an almost horizontal position.

Here, also, I had opportunity to improve a long acquaintanceship with another bird, the pectoral sandpiper. One of the pleasures of field study is that if you are not eagerly trying to identify a new species, you are often able to find old friends doing new things. A common name for the pectoral sandpiper is grass snipe, so-called from its habit of feeding in grassy meadows and along the margin of water. But the two I observed here stayed well out in the water all the time and fed wading belly-deep. They seemed to be bringing up something about the size of a small pea at every plunge of the bill. The pond was by no means clear; I found a piece of white note paper invisible when submerged to a depth of six inches. These birds were present on three successive days; and each day they were feeding out as deep as they could wade. Once one of them swam a short distance.

[4] J. Stokley Ligon, author of *Wild Life in New Mexico*, told me that he had seen flycatchers knock their young down in flight to keep hawks from catching them.

On two different occasions they were preening their feathers. They dipped their bills into the water every little while to keep the tip moist, or to cleanse or cool it, or maybe to take a sip of water with which to moisten the feathers and make them preen better.

A pectoral sandpiper directly facing you shows a white spot in front of each eye, extensions of the white lines over the eyes—longish spots they are, and each one is slanted down toward the other to make a broken *V* and give the features an oriental cast. Like the spotted sandpiper, this bird teeters, but more deliberately; and unlike the solitary sandpiper, he doesn't nod at all. I get from the books that in the breeding season the male inflates his throat to thrice its normal size to produce a resonant love note; and that even the downy-headed young make the vast flight from arctic tundras to Patagonia, almost from pole to pole, arriving there as early as the end of August.

Every so often, in my short wanderings about the camp, I caught sight of the solemn, triangular peak of Mount Livermore, sometimes from another peak, at other times from a comparatively low elevation. Now it appeared, lofty and massive, between and towering above nearer peaks. But the best view I got of it was from the bed of a deep canyon. Here, looking upward from crag to crag, out of the gorge, on and up, the eye finally rests upon the summit of this noble mountain which dominates and gives unity to the whole range.

I climbed Mount Livermore once, long ago, on horseback. At least I managed to get within about two hundred feet of the top on horseback, and the rest of the way crawling on all fours.

Legend has it that an Indian chief caused himself to be buried there on the topmost outlook, either to enjoy the grandeur of the view or else to be nearer the happy hunting ground which, in Indian mythology also, is up there some-where in the sky.

Excavation of this site began in 1895 under the direction of Mrs. Susan M. Janes, of El Paso. In the twelve succeeding years this heroic lady made seven trips to the top of Liver-more and recovered two thousand arrowheads. There were, however, in this cache no bones and no ceremonial speci-mens, which circumstance, according to the anthropologists, gives the well-worn fable a black eye. Messrs. Charles C. Janes, of El Paso, and T. A. Merrill, of Fort Davis, make a distinct addition to the lore of Livermore in their article[5] describing the collection, which is now in the museum of the Sul Ross State Teachers College.

A resident, an old-timer, tells me that at one time Mount Livermore was practically useless as a cattle range because of the prevalence there of wild steers. The outlaws, he said, corrupted the gentler stock so that they could not be driven from their mountain fastnesses. The original error was com-mitted by a Connecticut Yankee who bought the mountain in an early day and loosed thereupon a lot of yearlings. Being neglected, these cattle went native, and there was no way of getting them out. Then the ranchmen hired cow-boys with high-powered rifles to kill them on sight; and, concluded my informant, "the buzzards carried 'em out."

I made only one overnight camp on the way home in a pasture about halfway between Odessa and Midland. Ex-cept for the mesquite, all vegetation was in a bad way. Only two inches of rain had fallen in the last seven months.

As no birds appeared around the camp next morning, I strolled over to a windmill about a mile away, where I found a ground tank, drought-dried to the dregs, and at its edge a gigantic bois d'arc, or osage orange, a species once

[5]Publications of the West Texas Historical and Scientific Society, Sul Ross State Teachers College, Alpine, Texas, 2, 1930: *The Susan M. Janes Collection,* V. J. Smith, p. 7; and *Seven Trips to Mt. Livermore,* pp. 8 and 9.

nursed and petted by pioneers in vain hope that it would solve the fencing problem. This tree was gigantic only in comparison with the stunted growths round about. It was taking a lion's share of moisture from the damp margin of the dying pond, like a prosperous parasite upon an exhausted host. It cast a blighting shade upon plants whose ancient place in the sun it had recently usurped. In the natural order of things it had no business there, anyway, and gave me the impression of being disagreeably lush, displaying above the native vegetation, now dingy with dust, its dense masses of triumphant green.

In the dark shadow of this tree I surprised a whole family of Bullock orioles, western version of the Baltimore oriole, bathing in the dirty water. They made off in a panic, disappearing as flashes of yellow in the gray desert foliage. Much bolder, or maybe more accustomed to human associates, two matchless scissortails continued their ablutions. These elegant birds swooped down, breasting the water just deeply enough to cause a little splash. Time and again, until their feathers must have been quite wet, the bathers dashed their pearly breasts against the still water and fluttered out, flashing a glimpse of the salmon pink with which the under wing surface is lined.

A solitary mockingbird had taken possession of the bois d'arc and would permit no other bird to come near. Even the scissor-tailed flycatchers avoided his fierce and ill-humored dives. True to his character, he monopolized this one oasis of shade in a wide and withered landscape. A white-necked raven flew past, a species that serves this region instead of the crow, and difficult to tell from one except when his voice betrays him. His "shibboleth" will not pass muster: it is ragged and sore-throated in comparison with the brisk, rasping caw of the American crow.

I trailed back to camp feeling the futility of the morning's excursion. There was no bird life in the sky, and little life of any kind on earth except slick brown myriapods which last night's shower had made active, crawling everywhere. You could hardly walk without stepping on one.

Running over in my mind, or rather simply permitting the incidents of the past week to parade themselves in memory, I selected one feature for detention and dwelt upon it as the high point of my short stay in the mountains.

Late one afternoon, I had climbed to an altitude of about seven thousand feet from which vantage point the open character of the mountains permitted the eye to range far and away over great distances punctuated by peaks, scored by bluffs, interspersed here and there with lower elevations, smooth and rounded, and on downward by degrees to long, gradual valleys dotted with clumps of oaks, some bright green and some of a deeper bluish hue.[6]

On this lookout I experienced the effort of trying to lengthen out the sight, widen its scope, taxing it a little and a little more to extend its reach to the utmost through air so clear that distance did not obscure an object or fuzz up its outline, but only reduced its proportions. At the same time I felt the need of more expansive breathing. The struggle for oxygen and the greater visual effort were stimulating rather than unpleasant compulsions. It was delightful to feel the tonic effect of deeper inhalations while the eye encompassed the spread and pomp of this far-flung mountain scenery.

Even with no nature hobby to indulge, if one is enough of an East Indian, as I am, to enjoy periods of undiluted contemplation as opposed to intellectual effort of any kind or character, he may here, comfortably above the torpid life of the lowlands, "fleet the time idly" for a few summer days at least, drifting along such currents of musing as these cool solitudes may set going, and come out the fresher for it. Indeed, if William Wordsworth, as he solemnly assures us he did, completely cured a sore heel by giving up temporarily

[6]Groves of oaks here are rarely of one species only. The Emory and the gray oak (*Quercus griseus*) associate on the most intimate terms. In each motte both species occur, giving it two shades of green, and you rarely see an isolated tree of either species. The botanist can doubtless give a rational explanation, but to the sentimentalist it seems to be Nature's protest against exclusiveness or segregation. The leaf of the Emory oak is a bright, glossy green; that of the gray oak is bluish green, dull, almost dusty-looking.

the rigors of poetical composition, surely the rubs, galls, and abrasions of the spirit may be soothed, if not healed, by simple abandonment for a time of mental strife—a remedy made particularly easy in these open mountains where one may, with yoga detachment, immerse himself in the silence of sunset or of the rise of stars.

12. The Golden Eagle

Not until I was packing up to leave at the end of my stay in the Davis Mountains did I catch sight of a golden eagle. He was soaring and presently disappeared behind a peak not a great way from camp. Certainly the most disturbing bit of bird information I picked up while there concerns this very bird. No other flying creature occupies so large a place in the pages of history, poetry, and romance; but he preys upon lambs, and he is being slaughtered on a scale unparalleled in the long history of eagle-hunting.

The sheep raisers are banded into a defensive league against this bird whose depredations are said to menace the profits of the industry.[1] A skilled aviator armed with a sawed-off shotgun, flying a tiny monoplane, is employed full time. He reports killing 1,875 golden eagles within two years. I think there is no other record of eagle slaughter which anywhere near equals this one.

From the Guadalupe Mountains in New Mexico southeastward to the Big Bend of the Rio Grande, including the central portion of Culberson County, much of Hudspeth,

[1] Sutton and Van Tyne say the golden eagle is found throughout Brewster County, "and in many cases is exceedingly common. We saw six perched near one another in some low trees west of Mount Ord . . . Because of alleged depredations against sheep and other livestock, the local ranchers kill these splendid birds at every opportunity and hang their carcasses from the roadside fences as scarecrows or as evidence of their own prowess." *The Birds of Brewster County, Texas,* by Josselyn Van Tyne and George Miksch Sutton, University of Michigan Press, August 24, 1937.

and the whole of Jeff Davis, Presidio, and Brewster counties, is a territory roughly three hundred miles long and from fifty to a hundred miles wide, moderately mountainous, with rugged peaks, deeply dissected ridges, canyons, and other typical features of the Rockies, bordered by plains and interspersed with smooth, richly grassed, intermontane valleys.

Here for untold centuries, until the advent of the white man, the golden eagle, deer, antelope and the bighorn sheep had maintained a balance. The predators, including besides the eagle, wolves, bobcats, and mountain lions, kept these herding animals healthy by preying upon the sluggish, the unwary, the weakly, and the diseased, and took their fee for this medical service in fawns and lambs, which came along just at the right time to nourish the eagle's young with a supply of particularly tender meat. In the absence of "baby beef" these birds are known to offer the very young eaglets tidbits of liver torn from prey too tough for ready assimilation, to say nothing of the hazard of choking their offspring.

Eagles are much more careful than some human mothers about what they stuff down the throats of their young. In babyhood, they dish out only the tenderest tidbits, especially the liver of their prey, but never the entrails, which the parents themselves consume. As the eaglets get older, young rabbits are fed to them quite generously, if such prey is available, but even this delicacy is stripped of fur as long as the eaglets are in their downy stage. Later on the parents feed them rattlesnakes, being careful, however, to eat off the head before delivering the corpus to the nest.

The eagle conferred another benefit upon the grazers and browsers, after his young were reared, by returning to plain and valley to prey upon rabbits, prairie dogs, and other range destroyers, as well as upon the acorn-eating squirrel. A fair exchange in this golden era of wild life in the Big Bend was no robbery. No species got all it wanted, of course —no species ever does—but it got all that was good for it.[2]

[2]To say that no species *ever does* exaggerates. Occasionally, some animal quite noble in a feral state degenerates into parasitism by the

This balance or beneficent association between and among the fiercest enemies, superimposed and enforced by nature's foresight, turning enmity as well as mutual aid to her purpose, has the charm of a good poem or fine music, until man enters with a decisive discord.

In the present instance, Man, disturber of balances, began by exterminating the bighorn[3] and the antelope and introducing grazers and browsers more to his liking. Recently, as a commercial venture, he has taken deer into protective custody and reintroduced the antelope.[4]

Meantime the eagle was not made a party to all this jumbling-up of species in his native range. He is thankful for the reintroduction of the antelope and, though he pre-

---

interposition of man. For illustration, seagulls between San Francisco, Calif., and Catalina Island fed for fifty years on offal thrown overboard daily from fishing smacks plying between the island and the port, since the fishermen cleaned their catch on the return trip. Generations of gulls took this daily ration and waxed fat for half a century. Then, in the great depression of 1929, the operating company discontinued this line, and these gulls sat around and starved to death by the hundreds, too fat, too lazy, too little skilled in the techniques of normal gulls to gain a livelihood. Other instances of the disastrous interposition of man are found in the introduction of a species into a new habitat in which there is abundant prey and few, if any, enemies.

[3]At the conclusion of his classic description of bighorn sheep, published more than fifty years ago, Bailey says: "It is with some hesitation that I make public these facts as to the abundance, distribution, and habits of mountain sheep in western Texas, and only in the hope that a full knowledge of the conditions and the importance of protective measures may result in the salvation instead of the extermination of the species. It would not be difficult for *a single persistent hunter to kill every mountain sheep in western Texas if unrestrained.* (Italics supplied.) Not only should the animals be protected by law, but the law should be made effective by an appreciation on the part of the residents of the country of the importance of preserving for all time these splendid animals.—*North American Fauna,* No. 25, p. 75, United States Department of Agriculture, Biological Survey, Washington, 1905.

The eagle, having learned to depend upon the bighorn and the pronghorn for an extra supply of tender meat with which to nourish his brood, transferred his appetite and his attention to domestic sheep when offspring of the former were no longer available. When their young become self-supporting, eagles both young and old subsist largely upon jack rabbits, cottontails, prairie dogs, squirrels, and other small mammals, as well as upon rattlesnakes, of which the bird is particularly fond and quite adept at taking.

[4]Landowners charge the hunter $100 "per look"; that is, a fee of one hundred dollars is charged for hunting on a given property, the landowners furnishing the guides, horses, and so on, guaranteeing that the hunter will *see* an antelope or get his money back.

fers the young of the bighorn, he will manage to make out with the lambs of domestic sheep and the kids of domestic goats. Necessity now forces him to take whatever in the way of tender meat is available to satisfy his clamorous nest.

Thus this bird finds himself in head-on collision with a commercial interest, armed with a weapon against which all his accumulated eagle lore is of no avail. As long as his ancient habitat was merely a cattle range, the eagle might be tolerated, but sheep and goats are another matter. Indeed, a good case can be made for the eagle in a cattle country, since he destroys range-destroyers, and his occasional attack on a calf, hardly ever successful, may be overlooked.

Before the Air Age the golden eagle's habit of soaring was a protection since it kept him well out of gun range. His eyrie was once believed to be in heaven itself. Once his glory, this soaring while "kindling his undazzled gaze in the full midday beam"[5] is now his undoing. Soaring, he advertises himself to the watchful eyes of ranchers and their employees, who immediately telephone to the eagle hunter, J. O. Casparis, at Alpine, who is then off in a jiffy and on location in a matter of minutes. Maneuvering the bird into position, below and to his left, he turns loose the controls of the little monoplane long enough to pour a charge of shot into his victim at a distance of anywhere from twenty to sixty feet.

[5] Poor Milton! When he saw a noble and puissant nation rousing herself like a strong man after sleep, and shaking her invincible locks, and figured this mighty nation as an eagle "mewing up her mighty youth, and kindling her undazzled eyes at the full midday beam," no probing anatomist had been pulling the membranes of an eagle's eyes apart with his tweezers. Science, speaking through Sir J. Arthur Thomson *et al.* had not yet discredited this story. The eagle doesn't really, as is now common knowledge, "kindle his undazzled eyes," but carefully protects his eye from the glare by drawing over it a third eyelid, of which evolution has left man but a scrap, an inutile vestige. Without this special equipment called the "nictating membrane," the eagle could no more kindle his undazzled gaze in the full midday beam than you could. Of course, we use smoked glass.

It is obvious that no large bird which exhibits itself thus conspicuously can withstand the tactics of rapid communication, airplane, and sawed-off shotgun. At the present rate of killing, the golden eagle will probably be exterminated in the whole of the Big Bend, the Davis and Guadalupe mountains, and in a vast contiguous territory within a comparatively short time. He was driven from the eastern United States by a much less systematic persecution. But for a breeding range that includes most of the northern hemisphere,[6] and but for his solitary habits, this species might soon be exterminated.

It has been suggested that the eagle will eventually learn to avoid the airplane, as the crow has learned to keep his distance from man in accordance with the increasing range of the rifle. Can the bird acquire the simple knack of diving into deep and narrow canyons as the distant whir of airplane propellers becomes audible? I shall discuss this in another chapter.

Quotations I use herein indicate that naturalists generally are inclined to discount almost to the vanishing point the golden eagle's destructiveness in a sheep-and-goat country. Alexander Wetmore, who certainly knows his eagles, warns against overestimating the eagle's carrying power, and others take up here, doubting the bird's ability to make off with a lamb. But too many observers have actually seen it done. As for his inability to fly off with a lamb, he often lightens the burden in his talons by first eating the head and entrails. The weight-lifting experiments with tame eagles even when catapulted from a tower set the utmost limit of his capacity at eight pounds. But these experiments do not impress me. Birds reared in captivity certainly cannot have the wing strength of feral ones. As well expect a cage-reared coyote to keep up at once with a hard-pressed pack of wild ones running at full speed.

But ravages by any predator tend to be exaggerated. Mis-

[6]No account is taken of the seven races which have been distinguished, since the races interbreed wherever their respective ranges overlap.

cellaneous observations quickly build up into top-heavy totals. When one predator acquires a reputation for prowess, the evil deeds of others are loaded upon him.[7] The lamb dead at birth is torn by some vulture, and the ranchman who finds it chalks up another evil deed to the deadly eagle. The Davis Mountain eagle hunter declares that the same eagle may kill three lambs in one day, selecting only the fattest and most promising at that. But when all is said, when due deductions are made, and only the most reliable testimony is considered, we are compelled to admit that lambs and kids are killed by eagles each year, especially during the two or three months when the eagles are feeding their young. But we do not have conclusive proof of the extent of his depredations.

Until an adequate study by competent scientists is made of the pellets which these Big Bend eagles disgorge, best index of their food, I shall refuse to take as conclusive miscellaneous observations, so easy to exaggerate, concerning his depredations upon domestic stock. In disgorging pellets, the eagle writes his daily menu for the scientist as clearly as if it were typed out on white paper. The droppings of the wolf are almost as revelatory. Such a food study in a given range, covering not only a season but a whole year, of the eagle and of the coyote should be made before the wholesale slaughter of these species is permitted.

In continental United States, the Big Bend of the Rio Grande is now the eastern edge of the golden eagle's breeding range. He has become within the last century almost exclusively a Rocky Mountain bird, but retains a racial memory which pulls him eastward on occasional excursions toward the Appalachians. There are scattering records of his nesting recently east of the Mississippi, as well as instances

[7]It has always been thus with bears. The stockmen of New Mexico and of other western states would have exterminated the black bear as well as the grizzly on the records of depredations of a few individuals, had not knowledge with the law on its side intervened.

of his appearance far east of the Rockies in such an exhausted state that he is easily killed or captured. One was taken alive in the streets of Rochester, New York, a few years ago and placed in the city's zoo. Another was captured at Phillipsburg, New Jersey, in early November 1943. A golden eagle pursuing a hawk was electrocuted in the wires of a power line in Hugo, Minnesota, in 1935.

I have myself collected and verified several accounts of his appearance on the plains and prairies of Texas, and in nearly every instance the individual was in a starved or exhausted condition.

Before fences were common, the eagle had an extensive hunting ground far and wide over the plains and prairies. Rabbits, one of his favorite foods, were here easily taken. His manner of capturing running prey is conditioned upon open, unobstructed areas to give his swooping power its full effectiveness. Brushy country defeats him, and the introduction of fences into open country greatly interferes with his activities. The swoop of the golden eagle has been called "the swiftest thing, as it is the most magnificent, in the bird world"—all the more reason for its requiring clear spaces of considerable extent. It is my opinion that, still yielding to the instinct to hunt in the open country, the golden eagle, once out of the mountains, overshoots his mark and gets too far away from his base. His reach of wing literally exceeds the grasp of talon in a prairie or plain now littered with fences and other obstructions. Hunger drives him to desperation while his strength fails him.

I am reasonably sure that such was the plight of one which attacked a negro child near Jarrell, Texas, in October 1937. Before I could get to the scene of the attack, the body of the eagle had been destroyed; but from measurements taken and from the description given by those who saw the bird, I have no doubt that it was a golden eagle. I was not able to find the family of itinerant cotton pickers to which the child belonged. From the school principal at Jarell, U. D. Filizola, and from the farmer, Ed Sypert, upon whose place the Negroes were employed, and from others, I learned that during noon-lunch period, the girl, about thirteen years old and small for her age, was sent a distance of about one hundred yards out into the cotton field to fetch a jug of water. Presently she screamed, and the other members of the family saw her knocked down by a huge bird. They rushed to her aid, while the bird flew a short distance away with the child's large straw hat in its talons. There it stayed ravenously tearing at the hat until one of the men went to the farmhouse several hundred yards away for a gun, with which he killed it. All accounts agreed that the girl's ankles were badly clawed and that she was at first knocked down by the impact of the eagle's stoop.

Alexander Wilson records an attack by a bald eagle on a child who was left alone a moment while the mother was gathering vegetables. The fact that a piece of the frock tore loose and the bird made off with it, he says, probably saved the child's life. In both of these instances, a piece of clothing diverted the bird. The eagle is accustomed to attacking *naked* prey and so, when a piece comes loose, it is good to eat and he retires to enjoy it. It takes a little time for him to discover that human clothing is counterfeit.

Nearly all tales of child-stealing by eagles have the earmarks of myth.[8] Casparis says the golden eagle can carry a burden equal to his own weight, and that his average weight is twelve pounds. A newspaper report says he killed

[8]Ancient tales of child-stealing by the golden eagle are based largely on the ravages of the bearded eagle, or lammergeier, of Europe and Asia, a larger and much more ferocious bird, three and a half feet long with a wingspread of ten feet. James Bruce, in his *Travels*, widely read at the beginning of the nineteenth century, called the *lammergeier* the golden eagle and told hair-raising stories of the bird's preying on man and beast that have passed into folklore and have even been repeated as authentic by responsible authorities. The lammergeier, or lamb vulture, is the bird of Leviticus 11.13 which must be held in abomination by the faithful, and is called the ossifrage, or bone-breaker, from its habit of breaking large bones by dropping them from a great height. He also drops turtles to break their shells and Pliny accuses him of causing the death of Aeschylus by dropping a tortoise on his bald head which he mistook for a stone.

"There seems to be one authenticated case, at least, of a golden eagle attacking a child. Edward H. Forbush investigated this and found that a girl of nine had been attacked and her arm much discolored and cut before her father was able to dislodge the bird and the mother kill it with an ax. . . . Soaring at great heights he (the golden

one which weighed twenty-five pounds and measured ten feet three inches from wing tip to wing tip. If he is correctly reported, I think it is too bad that he did not have a taxidermist handy to preserve this specimen, since eagle experts without such evidence will doubt both the validity of the scales and the accuracy of the measuring tape.

There are, no doubt, babies small enough and eagles large enough to make baby-stealing possible, but whether the bird likes babies well enough to carry one off has not been demonstrated, and no one at present produces babies for such experimental purposes. One thing in this connection is quite sure: all stories of babies found alive in an eagle's nest are folklore, including the famous kidnaping of Ganymede, since every eagle kills his prey before delivering it to his young.

Another golden eagle far from his base was killed by W. S. Kuykendall on his ranch near San Saba, Texas. He tells me, in a letter dated December 10, 1938, that he had killed a Mexican eagle that had been preying on his lambs. "Mexican eagle" is the common name for the caracara; but, judging from Kuykendall's description—seven feet from tip to tip and weight eleven pounds—it could not have been a caracara, which is only twenty-two inches long. So, also, the bird reported killed by Herbert Stellewerk near New Braunfels, Texas, in April 1937, was called a Mexican eagle, but measured six feet from tip to tip.

R. V. Carnes writes me from Grand Saline, Texas, March 26, 1943, saying that he and his brother, Harold, roped an eagle three miles from Grand Saline. Mr. Carnes believes that the bird's wings were so wet he couldn't fly.

---

eagle) half closes his wings, shoots down upon his prey at full speed, and disables or kills it at a blow." *Bird Flight,* written and designed by Gordon C. Aymar, Garden City Publishing Company, Inc., Garden City, New York, 1938, p. 67.

The tenacity of this eagle, in holding on to his prey while being killed with an ax, gives some color to the Lap's story of a golden eagle which with one talon in the back of a reindeer and the other clutched to the limb of a tree, was torn in two by the struggles of the reindeer rather than release his hold upon either. Stig Wessler tells this story for the truth in his article, "The Golden Eagle, King of the Mountains," *The American-Scandinavian Review,* Vol. XXI, 1933, p. 94. The article is mainly concerned with the eagle's robbing trappers of ptarmigans caught in snares.

I got a positive identification of this bird, since the Carnes boys sent it to the Dallas zoo. L. B. Houston, Director of Parks, Dallas, tells me that it is a golden eagle.

Dan Pearson, trapper, caught an eagle in a coon trap on the Gus. F. Schreiner ranch near Kerrville in January 1941. He reported that a group of forty wild turkeys and five deer stood about the trap and watched the dying struggles of this great bird, whose wingspread measured eighty-one inches. It weighed twelve pounds. Pearson says this was the first golden eagle killed in Kerr County in five years.

A description of the golden eagle's reaction to the first appearances of airplanes could easily be made into a story calculated to drive the ultrascientific into a rage of denunciation as nature-faking, an imposition on the naturally superstitious, an example of sentimentality, literary skullduggery, and the like. Still, facts are facts, even though they seem to invite mystic or sentimental interpretation.

As soon as this great soarer was confronted far up in the sky, his native element, by man's noisy contraption—built more on the insect than on the bird model—he was infuriated and forthwith anticipated the kamikaze attack by dashing himself to pieces against the invading monster. It was as if he had a premonition of what the airplane was going to do to him. Anyway, as far back as the beginning of World War I, the eagle served warning that the airplane would invade his realm at its peril.

Casparis reports that early in his eagle-hunting career in the Big Bend, an enormous eagle crash-dived his plane before he could shoot, tore through the window, ripped off several feet of the fuselage and showered him with shattered glass. This incident may be dismissed as accidental, as the freak action of a crazy bird, as mere panic, or anyway you like. But at that, it curiously confirms reports of the reactions of the golden eagle to first appearances of airplanes in the skies of France. The French army authorities, on reports by aviators of eagle encounters, seriously considered training eagles to attack enemy planes, and a French aeronautical journal proclaimed boldly that no airplane could withstand such an avian offensive. The British Air Ministry issued official instructions to airmen on proper tactics to pursue when assailed by eagles. J. Wentworth Day reports a concerted attack by two eagles on a three-motored, all-

steel passenger plane near Allahbad. "The first eagle," he says, "flew straight into the middle engine, while the second dived from ten thousand feet, and went through the steel wing like a stone, ripping a great hole."[9] Of course, modern planes have little to fear from eagles or other birds individually, but the encountering by plane of migration flights, especially flights of large birds in considerable number, is said still to offer a considerable hazard.

Eagle slaughter in the Big Bend area is now complicated

[9]*Birds vs. Planes,* by Frank W. Lane, *Natural History,* Vol. LV, No. 4, p. 165, April 1946. Mr. Lane also discusses in this article the reactions of many other birds to the airplane.

by the imminent development of a great international park, eventually to include about two million acres, right in the heart of the golden eagle's territory. This eagle has become so rare in the more populous portions of the continent that the sight of one is a tourist attraction of great pulling power. Thus there will soon develop in the park area and in its environs another commercial interest which will naturally take sides with the eagle. Besides, nature-lovers and science generally "view with alarm" the destruction of a bird of this character, and the reduction of the species to accidental status in a region such as the Big Bend National Park where two nations have united, unique in national annals, in the promotion of a project having as one of its chief purposes the preservation of wild life. Just what compromise may be worked out to preserve the eagle in the park and still protect the neighboring sheep-raising industry from his spring depredations cannot at present be stated.

The Enabling Act that created the National Park Service, as well as the one that established this particular park, provides that all wild life be protected. The golden eagle, mountain lion, bobcat, coyote, snake, and every other form of wild life are included. It is only when some form presents a hazard to the lives or safety of park visitors that the park authorities are permitted to destroy it. By special permission of the Secretary of the Interior, a reduction in the number of animals may be made if it is found that excess numbers threaten the health of that particular species.

Predators that venture outside the park boundaries cannot, of course, be protected. A rancher or farmer is permitted to protect his livestock so long as that protection is on his own property.[10]

[10]"It is, of course, difficult to determine the size of the hunting area of a nesting pair [of golden eagles]. I have seen eagles fly off four miles from the nest site in a few minutes. It would seem highly improbable that eagles confined their activities to an area less than ten miles in diameter and I expect they may cruise considerably farther afield at times, especially when carrion is available." *The Wolves of Mt. McKinley*, by Adolph Murie, Fauna of the National Parks of the United States. Fauna Series No. 5, 1944, p. 224.

The author goes on to cite assemblages of eagles around carrion, and concludes that many eagles feed over a common territory and that their ranges are quite extensive.

As long as there is not sufficient food for his young inside the Big Bend National Park, the eagle, having wings, will certainly seek it outside the park boundaries, and there, just as certainly, he will be killed. An eagle having an eyrie in the Chisos Mountains can be purloining a lamb on a neighboring ranch within fifteen minutes after leaving his nest. If he chooses to soar, he will soon be soaring above private property where he becomes a legitimate target for the airplane hunter. A price is upon his head.

The only way to keep the park eagles from preying outside the park is to provide food within the park. When range conditions become somewhat restored, it will be practicable to reintroduce both the antelope and the bighorn sheep and perhaps re-establish the ancient balance among these species. This, I understand, is the present intention of park management. It may be necessary to favor one or the other species by artificial means in order to maintain the balance, but that is feasible and certainly worth-while.

Whether as eagle food or not, the Rocky Mountain sheep should be restored as a part of the fauna in this great national park. Not only is this species loaded with pioneer lore, but his tradition goes far back and beyond frontier times or even the first appearance of the white man in his range. Near by in New Mexico, the bighorn was evidently a favorite of the Zuni in pre-Columbian times.

In one of its circulars, the Laboratory of Anthropology, Sante Fe, New Mexico, reproduces in natural color the head of a mountain sheep carved in serpentine, which "was probably made to serve its owner as a hunting fetish—to safeguard him, to bring him luck. It was found among a collection of fetishes from the Pueblo of Zuni, but its character and material indicate an origin farther south; and in date, either 14th or 15th century." This particular relic may have come from the Big Bend area itself "when the most southerly sedentary peoples of our Southwest abandoned their homes in the 15th century."

13. The Golden Eagle: Soarer

As a species the golden eagle is tough. He hangs on with surprising tenacity in the face of persecution. In Scotland Seton Gordon reported[1] that, although the osprey, goshawk, kite, and erne had been exterminated, the golden eagle was still holding his own in the face of a market price on his eggs of five pounds per set.

"A Census of Pleistocene Birds," taken on the remains available in the Los Angeles, (Calif.), Museum by Hildegard Howard[2], revealed that the golden eagle was ages ago, as he still is, more abundant in a certain section of California than all the other accipitrids taken together.

Nevertheless, the golden eagle cannot survive systematic, continued, and unlimited killing by airplane in a range as narrow as that to which this bird is confined in the Davis Mountains, the Guadalupe Mountains, and other small ranges including those in the Big Bend of the Rio Grande.

This war on a species, killing at the rate of a thousand individuals per year, which also destroys nearly as many eaglets per year, is but an incident, however, or skirmish in the general onslaught commercial interests equipped with an improved technology are now prepared to wage against wild

[1]"The Golden Eagle," Seton Gordon, *The Nineteenth Century,* 101:574–81, April 1937.
[2]*Condor* XXXII:87, March 1930.

life on a hundred different fronts, wherever killing pays directly or yields a profit indirectly in mitigation of a pest.

From the Stone Age on, the weapons of war and the chase have been interchangeable, and one activity has been a preparation and training for the other. In modern war we learn to kill each other at great distances and on a scale which actually threatens the life of our own species. In intervals of peace we proceed to turn the technology so developed and the skills so acquired against the lower animals. Competition in war and in the chase not only develops unbelievable ingenuity in the creation of weapons but toughens the conscience to tolerate their most diabolical applications.

Whaling expeditions are now fitted out with the elaborateness of a land-and-sea operation against an enemy country. Optical instruments, long-range guns, airplanes, radar, radio, and all the ghastly paraphernalia of human carnage are turned against one species or another for commercial profit or for sport. But those animals of which the slaughter provides either sport or profit still have a better chance of survival than those considered pests, since neither sportsman's nor business' interests care to kill the goose which lays the golden egg. Sportsmen are well-organized even across national boundaries to preserve game, and they often do a splendid job. The sperm whale, scientists say, would be exterminated in a few years if uncontrolled competition for this golden harvest were permitted. Commercial interests have succeeded in getting whaling nations together to subscribe to certain rules which, if enforced, will probably give this monster mammal of the deep a long lease on life. These are stirrings of conscience; the nerve-endings are in the pocketbook.[3]

[3]Hunters were first to discover the dangers of modern technology in the realm of sport. They saw that it threatened not only the extinction of game animals but destruction of sport for sport's sake. Plato discussed this very point twenty-five hundred years ago, and roundly condemned the use of "lazy contrivances" such as nets since such devices killed the very spirit of sport and impoverished the educational returns from participation in it. Hunters have placed on the modern statute books many laws forbidding under severe penalties the use of "lazy contrivances." "All things are with more spirit chased than enjoyed," expresses the very essence of sport. Technology by making

But pests—that is, animals which do, or are accused of, damage to commercial or sportsmen's interest—against these is waged relentless war. The people who love these pests are many but unorganized, and are in no position to make their influence felt. They are even derided as sentimentalists, and mewling souls by the big he-men who, scorning such weakness, nourish in their hardy souls a genuinely masculine lust of slaughter.

The National Park Administration and various voluntary organizations make up the only nuclei of resistance to what is often ignorant and indiscriminate persecution. The great unorganized mass of people who simply love wild creatures, and glory in the vast variety of nature, and consider the extinction of any species of life a catastrophe of major proportions—in short, people who believe that the educative power of nature is almost, if not quite, indispensable to the forming of a genuinely moral character—these have no machinery for effective action and few organs of protest, even.

Before the age of modern technology, animals had time to learn to recognize new enemies and how to cope with them. Changes of natural environment usually came slowly enough to permit an evolutionary accommodation of their ways of life to new conditions. Marsh-forming or marsh-drying, for

killing easy satisfies a kind of primitive blood-lust but deprives sport more and more of the high spiritual values claimed for it in hardier times among the great races of men.

Under the present system of "deer leases," plus legal protection, deer multiply, but deer-hunting as a sport tends to become decadent. It is too easy. On one great ranch in Texas the hunter is not allowed to leave the automobile. He pays his fee and is then conducted to the herd by a chauffeur-guide. The buck being selected by the guide, the hunter rests his rifle on the window frame of the car, kills the animal at a distance of rarely more than sixty yards, and the hunt is over. Actual money is paid for the privilege of hunting after this fashion. For eleven months out of the year these deer have been taught not to fear an automobile or a man with a gun. They associate with domestic cattle and become almost as gentle. They have been thus conditioned to easy hunting. Lazy contrivances vitiate sport. They deprive it of those disciplinary values Plato prized, and they must also leave any poet cold. "The stag at eve had drunk his fill"—and, being discovered by a chauffeur-guide, was shot by a chaperoned hunter—is rather uninspiring. I doubt if any modern Scott is going to make much of a poem of such an incident.

illustration, was a gradual process. Now marshes are made or dried up overnight. Grassy plains are converted as suddenly into plowed fields; physiographic features are radically altered, giving no time for those slow, evolutionary transmigrations of wild life, or for it to adjust itself in any other way. The duck with her brood of new-hatched ducklings, striking out across a desiccated prairie in hopeless search of the ancient but no longer existent marsh, stands as a symbol of what these man-wrought cataclysms mean to wild life.

Game animals learned to keep their distance from man through the long ages of evolution in his weapons from stick and stone to sling shot or boomerang, and from dart to bow and arrow. But now no time is permitted. Airplane, radio, radar, increasing range of gunfire, optical instruments —all burst pell-mell from a thousand factories to be turned at once against "the great whales and every living creature that moveth . . . and every winged fowl," which, says the author of Genesis, when "God created" He "saw that it was good."

Nevertheless, a whole species sometimes readily adapts itself to technological changes which impinge upon its way of life and seem seriously to threaten its very existence. There are amazing instances of the teachability of both wild and domestic species when confronted suddenly by some menace of man's making. It was freely predicted fifty years ago that barbed wire could never be used for horse pastures. Horses in fear or frolic dashed right into it, cut their own throats, tore great slugs of flesh from their breasts, while wounds not fatal or mere scratches became infested with screwworms. I can remember the time when there was hardly a horse to be found in Texas farming or ranching sections that was not scarred up from encounters with barbed wire.

When automobiles first appeared, horse-drawn traffic was disorganized. The more considerate autoist would drive out of the road and cut off the motor immediately a team of horses hove in sight. Not only that, the motorist would get out of his car and help the driver lead the rearing, snorting horses by it. Many the vehicle wrecked and many the neck broken in making the introduction of horse to automobile and establishing his tolerance for it. Loud were the demands for laws to keep automobiles in their place.[4] But in half a century the horse has learned to avoid barbed wire. Colts rarely dash into it. The whole species has been taught a new fear.

Domestic stock generally have lost their original fear of both the locomotive and the automobile, although those animals both wild and domestic which depend upon speed for their safety will course down a railroad track in front of an approaching train until it bumps them off, apparently unable ever to learn the connection between the oncoming locomotive and the two rails which demark their fatal course. Here, it seems, is a lesson too complicated to be learned, viz., that the locomotive or the automobile cannot leave the track which has been built for it.

The jack rabbit hasn't learned this, either. Oblivious to the fact that the automobile is tied to the pavement, this fleet hare undertakes to outrun it straightaway and often comes to grief, as the litter of dead jacks along any highway in jack-rabbit country attests. His instinct holds him to smooth running areas which in a state of nature have always yielded an advantage over terrestrial pursuers. He dodges only after being pushed to desperation, and hardly ever then. Attacked from the air, however, the jack rabbit seeks cover. I once saw a young jack darting from cover to cover like an artful and seasoned dodger to avoid the stoops of a prairie falcon, although there was plenty of open country

[4]Senator Joseph Weldon Bailey, champion of both the farmer and the horse, introduced into the United States Senate a bill forbidding automobiles access to the public highways, in support of which he said, with his accustomed oratorical flourish: "If my friend, Senator Warren, wishes to use one of these newfangled devices inside the confines of his own ranch in Wyoming, no one shall say him nay, but not on the public road. The horse has an ancient and prescriptive right to the highways."

to run on. A Wyoming rancher told me that a jack rabbit, attacked by a golden eagle in the open country, makes immediately for a fence, if there is one handy, and courses down it until the eagle gives up pursuit. Thus the jack rabbit has a different defense against the eye of the eagle from that which he employs against the nose of the wolf.

It is almost a rule that when the young of any species in association with adults experience a new danger and live to get away, they acquire through imitation a protective fear. This, of course, happens oftener to gregarious than to solitary animals, but only when the new menace does not run afoul of a fundamental instinct. The antelope, for instance, cannot be taught to hide. It has depended too long on sight and speed. "Its sole aim is to be able to see its enemies, and it cares nothing whatever about its enemies' seeing it." Hence, valuable game animal that it is, it could not without legal protection survive the use against it of the high-powered rifle with effective range exceeding the animal's vision. But even before the introduction of long-range guns, the pronghorn's insatiable curiosity threatened it with extinction. I have heard old hunters tell of lying flat aback, feet in air and rifle between legs, until the antelope's curiosity drew him within range.

The armadillo depends for his safety more upon his ears and nose than upon his eyes. His hearing is good, and at a strange sound he stands on his hind legs and sways his body from side to side, giving his nose a wide arc in which to verify the odor of a possible enemy. This habit helps against his natural enemies but greatly increases the hazard of his crossing an automobile highway. The rumble of an approaching car causes him to rear up and sway his body from side to side. In this position his head is just high enough to be cracked by the bumper, whereas if he had proceeded across the highway, instead of stopping to smell out the danger, he would have escaped unhurt. Or if he had done his smelling on all fours instead of in an upright position, the chances are that the car would have passed over without injuring him. Will he ever learn to keep on across the road when he hears a suspicious sound or, having paused, will he ever learn to use his nose on all fours? I think not.

Animals absorb fears from their parents. They are not born with them. The reason the mare is able to teach her foal the danger of barbed-wire fence is that she shows this fear herself in the foal's presence and the foal imitates her physical reaction to it. The mare has learned from experience or from her own mother that the fence is dangerous, and therefore in her plays and gambols avoids it. The colt running with her checks up also in imitation and thus, during his association with his mother, establishes a habit of avoidance which appears to us a fear. This teaching is passed on from generation to generation as a social but not as a biological inheritance. The colt also learns tolerance of the automobile in the same way, and we no longer have breakneck runaways every time a team of horses meets an automobile on the highway.

Many of the delicate physical reactions of the mother by which she imparts to her young the fears, attractions, repulsions, indifferences, and curiosity, and the various gradations and minglings of these important emotions, long escaped the attention of animal psychologists. Too much was attributed to inheritance. The young is for the gestation period physically a part of the mother. This ends, of course, with birth, but there persists a mysterious psychic connection long after the physical tie is severed. The whole being of the infant animal is attuned to the mother so sensitively that it still seems to be physically a part of her, and its nervous system, particularly, merely an extension of hers.

At the approach of danger, how instantaneously the fawn bounds away with the doe, as if set on an identical spring; and how quickly the kitten learns to spit in unison with its mother and with the same facial expression! Within three weeks after birth the foal has learned to wheel, back his ears, and kick in exact imitation of the mother, a coordinated action of considerable complexity. The young animal at first merely imitates the actions of the mother and only gradually comes to feel the emotion to which he has already given physical expression.

This teaching by imitation—or through some mystic psychic connection—is, of course, not confined to the animal world. Much of the education of children referred to as absorbed with the mother's milk is transmitted by the same method by which the kitten learns to spit its displeasure or the pup learns to wag its welcome.

I knew a mother of twins who, having lost one by death, alienated the affections of the other by continually weeping over him in memory of the one who had died. After a month of this the little three-year-old boy not only avoided his mother but often burst into tears at her approach.

The wolf's pup snarls at the odor of man long before he has experienced any injury or discomfort at the hands of man. He snarls because his mother snarls, and the physical mechanism set up in him flowers as distrust, anger, hatred, belligerency, and so on, even though the kindliest treatment is accorded him by his human keeper.

It has been demonstrated by actual experiment that the pup of a wolf suckled from the first by the bitch of a domestic dog has no fear whatever of man and is quite as docile as the pup of a domestic dog. Reverse the relationship, however, and give the pup of the domestic dog to the wolf, and as the pup grows, he absorbs and exhibits the reactions of his foster mother. Reared by his own mother, he is soon "wilting" his ears and wagging his tail at the odor which, under tutelage of his wolf mother, brings up his bristles and unsheathes his baby teeth. In a state of nature, by weaning time the wolf pup absorbs into himself all, or nearly all, of his mother's reactions, learns what animals he must pursue for food, which ones must be avoided, and those which are neither good nor dangerous. He must know them by sound, sight, and smell—he must be a postgraduate in the lore of wolfdom, for one little slip on examination may mean his extinction.

The gregarious animals have a long period of tutelage. They are absorbed gradually into the flock or herd. Solitary animals, of which the eagle is one, are graduated more abruptly. Gregarious animals generally seem to be smarter, at least more teachable, than solitary ones, but the difference may be due to the longer period of schooling the former receive, and to the advantages of a larger faculty.

The wise and gregarious crow has accurately spaced himself from man to accord with the improvement in the range of rifle fire. He knows just when to take off, as man approaches rifle in hand, and the young pick up this useful knowledge by association with adults.

For years I have had difficulty in getting near enough to several different species of hawk to identify them. On foot they can rarely be approached at all, not even near enough to bring them into range of ordinary field glasses. Like the crows, they have learned almost to a yard how far a rifle ball will carry. They have learned something else about the automobile, and that is that a moving car is harmless, while one that stops is dangerous. Often I have passed within a few yards of an interesting hawk sitting on a fence post, staring at the moving automobile from a distance of a few yards. Having learned his fear, I pass on to a distance of a hundred yards or so before stopping to take a look; and nine times out of ten, the moment the car stops, the object of my interest takes wing and sails safely away. Hawks must have learned this in a comparatively short time.

Theodore Roosevelt reports three antelope fawns suckled by a sheep, which became so gentle that you actually had to kick them out of the way.

Along new automobile highways in the Jewish state of Palestine, the little African wood doves, there only for the nesting season, have not learned to associate danger with an automobile, "so they can be picked off the telephone wires with perfect ease."[5]

It was a common belief among Texas ranchmen of the

[5]Paula Arnold, "Wild Life on a Palestine Farm," *Contemporary Review*, 154:470-7, October 1938.

early days that the calf of the wild longhorn was born with more intelligence than the calf of any of the gentle breeds, which showed no fear of man and would follow a dog or any other farmyard animal around, even trying to suck it. Such an inference fails to take account of the fears instilled by the reactions of the longhorn mother who either threw herself into an attitude of defense immediately at the approach of a man or any other enemy, or else fled. The calf imitates her reactions and, imitating them, comes to feel the emotion of fear. As Professor William James used to point out to his classes fifty years ago, "You are frightened because you run rather than run because you are frightened." The physical reaction precedes instead of follows fear or any other emotion. Certainly it does in the young of animals who reflect with an exquisite sensitiveness every physical reaction of the mother; the widened nostril, the tremor, tensing of muscles, the lowered head of belligerency in the bovine tribe; the backed ears, wheel, and kick of the horse, and so on.

I have heard it asserted, also, that range horses are more intelligent than those reared about the farm, but I doubt it. Of course, farm-reared horses know less of how to take care of themselves on the range than horses native there, but that is not evidence that they are less intelligent. The colts of the range mares pick up the knowledge of how to care for themselves by imitating those with which they associate; the horses of the barnyard pick up different information and acquire different habits from barnyard animals.

During the blizzard of January 1–4, 1947, the whole of west-central Texas was covered with snow and sleet for four days, a very unusual spell of weather in this latitude. I was caring for two brood mares, one colt, and two three-year-old range fillies. The two brood mares stayed around the shed the whole time and begged for food every time I appeared. They didn't even try to find food on their own account. The two range fillies, on the other hand, disappeared the day the blizzard struck, and I saw no more of them for three days. I knew they could take care of themselves, but finally became uneasy and went to look for them.

In the far end of the pasture, among the scrub oak and cedars, I soon found areas each several yards square on which the crust of sleet and snow had been broken, pawed away, and the grass underneath closely grazed. I saw that they had been caring for themselves. Continuing my search, I found these two "rustlers" on a plateau grazing among rubble, that is, loose stones from four to ten inches in diameter, scattered about. The careless grazers which had preceded them had grazed only up to the edges of the boulders, leaving blades and tufts of grass hugging the stones too closely to be cropped. These fillies were nosing over the boulders, cropping the tufts of grass thus exposed, and making out very well.

Pawing the crust away for the grass underneath and nosing boulders to one side—a thaw had by this time loosened the stones—require intelligence, but I am convinced that if the brood mares had had the same schooling as the fillies, they too would have been out pawing away the crust and nosing out bits of grass among the stones. And if the fillies had been reared about the barnyard, associating from colthood with animals which had got their food by whinnying every time a man appeared, their intelligence during this cold spell would have been exercised in exactly this way. The rural-reared youngster is amazed at the stupidity of the city chap who is visiting him, but when he returns the visit, he leans heavily on the "intelligence" of his city pal to find his way around.

But with all the teachability of wild animals, an invention which permits man to take advantage of some basic instinct in killing them gives him power of life and death over the species itself. The little Carolina parakeet, a pest, whose instinct was to succor a wounded member of the flock, brought the whole of any given flock within range of the deadly shotguns of farmers whose crops they were devastating. The passenger pigeon's instinct for compact roosting which permitted hunters literally to thresh the birds out with flails was largely responsible for the extinction of that species. They couldn't learn solitary roosting or even learn to scatter themselves about a little.

The alligator whose eye cannot suddenly adapt itself to a bright glare at night is threatened with extinction by the use against him of a simple bull's-eye lantern and buckshot. One hunter on one southern plantation is said to have killed two thousand in a single season.[6]

The armadillo will never learn to duck under an approaching automobile for the reason that the young have been taught to rear up and sway the nose from side to side at a suspicious sound before they ever come into contact with an automobile and after they have been graduated from the care of adults. This particular animal, being neither game nor pest nor commercially valuable, is marked for nothing more than accidental slaughter. It is the animal falling within one of these three classifications which is in danger of extinction whenever a basic instinct of his meets head-on one of those deadly devices which technology is now supplying in ever-increasing variety and volume.

Soaring is the basic instinct which renders the golden eagle a ready victim to the kind of attack described in the foregoing pages. But for it, he could not be located so easily and, once located, he would be more difficult of approach by plane. He has the power of hedge-hopping. Often he dashes up one slope within a few feet of the ground to surprise his prey on the other slope as he tops the hill. The squirrel, one of his favorite foods, is taken this way. A hedge-hopping flight would completely frustrate a pursuing plane.

Soaring, the eagle discovers his food; soaring, he courts and attracts his mate. He is thus tied to soaring by the two most fundamental instincts, food and sex. A non-soaring eagle would starve; and even if he didn't starve, he could never mate.

Having mastered the upper air, having ruled there for

[6]Herbert Ravenel Sass, "Dragon Music," *Saturday Evening Post*, 219:22–3, December 21, 1946.

countless ages, it is his instinct to fight any intruder. In this, his native element, he cannot be taught to fear or flee.

But even if an individual eagle could be taught to cope with an airplane, the skill could not be transmitted, since the eagle is solitary. He associates with his young for only a brief period after they have learned to fly. A group of ten or fifteen may gather around a carcass, but immediately their hunger is satisfied, they disperse. So, in any given range, it would seem that the golden eagle can be quickly exterminated by methods now in use in the Davis Mountains.

It is one of those curious ironies that the soaring habit, which has been mainly responsible for the golden eagle's world-wide fame, now renders him an easy victim. It is soaring, more than any other characteristic, which has glorified the tradition of this magnificent bird. He more than any other flying creature first set man adreaming of flight. He fledged the arrow of man's ancient longing, and now,

"on the shaft that made him die,
Espies a feather of his own."

Some birds sing; others soar. While the diurnal birds of prey are not so dumb as their kin, the vultures, still their range of sound is strictly limited. A shriek in anger or in triumph, the noise of flexed wings cutting the resistant air in a three-mile-a-minute plunge for prey or pleasure, a few uneuphonious calls or screams in courtship—these about exhaust the list of their sound-producing abilities. But there are compensations.

That picture of wintry desolation created by Keats in the phrase, "and no birds sing," is somewhat relieved if there are soarers present, as this same poet indicates with the line,

"Eagles may seem to sleep wingwide upon the air."

Their art is pictorial rather than musical. If art is essentially play, and a manifestation of exuberance of life over and above the amount required, soaring is as much an art as singing. It, too, is a working-off of excess energy, inspired by the sheer joy of living. Thus the eagle, his brood fed and safe from attack, his own hunger appeased, an adequate food surplus cached, joy in his heart—thus conditioned, he elects to soar for soaring's sake, pleased to the great hollows in his bones with the very inutility of action, else why should he plunge two, three, four thousand feet, only to mount again? Why should he experiment, descending rolling over and over sideways, winding up, so to speak, and halfway down, reverse and unwind, as one observer describes his doing? Why should he still soar at nightfall as the earth darkens and obscures any possible prey?

At the mouth of St. Helena Canyon on the Rio Grande, an area now included in the Big Bend National Park, I saw a golden eagle take off from a promontory just at sunset. I followed him with my field glasses in ever-ascending circles as the sun sank lower and lower beneath the horizon. Higher and higher he rose, and still I held him in the field of my binoculars even at the peak of his flight, a fleck of sunlight in a sky almost ready for stars, and after the songsters in the darkened valley had gone to roost.

14. Nature Lore
in Folklore

Even the humblest naturalist soon finds himself becoming a folklorist of a sort, for he depends upon folks for much of his information. In the nature lore of the people he finds much truth that is stranger than fiction, and also much fiction in excellent disguise. The wheat he harvests from this field is cluttered up with much miscellaneous rubbish which somehow must be got rid of, and in the processing he passes not only on the reliability of witnesses but on the credibility of the story itself. Nor can he simply discard a liar out of hand as soon as he discovers one, for unreliable witnesses are often repositories of valuable information, as any lawyer knows. He finds himself studying beliefs in general, irrespective of their truth or falsity, because they furnish clues.

Thus when Thoreau, a specialist in beliefs, was told by the natives that Provincetown cows ate codfish, he was interested but skeptical. He could find no actual eyewitnesses to this contradiction of bossy's herbivority. He didn't himself notice any more interest on the part of Provincetown cows in fishy food than on the part of Concord kine with which he had long been associated on intimate terms as a yardman. While doubting the story, he set himself to find the reason for the belief, for it is almost an axiom of folklore that any widespread belief, though in itself absurd, still has some reason for existence.

He kept inquiring around until he found an "inhabitant"

who assured him that *sometimes* the cows thereabouts did eat cod's *heads* but not *often*. He might live there his whole life and not see one eat a piece of codfish. A less easily satisfied person might have taken this for an answer, but the conversation continued, and presently the inhabitant volunteered the information that sometimes a cow wanting salt would "lick out all the soft part of the cod on the flakes."

With this cue Thoreau runs back over all the tales he can find handed down from Oelian, Pliny, Nearchus, as well as those from more modern chroniclers—Braybosa, Niebuhr, and others—concerning this perverted bovine appetite, suggesting by implication that the whole cow-eat-fish cycle might be nothing more than cow-licks-salt. For my own part I have seen many instances of cow-eat-gunny-sack, especially gunny-sacks which had contained salt. This kind of prodding-around the naturalist is bound to do all the time.

Alexander Wilson carried the brains and entrails of a Carolina parakeet in his pocket "until it became insufferable," trying to find a cat to eat the mess in an effort to confirm or discredit the general belief that entrails and brains of the parakeet kill cats. But experimental material was scarce, and he had too much faith in the story to try out a dose on household pets in the homes which extended him hospitality. He thought it worth while to record that one witness declared that it was not the entrails themselves which were lethal, but the seeds of the cocklebur. This was reasonable since everyone knew that parakeets preferred cocklebur seed to any other food and that their entrails were usually stuffed with them. The brains dropped out of the story unnoticed. The parakeet is probably extinct and this bit of folklore now seems safe from experimental attack. There are plenty of cats and plenty of cocklebur seed, but no entrails, and entrails may be an essential element of the mixture.

The first time I heard of a frog's swallowing a humming-bird, I dismissed it as a fiction at once. The frog, said I, is a favorite with fablers and, like the toad, may wear a precious jewel in his head, and his toe along with "the eye of newt" is still essential to the potency of any witch's broth. I re-examined the testimony, however, when a credible witness told me that he saw a frog swallow the head of one of his ducks. Then I ran across several indisputable records of other Calibans swallowing other Ariels, and of one Ariel playing Jonah to a trout.

But when an eminent folklorist published a letter from a correspondent living in Mathis, Texas, saying that she saw a praying mantis catch, hold, and eat a hummingbird, I said this was too much. A frog, yes; a mantis, no! Hummingbirds are the least birds, and folklore always exaggerates any outstanding characteristic, like the cleverness of the fox, the stupidity of the ox, the affection of the dog, the tininess of the hummingbird. This is a perfect case: frog swallows one, devil's horse chews up another, and we shall next hear that a Texas-coast gallinipper made off with a struggling hummer.

During my consideration of this matter, I happened to remember a scientist who had been breeding and rearing the praying mantis for years in order to study a parasite to which the mantis is host. I told him the story and expected an immediate repudiation, but he was not at all surprised. Indeed, he said it might very well be true. "They capture large moths, hold down their wings with their powerful front legs, and devour them with jaws quite strong enough to masticate the flesh of a hummingbird." He then inquired where this incident was said to have occurred, and suggested that there might be a larger species of praying mantis there than the one I was accustomed to seeing. When I told him of the extreme depth of the breastbone of this little bird and of its large and powerful flight muscles operating wings which carry it all the way from Alaska to Brazil, sometimes beating out two hundred strokes per second, and pointed out that surely with such power and action the hummer could easily shake off any insect, he was still unimpressed.

Then I wrote a scientific journal, and the editor replied by citing me to the record of a South American praying mantis capturing a hummingbird[1] but expressed the opinion that if it happened at all, it was not a normal procedure. My first skepticism was considerably jarred and it is still shaky, especially since finding the record of a dragonfly's taking a hummingbird, and of another one's becoming entangled and held in a spiderweb.

Since we are speaking of hummingbirds, hardly a year passes that the press services do not put out as a fact, giving names, dates, places, and other circumstantial data, an account of a hummingbird's hitch-hiking on migration, concealed in the feathers of a larger bird: the stork is his usual victim in Europe and the goose in America. Science refuses to countenance this one at all, but folks are determined to have it anyway. I wrote my science editor about it and unfortunately he published my letter. Among the replies I got was one from a woman who assures me that the hummer is indeed and in fact a hitch-hiker:

> Noted your letter. It is common for small birds to ride on the backs of big ones in this locality. I see them doing so in spring and fall. Suppose they are migrating. This fall I have seen kinglets and hummingbirds riding on the backs of crows, hawks, and buzzards.

[1]*Entomological News*, Vol. 44, p. 39, February 1933.

Another letter is from a gentleman apparently enraged that I should even raise such a question, and he proceeds to vent his disgust with my credulity by resort to caricature, spoofing me thus:

> Referring to your inquiry, I shot a lovely specimen of the great horned owl two days ago. Imagine my surprise and delight when fourteen tiny hummingbirds tumbled out from underneath the old owl's wings and side-pockets. One of them sung out very distinctly just before the owl fell, "Straighten up and fly right." You are partly right, the hummingbirds don't ride on the *backs* of big birds, but are tucked in *under the wings* which form side-pockets as it were. Have never seen them standing up on the big bird's back and holding on with their feet. Am shipping dead owl to you express collect, with three hummingbirds.

I can't quite see myself how such a travel bureau could function, since the hummingbird must have blooming flowers from which to suck nectar along his route or else die of starvation. The goose is quite independent of flowers and often lands ahead of the nectar-producing season. If the goose should deliver his hummingbird here in this part of the Edwards Plateau before the buckeye blooms, his passenger would certainly perish of hunger.

But it makes little difference how many facts kick this story in the head, it will not die. It is too pleasing a fancy, too human. The poor hummingbird, so small, so frail, and such a long, long journey and cold, too. And here is a great big stork or goose, powerful, majestic, just ready to take off for the very place to which the hummingbird wants to go. What more natural than that he should conceal himself as a stowaway on this great ship of the air and ride safely to his destination! Of course, the big bird flies high and it's cold as Christmas up there, but what cares the little hummer snuggled down in goose feathers, warm and comfy, with his long bill sticking up through the feathers for air, of course. The little fellow has to have air. The other element which gives this story vitality is that it permits the weak a victory over the strong, as in the fable of the lion and the mouse. Folks like that. "The meek shall inherit the earth." It is the kind of thing folks will not willingly let die.

Some of the soldiers and sailors returning from islands in the Pacific tell about the myna's "courts of justice." Since Aristophanes and perhaps before his day, there have been tales of government by birds, legislative, judicial, and executive. Chaucer announces a Parliament of Birds to try the cuckoo. Fiction, fable, folklore, and straight-out faking all exploit this fancy, so the seedbed is ready for any germ of observed fact to sprout, grow, and luxuriate. There is a considerable volume of serious literature touching the matter.

The myna story is that one bird accused of having committed some offense against the social order is tried and, if found guilty, executed. The myna's court omits nothing. There is prosecution and defense, judge or judges, executioners, and all the pomp, ceremony, and functionaries of a human court of justice. I wrote the young Lieutenant Commander who told me this story, expressing my doubt and asking if he had ever actually seen a myna tried, convicted, and executed. He replied, as follows:

> The myna story may well be folklore, but: (1) While I have never seen the full story acted out, I have seen a conclave of squeaking mynas surrounding one of their number, all beaks pointing inward and the air rent with their racket; (2) I have picked up a bloody myna with a bit of life left in him, whose head had been pecked viciously, so weak he could not stand up on his legs.

There is basis in fact for this story, but on the foundation of fact is an old, old story built as high as or higher than ever before. The fact is that the mynas have playlike brawls in which a tough fight is simulated but none of the combatants is hurt by so much as a permanently displaced feather. The authorities are agreed on this. But the superstructure reared hereupon is made up of materials gathered over a wide extent of space and time. Goldsmith's *Natural History* cites Mrs. Starke's "Letter from Italy" telling of a wild stork which was brought home by a farmer to be companion to his tame stork. The tame bird resented the intrusion and tore the wild one nearly to pieces before he escaped. Four months later, according to Goldsmith's informant, the wild stork returned to the farmer's barnyard with three companions and all four fell upon the tame stork and killed him on the spot. Justice was done. Moral: "Be not forgetful to entertain strangers, for thereby some have entertained angels unawares." Folks like this, too.

Reverend G. Gogerly quotes a missionary, Mr. Lacroix, who says he saw flamingos hold court and kill a criminal. The usual court machinery is here present: crime, assembly, prosecution, sentence, execution.[2] Here also Bishop Stanley quotes a French surgeon who touches up the tale with sex interest. It seems that a hen's eggs were placed under a brooding stork in place of her own. When the chicks began breaking through their shells, the male stork left home in a rage and returned in a couple of days with large numbers of storks who proceeded to try and execute the faithless female. Rev. F. O. Morris tells this same story, but changes hen eggs to goose eggs—betrayal still more heinous!—and lays the scene in Berlin. In this trial five hundred storks participated, and "one after another addressed the assembly." The upshot of the affair was that the female was found guilty and executed. The Reverend Morris reports another case with a happier ending: the two storks, male and female, joined in exterminating the chicks as they hatched out. In this case circumstantial evidence failed to convince, and the moral is implicit for jealous husbands. Folks like this, too.

Storks have a way of gathering together in great flocks

---

[2] This story is quoted in an unsigned article, "Bird Courts of Justice," *Popular Science Monthly*, Vol. 33, p. 834, 1888.

after the young are reared. They concentrate in stubble fields and a great clappering of bills takes place. This is called the "council of storks" and according to legend the date of departure on migration is set. They are also said to kill off those individuals unfit for the migration flight. At any rate, great numbers of storks gather in from miles around for a great premigration powwow. Possibly this council is the basis for courts-of-justice stories, and the fact that crows have a way of getting together to do a lot of cawing has fastened this story upon them also.

A generally accepted belief, like a modern automobile highway, has its ancestors. Fifty years ago a wagon road followed the same general course, and off the modern highway here and there are vestiges of ruts or a little primitive grading. Scratch a little deeper and you may find a pioneer trail by which the traveler went from one water hole to another, or from mountain pass to ford of creek or river after crossing which, the trail veered this way or that to escape a marsh. The savage bequeathed this trail to the pioneer, while a still more ancient animal trail probably fathered the Indian trail. So it is with beliefs, especially in the field of folklore: folk-thinking turns and twists and veers about. Perhaps there is only one field of modern thought in which old trails and weathered ruts and gradings are completely scorned, and that is in the field of pure mathematics.

Since the wood duck nests in the hollow of a tree ten, thirty, or even fifty feet above the ground, the method of descent of the ducklings has been a matter of considerable controversy. Some say they climb up the hollow to the opening and simply tumble out. Others say the parents carry them to the ground. All except one observer agree that if the nest is above water, the ducklings tumble out.

Audubon *asserts* that the mother carries the ducklings down, but *records that he saw* them tumble from the nest. If they are carried, how does the parent carry them—in the bill or on the back? The back and the bill—each has its partisans and its eyewitnesses. Mr. Bent's[3] correspondents have seen the wood duck in flight carrying the duckling, and they have seen the duckling carried in the bill and between the feet, as well as on the back. Dr. T. S. Roberts[4] inclines to the tumbling theory and quotes Joseph Dixon's[5] study in which out of twelve nests under observation, eighty per cent of which were over water, he actually saw the ducklings tumble out of three of the nests. None were carried. Those who have seen a little one riding on the back of the mother say that as soon as she gets over water she throws her body into a vertical position and thus dumps the duckling.

The anatomist makes his contribution by observing that the wood duckling is hatched with long, sharp toenails, which would seem to indicate that nature knew that he would immediately have some climbing to do. The duckling is also supplied with an unusual amount of down. He is described as an unusually fluffy duckling, which would seem to anticipate some sort of fall, but whether from the nest or from the mother's back or beak is not indicated.

Evidence comes from a very high authority in England. Viscount Grey, of Fallodon K. G., in *Fallodon Papers*[6] tells of setting his gardener, a Mr. Henderson, of unquestionable integrity, to keep watch over a brood of wood ducks in a nest thirty-one feet above the ground. Henderson saw the parent duck on hatching day fly out of the hole and take her position in the grass and utter a peculiar call. Then one after another of the ducklings climbed from the nest up two feet to the entrance and tumbled down into the grass. Whereupon the mother assembled her brood and led them through the grass to the water three hundred yards away.

Of course, it is possible that two methods are used, but

[3]Life Histories of North American Wild Fowl, Bulletin 126, pp. 162–4, 1923.

[4]*The Birds of Minnesota*, 1:248, The University of Minnesota Press, Minneapolis, 1936.

[5]"Nest of the Wood Duck in California," Joseph Dixon, *Condor*, 26:41–61, March–April, 1924.

[6]Constable & Co., Limited, p. 121, 1925.

unlikely, since it is the nature of an instinct to discharge itself in a definitely restricted channel. There are few alternatives. Choice, the great stimulus of rational thinking, confuses instinct.

To me, the claws are the most marvelous thing about the whole story. Two days out of the shell, the duckling has developed claws long, sharp, and hard enough to enable it to climb a perpendicular wall of wood two to four feet high, roughly twelve to twenty-four times its own height. Coincidentally with climbing hooks it has developed enough feathers to break a fall of thirty feet. I am inclined to reject the carrying story, since folks like the motherliness of safe-conduct, especially by air, and resent the idea of a mother hard-hearted enough to call her babies off a high place to fall hit or miss, bumpity-bump, to the ground. Surely folks don't like that, and to avoid it the story takes off on an old trail.

But it is folklore about the owl which is really immortal. The ruts of the old trails in the popular mind are deep—ancient trails, even animal trails. Fear of the night: the owl is the child of the dusk—flies and hoots and hunts by night. It loves darkness because its deeds are evil. Its face caricatures the human face and thus acquires a weird power over human destiny. It is secretive and, as night falls, wings its way in soft, snooping, noiseless flight to plunge deadly talons suddenly into its unsuspecting prey. In the tower which broods over the churchyard with its "magazine of bones," the owl mopes by day and at night "doth to the moon complain." In deep woods one often has a sense of uneasiness; at least, I do. Someone is watching from a hiding, and presently this bird of ill omen from a recess in leaves or camouflaged against the trunk of a tree is staring. Owls don't look; they stare.

And since people—or rather the waste foods people leave lying about—attract rats and mice, owls haunt human habitations. The rats and mice den up in secret places in the house and barn, and the hungry owl stalks them there, in which pursuit the owl gets the reputation of being sly and stealthy, whereas it is his prey which is. But the mouse-rat-owl linkage is ignored, and the owl is believed, on his own motion, to haunt homes and sneak about in obscure corners. Why so surreptitious, if not for some malign purpose?

While ordinarily silent, on occasion they utter eerie and sometimes bloodcurdling sounds. The shriek of the barred owl is of this character.[7] I was camped out in a creek bottom not so long ago with a man of limited rural experience. He had been reared in a large city and although a very sensible person of good education he didn't know the difference between a sheep and a goat. On this very trip he had asked me naïvely if the goat was not the male sheep. I asked what put that idea into his head, and he replied that the goat seemed to have whiskers.

We had retired to our cots well-protected by mosquito netting since these insects were numerous and hungry. Hardly had we got to sleep when a barred owl on a limb not ten feet above my companion's cot uttered his shrill, wild cry as if in fright or horror or anguish. My friend forgot all about the mosquito netting which enclosed him, and plunged into the underbrush with it hanging about him, impeding him and finally stopping his progress. This detention increased his fright, and I found him in the glare of my flashlight flouncing frantically to free himself like a very athletic fish in a quite adequate net.

I can well understand what an evil reputation a bird or any other animal, for that matter, with such a voice and such erratic and unseasonable delivery must gain among a primitive people, especially with a tribe on trek for the first time across this bird's range and hence unfamiliar with his habits.

That the owl is a messenger of death is one of the oldest and most deeply rooted of all popular superstitions. My

[7]George Finlay Simmons describes the barred owl's voice as, "A wild mixture of hoots and bloodcurdling shrieks, screams, and loud, terrible, mocking, maniacal laughter."—*Birds of the Austin Region,* The University of Texas Press, 1925, p. 114.

fondness for having owls about, particularly the little screech owl, has brought me into conflict with my neighbors more than once. He is a friendly little bird, likes people—or the mice people attract—but his quavering voice at dusk, answered from far away like an echo or some ghost voice from another world, upsets the nerves of those who have not accustomed themselves to listening for strange sounds in nature, or cultivated an appreciation of the eerie.

> "Yon screech-owl," says the Sailor, turning
> Back to his former cause of mourning,
> "Yon owl!—pray God that all be well!
> 'Tis worse than any funeral bell;
> As sure as I've the gift of sight,
> We shall be meeting ghosts tonight!"

In New Mexico, a number of years ago, I noticed a pair of the little Mexican screech owls flitting about my yard now and then. As they remained past the time when owls should be off in the woods mating, it occurred to me that they might be depending upon me to provide nesting facilities. I put up a box of prescribed dimensions with two compartments and an entrance on each side, for I didn't know whether they preferred an east front from which they might observe the sun rise, or a west one from which they might watch the fading day and be the better able to judge just the moment when they should be off for the night's hunt.

Unfortunately I had to place the box between my back yard and that of my neighbor to the east, with only an alley intervening. The owls chose the west side of the box, nested, and reared four little ones, much to the discomfiture of my neighbor across the alley, a retired merchant and a man of great common sense but curiously afraid of owls. He protested, saying that owls about brought death, and asked me on a number of occasions to take the box down. I told him that the owls had chosen my side of the box, hence if any ill luck came, they meant to bring it to me and not to him. I could see that he was unconvinced. Other neighbors became apprised of the controversy and there developed owl and anti-owl factions, but in all good humor. As one wag put it, "Sometimes one side had the bone and sometimes the other."

When the next nesting season arrived, my neighbor across the alley again became restive. He insisted that the owls should not be permitted to nest in the box again. To make matters worse, they chose his side of the box. But I was really stubborn about it. I justified my obstinacy by telling myself that it was a good object lesson. It would help cure this silly superstition. How much of this was *pro bono publico* and how much because I simply like to have the owls about, I can't say.

One spring afternoon a few of us were gathered on the edge of a vacant lot, engaged in neighborly chat under a low and rather scrubby tree. My owl-fearing friend, in excellent spirits, had just told a good story when I happened to look up—and there not four feet above his bare bald head sat my two owls. I could not withhold an exclamation of surprise which startled the birds from their dozing and stimulated in one of them the usual reaction to sudden fright as it left the perch. My friend looked up just as the owls dashed away ... and I, feeling a kind of responsibility, came to his rescue with my handkerchief. He said no word, but his face flushed and his bald head slowly reddened. He turned and walked quickly into his house, entering by the back door which he closed violently, and I wish this might close the incident, also. But the next day I found him in bed with a high fever. The day after, all company was forbidden. The doctor called it by some unpronounceable name. Two weeks later he died.

Occasionally I check up on my notebook recordings, suspecting them of having absorbed unreliable data from the accumulation of fictions I pick up here and there and set down along with notes of factual observations. Such a doubt of the validity of my own observations evidently occurred to me on August 2, 1940, for I find a note of that date addressed to Dr. Harry C. Oberholser, greatest authority on Texas birds, which reads as follows:

> A couple of years ago I saw a cardinal with a black head on the Schieffer Ranch between Johnson City and Marble Falls, Texas. His whole crown and cheeks were black. I followed this bird around for a couple of hours, trying to make him out. I couldn't tell whether the feathers had fallen out and the skin was black or whether the feathers themselves were black. I thought maybe the bird was diseased. Now, curiously enough, there is around my home a cardinal with the same peculiarity, or disease. Can you give me some light on this dark head?

After writing this note and before receiving a reply, I got closer to the bird and saw that the head feathers including crest and upper neck had molted and that the head appeared black on account of the very dark skin.

Dr. Oberholser's reply suggested that the black-headed redbird might be a Brazilian cardinal escaped from captivity. Once in a while, it seems, a caged bird from a zoo gets loose and mystifies the amateurs. He said that a Brazilian cardinal escaped from captivity frequented the grounds of the Department of Agriculture in Washington a few years ago. He suggested further that it might be a case of partial melanism.

His second guess almost hit the bull's-eye, and convinced me that at least I was not just seeing things. The case rested here about a year when I picked up a copy of *The Wilson Bulletin*[8] giving several instances of bald-headed redbirds. This turns out to be a freak molt, for the feathers usually come back in a few months. The note is by Josselyn Van Tyne and concludes: "Thus we have a record of a cardinal at least eight years old, losing all of the feathers from its neck and head in June, remaining bald, but living normally through the whole summer, growing a complete new set of head feathers in twenty-eight days, and remaining fully feathered during at least the following ten and a half months."

[8]Vol. 55, No. 3, September 1943, p. 195.

I made inquiry now and then among out-of-doors people, hunters, farmers, and ranchers, to see if there had been any other black-headed cardinals around. There were none, but I received several times in explanation of the one I saw the suggestion that it was probably a cross between a cowbird or a grackle and a redbird. Perhaps partial melanism or partial albinism, or partial molts may be responsible for the common folk belief that interbreeding occurs between different species of birds or even between different genuses. The mottled appearance of the young summer tanager, red feathers mixed with feathers of orange or buff, often causes it to be identified as a "cross."

I have been accused of nature-faking also on account of an observation I made and duly recorded which I refer to as "the mother redbird teaching her young table manners." I realize that this is a suspicious title for a serious observation, but here are the facts.

Cardinals are fonder, I believe, of watermelon seed than of any other food. During the watermelon season I keep and cure the seed for feeding redbirds about my yard. When the young are following the mother about the yard I have noticed that she has a definite procedure in feeding watermelon seed. The nature of the seed is such that it takes her some time to crack it, extract the kernel, and nip off a small bit for the young.

While she is thus employed, the little ones gather around in front of her in a half circle. They are quite impatient. She feeds them by turns; at least she does sometimes. I watched the feeding one morning and noticed that one of the young was more aggressive than the others and kept rushing forward out of his turn to get the tidbit from the mother's bill. Presently she gave him a severe peck on the head and drove him out of the circle. It is stretching this a little to call it teaching table manners, but it's not far off. After a while I quit telling this story, thinking that it was perhaps an accident and without any particular significance. But I took it back into my good graces on May 31, 1942, when Mr. A. C. Wright, Manager of the University of Texas Press, a lifelong out-of-door man whose reliability in nature observations no one who knows him will question, told me of a similar instance.

I give it as nearly as I can in his own words: "In our yard a male redbird was preparing to feed a young bird from a scrap of hard toast. In working on the scrap he turned his back on the young bird who stood begging at a respectful distance. Then an English sparrow flew up from behind and, as he went by, snatched the piece of toast from the redbird's bill and made away with it. The redbird wheeled quickly, showing every evidence of anger, and fiercely trounced the young bird, completely unaware that it was the sparrow that had committed the larceny."

I am indebted to Mr. Wright for another sparrow-cardinal story. There was a young sparrow begging around a redbird which was feeding on crumbs at his doorstep. Presently the redbird gave the young sparrow some crumbs, feeding him exactly as he feeds his own young. I will close this on a folklore note and call it "returning good for evil." But be warned that any improbable nature story which has a popular moral neatly done up in it is probably false. This one, however, happens to be true.

15. Folk-naming of Birds and Flowers

Ruskin was fond of saying to his beginners in natural history, "Consider first what has been beautifully thought about a creature." Much that has been beautifully thought about birds and flowers will be found bound up in their folk names, for always among folk are those who have a genius for naming things. Hence I go searching for names, those names which are current locally as well as the ones already widely accepted and listed in the books. It's true that this is a meandering and indirect approach to what has been beautifully thought about a creature, but pleasant going at that.

There are other repositories of beautiful thoughts, aptly and beautifully expressed. There are the literary scientists, poets, straight-out naturalists, naturalist-philosophers, artist-naturalists, all to be considered, not to mention literary men and women with only a naturalist side line.

Genuine classics are available about the humblest creatures from the earthworm up and from the earthworm down. Darwin himself thought beautifully about the earthworm; and William Morton Wheeler thought not only beautifully, but scientifically and humorously as well, about a certain wood-burrowing insect, the termite.[1] Many good

[1]William Beebe has lately rendered good service in bringing together into small compass much that has been beautifully thought about various creatures in the anthology, *The Book of the Naturalist*. Alfred A. Knopf. New York, 1944.
This book includes the Wheeler essay just mentioned, pp. 250–262.

science instructors are not unaware of both approaches—
folk and classical—to the great storehouse and use them to
good advantage.

Not only do folk names yield beautiful thoughts, but also
folk whimseys droll or humorous, morsels of straight history,
curiously crooked thinking, and much delightful misinfor-
mation. Ageless superstitions bob up unexpectedly like gar-
goyles nooked in here and there to relieve the solemnity of
some ancient pile,

> Not unbecoming, of grotesque
> And uncouth fancy.

Almost any true folk name is a tight little package, the undoing of which discloses a lot of lore. It's the people's choice
from a multitude of random suggestions, the result of a
selective process by folks who have lived in intimate contact
with the thing named, hence judge not by criticism handed
down from above but by constant reference to fresh, first-
hand observation. The acquisition of its folk names gives
the bare idea of the creature nourishment in a seasonable
and natural way. The cluster of ideas already formed about
a natural object, called by the old psychologists an "apperceptive mass," is thus fortified and enriched.

Who in England named the field camomile the "oxeye"
for its conspicuous disk and marginal rays? And why did
New England folk, not satisfied, affix to a species with the
same external characters the name "black-eyed Susan"? No
cloistered taxonomist did this. In *Rudbeckia bicolor,* which
has captured this name in Texas, there is a gentle droop of
the flower head and a hanging-away in provocative shyness.
The black eye is fringed with long, drooping lashes. Black-
eyed Susan, I am sure, was quite a rustic belle. This all van-
ishes into thin air if one is the least critical, but the name
sticks and has spread from New England all over the country, child's play though it be.

Every time I see a house finch fronting me in a strong
light, I think of the border Mexicans' name, *pajarito dego-
llado*—"the little bird with his throat cut." The tragic stain

comes down on the breast as if with the accidental splatter and chance distribution of blood jetting arterially from a slit throat, fading out on the belly. Presently he sings and then comes the pleasure of being reassured. It's all right, after all.

But I do have a genuinely surgical memory of this finch, curious as it may seem. It is the only bird I ever saw performing an operation on its young—a throat operation at that. The patient was gagging and choking and near falling off his perch altogether. The mother approached gently and inserted her bill down the young one's throat and began pulling out gummy, viscous-looking material. She had to dig down deep to get it, but she was tender and patient about it, and the patient was quite patient, too. The little fellow clung to his perch, gaping, gagging, and apparently a bit groggy, while the old bird probed deep and deeper, withdrew, wiped her primitive instrument on a limb, probed and wiped and wiped and probed, repeating time and again. I can't be sure that the operation was successful for presently both birds flew away.

Folk names prove themselves by sticking—sticking and spreading. The botanists assign fearsomely cumbrous names, sometimes two or three, each cluttered up with the name of the individual who fathered it, and they are all duly frozen in print for the great convenience of scientists scattered about over the world; but you can't use these names in a flesh-and-blood conversation. The official list of scientific bird names is more liquid, being officially revised every so often. It is subject to continual tinkering, and a name in it may be in good standing today and out-of-date tomorrow. But some of the folk names for birds and flowers which Chaucer used are still current among English-speaking people the world over.

A folk name in natural history ordinarily seizes upon some memorable aspect, usually an external character that strikes one of the five senses right in the face without use of artificial aids—dissecting knife, scalpel, field glasses, microscope or the like. The bare thing comes up against the bare sense and delivers its message direct. Folks scorn the logic of one name for one thing. Let's have a dozen or a hundred names for the same thing, if it so pleases. One bird or flower is richer than another and requires more naming.

If a mistake is made, it is usually a nimble-witted one worthy of attention. Its ingenuity makes it memorable. Explaining such errors, we say, "People once thought thus and so about it," and what, pray, is more interesting than what people, as a whole, once thought?

Why are our nighthawks called "goatsuckers"?

Why is a certain barn-inhabiting reptile a "milk snake"?

Why was the Greek folk name for kingfisher "Halcyon"?

Why "barnacle" goose?

Whence comes "brant"?

Nearly all of these are mistakes, but each one makes a pretty little story of such tenacity that all the big dictionaries record them. After the story is known, the bullbat, the milk snake, the goose, the brant, mean more: the apperceptive mass is richer. This is lore, really and truly.

Mistakes, especially botanical errors, are sometimes corrected in rough-and-ready fashion by the simple application of the word "false" to the name. For instance, a certain plant is called at first a thistle, but to distinguish it from another thistle, color is added and it's a purple thistle. But the trouble is, a different plant already goes by that name and confusion arises. Then the new claimant to the name is discovered on closer inspection not to be a thistle at all, so it is named a "false" purple thistle. And so on. Some ten or fifteen "falses" are applied in this way to species in central Texas alone.

Folk names germinate, scientific ones are thought out: one grows, the other is constructed. Only an infinitesimal proportion of folk names survives. They die and are born like living things, "with decay restless, and restless generation." Dictionaries are sown with fossil forms, and many died before reaching dictionary dignity. Throughout nature,

as fecundity increases, individual fatalities multiply, and so
it is with folk names. One survives in one environment and
not in another, and thus arises the horde of local names.

I wish the names for the cormorant might quickly die, but
they show no signs of mortality. Perhaps they have an eso-
teric applicability that I am unable to appreciate. This good
bird has been named to his hurt both in Europe and in the
Americas, in ancient and modern times. On the New England coast it's "shag"; from Florida around the Gulf coast to
Brownsville, Texas, it's "nigger goose"; from Brownsville
south along the Mexican coast, it's *pajaro burro,* or donkey-
bird. The common names indicate that it is generally de-
spised. The cormorant is also called a black swan, in
derision; a water buzzard—he eats no carrion; and a water
turkey, an obvious mistake in identification, since "water
turkey" is the well-established name for the anhinga.

English derives "cormorant" from an old French word
meaning "sea raven," a slander, since he is a far nobler bird
than the raven, captures his fish in a legitimate fashion by
overtaking it in a fair race under water, and eats only live
prey. A raven will eat anything.

As far back in English history as the Druids, the cormorant
was a bird of ill omen:

> And toward the mystic ring
> Where augurs stand . . . .
> Slowly the cormorant her heavy flight
> Portending ruin to each baleful rite
> That, in the lapse of ages, hath crept o'er
> Diluvian truths, and patriarchal lore.

In short, the whole folk conception of the cormorant is
false, to my way of thinking. He is not a raven or anything
like one; not a buzzard or anything like one except for black-
ness and a hooked bill; not bald as the old Greek name im-
plied; has no family ties with the anhinga; doesn't stand,
swim, or look like a goose; and possesses no swan-like char-

acters whatever. Still he is a black goose, nigger goose, water buzzard, and sea raven, and will be until the end of time. The names are mostly derisive.

And just to fix this bird forever in the evil estimation of the English-speaking world, John Milton uses him to encase Satan himself when, "confirming himself in evil," the "arch felon" enters the Garden of Eden. This bringer of all our woe, even Satan, is described journeying toward "God's fold," meditating dire things for the upstart race of men. In the mighty Miltonic line he is a "prowling wolf," "a thief," who "in at the window climbs." "So clomb this first grand thief . . . as into the church lewd hirelings climb":

> Thence up he flew, and on the tree of life
> The middle tree and highest there that grew,
> *Sat like a cormorant.* (italics supplied)

And there he perched, "devising death," and, still sitting "like a cormorant," soliloquizes, revealing his dastardly intentions toward our first ancestors.

Thus science (*Phalacrocorax*—bald raven), folk-naming, and classical literature all combine to perpetuate errors and superstitions.[2]

The Mexican cormorant of the Texas coast has freshwater leanings. When Marshall Ford Lake in central Texas, two hundred miles from the Gulf, filled up a few years ago, a colony seized upon the unsubmerged tops of pecan trees as a nesting site. They were shot at and harried by fishermen,[3] but finally succeeded in bringing off a considerable

[2]Poetry is, of course, the great repository for abandoned myths and vestigial superstitions, but it is curious to find a folk belief long ago exploded in a scientific work like the *Larousse* Dictionary (*Pequeno Larousse*, Claude Auge and Miguel Toro G. Paris. 1924) which in explanation of a folk name for the hummingbird, *pajaro resucitado* (brought to life or resuscitated), says it is "because it sinks into a lethargy in winter and comes to life in the spring." This is stated not as an erroneous belief but as a fact of nature.

[3]One greasy outfit prospecting for oil in the coastal waters along the Texas shore does more damage to commercial fish and to fishing for sport than all the cormorants from Key West to Brownsville. Yet fishermen abominate this bird as a rival. Food studies have shown that the cormorant consumes few fish of any economic importance. Of course, if an individual begins haunting a fish hatchery, that is another matter and demands surgical treatment.

number of young. Two huge rattlesnakes were guarding one of these nests, a perfect one that I wanted as a museum specimen, but I punched them off into the water and took it anyway.[4] J. Stokley Ligon tells me that a colony of this same species did the same thing when Elephant Butte Lake in New Mexico filled, leaving treetops exposed above the surface.

But for this great body of false folklore and mistaken naming, we might have made the same joyful use of *Phalacocorax Mexicanus* on Texas coastal bays and estuaries that the Chinese have made of their species from time immemorial; that is, as pets to catch fish with. In England a few hundred years ago cormorant-fishing was a great sport. Indeed some of the birds were trained not to swallow the catch even with no ring on the neck. If in the beginning someone had simply named the bird a "water falcon," water falconry, using the Mexican cormorant on the Gulf coast, would probably be an established sport and we should now be getting a lot of fun and fish out of him. There is much in a name, especially in a folk name.

First settlers on western prairies called a ground squirrel a prairie dog. But this error gave the species a little longer lease on life by rendering him unacceptable to the pioneer stomach through long meat-hungry periods on this frontier. The vocal protest which these creatures make at any approach to their towns was labeled a bark, and from the bark comes the "dog." The bark proved more effective as a defense than the bite, although this rodent has wicked teeth.

The pioneer stomach stood for almost anything, but it couldn't be quiet as its owner asked someone at the supper-table to "please pass a piece of the dog." The adult prairie dog is tough, it is true, but no tougher than an old jack

---

[4]Those who believe that the rattlesnake can't swim should have seen these two wriggle away through the water, apparently as much at home as moccasins.

rabbit, and on occasion I have found young ones quite palatable. However, these cunning little animals have now been about gassed out of existence, and they are taking their interesting tenant, the burrowing owl, along with them.

On the other hand, palpable mistakes, a typographical error, mispronunciation or a fool translation, sometimes produce a good name. "Redstart," a corruption of *rothstert,* literally "redtail," is better than the original. Before I knew the origin of the name, I thought redstart was particularly apt for the bird to which it is applied. The flash or start of red or reddish orange amid the greenery, sudden, vivid, as the lively little warbler darts about, seemed to be ample justification for redstart, a sudden flash of red. I think this corruption persists because of its appropriateness.

Scholars point out that misprints have given us good words, and mispronunciations do, too. In the old days when they were the literary fashion, a Browning Society I remember delighted to gnaw the bone of some obscure phrase right down to the nub. On one memorable occasion the Society exercised itself long and arduously on the interpretation of "slet of the sea." "Slet," of course, was a Browning coinage. "Slet" was not to be found in any dictionary, but how Browningesque, how it suggested the mood—or the moodiness, so to say—of the sea, how vivid! "His genius moves out beyond the bounds of language," observed one enthusiast. Everyone present was swept away in gusts of ecstasy except one person who looked puzzled and said nothing. Finally the leader turned to her and asked for an expression. "I can't find the word," she said timidly. Then much mustering of books, comparing, verification, and many talking all at once. It turned out that the timid lady's book was a different edition from the one the Society as a whole was using, and in her book the phrase read "islet of the sea." Had this misprint occurred in a first edition, instead of in the tenth or fifteenth, the English language would probably have garnered another word. I'm sorry it didn't. I like slet, especially the slet of the sea.

In certain parts of this country the mallard is called a

stock duck, I suppose because it is so often domesticated, hence is of the stock of a domestic duck. A similar error is embalmed in the name "stock dove" of Europe. The word "stock" is held by some to apply to this dove because at one time it was believed to be of the stock of the domestic pigeon. According to another belief, it is a stock dove because it nests in "stocks," or trunks of trees.

A bird or plant of many folk names is generally found to have surprising habits, wide range, well-marked individuality, striking shape, color, design, or all together—in short, outstanding features to attract attention and give the folk fancy something to play with.

The ruddy duck has fifty-nine common names. The much-naming of this creature is due largely to its wide range. Breeding from Hudson Bay to northern South America, it comes into contact with more folk than the average duck does, and in different localities exhibits different characteristics. In nuptial dress the male is exceedingly gaudy. Although one of the smallest species of duck, it lays the largest eggs and so many of them that they are sometimes stacked three deep in the nest for convenience in hovering. Occasionally the ruddy, quite a fighter, appropriates the nest of another duck or even that of the pugnacious American coot. Ruddy ducklings just hatched dive for their food, another innovation in the duck world where well-brought-up ducklings are supposed to be surface-fed for quite a time. Nevertheless, the ruddy duckling dives right out of the shell. The bird swims deep, more like a grebe than a duck, and also has the grebelike habit of simply sinking out of sight instead of plunging headfirst in conventional duck fashion. One folk name will emphasize one characteristic and another, another. A number of names have to do with his tail, feathers of which are stiff and spikelike. At rest in the water it carries them fanwise at right angles to the back. The generic name *Erismatura*, prop-tail, emphasizes this feature. But it is inapt since the tail is not used as a prop. Swifts and woodpeckers use tail props; the ruddy duck *props up* his tail. This little duck assaults folk attention from a dozen different angles over an enormous range and earns legitimately his fifty-nine different names.

Nicknaming of human beings follows the same principle. One individual invites a nickname, another does not. Many names have been listed in various parts of the country for the flicker, also a bird of striking physical character, pronounced individuality, and country-wide range. A study of each of the more than one hundred names for this popular woodpecker would give a completer picture of the habits and character of the bird than any life history—a pleasanter form of research, too.

It is in naming plants that folk fancy simply runs riot. Here is a plant called in folk talk indifferently Queen Anne's lace, beggar's ticks, and bird's-nest. Royalty, beggars, and birds are mixed up in the naming of this carrot. It probably comes about thus: In bloom the plant displays a delicate tracery of tiny flowers in a design generally suggestive of lace and a fine quality of lace at that. So let's call it Queen Anne's, as she doubtless had fine lace. Then, as the circular, flat-topped cluster matures and seeds, the middle of it sinks, creating a uniform depression with a firm rim around it. So it's a bird's-nest. It certainly looks like one. Finally the seed are equipped with tiny hooks which nature provides in the hope of getting them distributed by catching hold of some moving object. And do they hold on! They're tiny and stick like ticks, and since a beggar's tick is supposed, for reasons not disclosed, to stick tighter than a tick on a wealthy person, we call them beggar's ticks. Maybe another advantage of being wealthy is that you shed your ticks more easily. I am not enough of a historian to know why Queen Anne was such a great name-giver: Queen Anne's bounty, Queen Anne pocket melon, Queen Anne architecture, Queen Anne's War, Queen Anne Period in English Literature—certainly more names than her importance as an individual would seem to justify. "Elizabethan" is another matter.

There is a common iris called blue-eyed grass. I have never heard it called anything else. When not in bloom, it looks like grass. In spring comes a definite and beautiful flower. But folks don't care if no grass in the world blooms like this. Grass it is because its blades are long, narrow, and sheathe the stem, and because it grows in green and grass-like bunches. Now the iris of the eye is blue, and the pupil is yellowish or golden. So the grass is "blue-eyed" because the corolla, corresponding to the iris of the eye, is blue and the center, corresponding to the pupil, is yellow, as in human beings—logical enough. But here's another flower blooming right alongside which is named "Golden-eye." Since the flaring corolla, or iris, of its eye, is also blue, why shouldn't it also be a blue-eyed something or other? That would be logical. But no, blue gilia is "golden-eye" from its pupil, the other "blue-eyed" from its iris, and please ask no more questions about it.

A few years ago I was traveling by automobile over a considerable portion of eastern Texas—Marshall, Gilmer, Gladewater, Tyler, and on down Highway 79 to Thorndale. There was at that time an enormous weed luxuriating in cutover lands and deserted fields, especially in the poorer sands. It grew in huge clumps often ten feet high, and the heads were filmy like huge feather dusters. It was called by the natives "sand weed." Eula Whitehouse[5] makes the following note about this plant: [It is a] "pernicious weed in eastern Texas and soon covers cut-over pinelands. The dried flower-tops of several species were used by pioneers as a fever medicine. One of these plants was called 'joe-pye weed' in honor of the Indian doctor, Joe Pye." The scientific name is *Eupatorium compositifolium*. "Sand weed" is an excellent name because the plant grows better in the sand than in any other soil, poor sand at that. It luxuriates in sand so poor in nutriment that other species are dwarfed. It likes

[5]*Texas Flowers in Natural Colors,* privately published, 1936.

the sand and the name thus stands for an ecological fact. Joe-pye weed adds a pioneer interest, perpetuating the name of an Indian doctor, and also ties into it a bit of folk medicine. I mastered this lore quickly, and you, reader, will be able to repeat most of it when you have forgotten completely the scientific name. None of these important matters is suggested by the scientific name, as valuable as that name may be, placing the plant in its proper niche in the botanical scheme of things for one who makes a profession of botany. A person interested in natural history, however, should stay with these folk names, and add one more, "Yankee weed," for I suspect it contains a bit of history or a folk prejudice of some sort. It doesn't matter how many names a species has, so long as each name suggests something germane and memorable. The more, the better. Let it have one name for its flower or some peculiarity of its shape or color, another for its seed, one for its root system or for its general conformation, favorite habitat, odor, medicinal properties real or supposed.

In Texas the accidents of history have brought four racial groups together—whites, American Indians, Mexican Indians and Negroes. Anything black is likely to be called "nigger," as nigger-head, nigger-goose, and so on. Anything noticeably small or stunted will probably earn the "Mexican" prefix, and I think there is a dash of genuine racial prejudice in this. On the other hand, folks all over America quickly forgave the American Indian and converted him into a pleasant legend. It is easy to forgive the exterminated: the greater their prowess, the greater glory of the exterminator. We hold no grudge against the grave, but the Negro and the Mexican persist as elements of the populations, and it is here that folk psychology in the naming of natural objects seems loath to idealize and even reluctant to be just.

Our most beautiful flowers are named Indian this or Indian that. An amazing bit of color contrast, the gaillardia, is the Indian sunburst, or the Indian blanket. The red sage that enlivens the roadsides, blooming nearly all the year in great areas of Texas, is called Indian fire. In early spring the traveler in the south-central portion of the state sees a vast hillside of intense scarlet-red due to a thick stand of a plant whose broadened floral leaves have taken on this color. If it happens to be mixed with bluebonnets or phlox, the effect is still more striking. This general favorite is called Indian paintbrush or Indian pink. The red Texas star which grows along the roadsides, especially in the limestone country, holding high a spike of brilliant tubular flowers in flaming masses, is called Indian plume. One lovely buckthorn is Indian tea, and the graceful wild cherry is Indian cherry. It is almost a rule that "Indian" connotes something beautiful and is used for favorites, especially for the more colorful native flowers.

Exactly the reverse is true of "Mexican," which, so far as I know, is not given to any attractive or useful plant. The name belittles, thus: Mexican persimmon bears globose fruit about the size of a large marble; Mexican walnut, a dwarfed tree of small, hard nuts; Mexican tea is a croton which covers worn-out, deserted fields, a kind of poverty-weed. None of the gorgeous mallow family is called Mexican except the Mexican apple which bears an applelike fruit about the size of a hazelnut. Here the term is clearly used as a diminutive. But there is a flower and a poor one, called Mexican mallow, which does not belong in the mallow family at all. Of two wild plums fairly common in central Texas, *Prunus tarda* and *Prunus minutiflora,* the former is called the Mexican plum and the latter the dwarf or hog plum. And then there is a member of the genus *Astragalus*—not a plum at all, of course—which goes by the name of the Mexican ground plum.

Folk estimates of national character are found, also, in folk names. We call the shrike a French mockingbird. Why? At a casual glance the migrant shrike looks like a freshened-up, elegantly dressed-out mockingbird. The quiet gray of the mocker becomes a lively pearl gray, quite vivid, contrasting sharply with the jet black of this winter resident. Instead of the leisurely flight of the mockingbird, the shrike flutters his wings, and instead of the mocker's level progress the shrike makes a sweep downward from one perch nearly to the ground and rises to another perch of the same elevation, say from one telephone pole to another, describing an arc of a circle. Everything about this bird seems artificial, flashy, meretricious, formal, chic, in comparison with the dress and manners of the mocker—hence, a *French* mockingbird. Thus we are inclined to estimate the French, irrespective of how this folk-thinking has been corrected by formal instruction and study.

The callicarpa is a formal-looking bush. Its branching conforms to a general design, and each limb of it taken separately is a symmetrical unit. The leaves are large and uniform and definitely placed in the leaf scheme of the plant. In the fall there comes a cluster of fruit not placed normally on the ends of twigs or pendant, grapelike, on a special structure, but curiously massed together in the axils of the branches; and since the axils are evenly spaced one from another, so are these clusters of color, a shade of red never seen elsewhere on land or sea. Again there is formality, apparent artificiality, flashy appearance, and so folks call it the French mulberry.

We conceive of the Spanish as a particularly graceful people; hence the most beautiful moss in the country, long, swaying gently in the breeze, festooning the ancient live oaks, is "Spanish" moss. The long, keen, spearlike, excellently proportioned and needle-sharp blades of a certain species of yucca give it its name—Spanish dagger, or Don Quixote's lance.

Any plant of evil odor is likely to be called a skunk bush or skunk weed—there is even a skunk daisy—think of it!— growing appropriately in waste places, particularly in the alleys, near sheds and outhouses. "Bear" and "buffalo" are reserved for big, burly, coarse plants and are general favorites. Any tough, spiky grass growing anywhere in Texas is apt to be called locally bear grass. Fake fruit takes the name of "possum," perhaps because it is a general belief that the opossum feigns death, shows fight when he means flight, and is a slow-witted faker. The little yaupon berry, that looks like a haw but certainly doesn't taste like one, is a 'possum haw; and the black persimmon, whose plumlike appearance makes the mouth water, is a 'possum plum. Any fraudulent fruit is likely to earn this epithet.

So, things black, nigger; stunted, Mexican; colorful, Indian; graceful, Spanish; formal, meretricious, French; stinking, skunk; tough, bear or buffalo; fake, 'possum.

Few birds are tagged with "angel" or "devil" or "snake," but many plants are. Texas flora has a considerable sprinkling of "devils," principally reserved for different species of cactus. A comparison of angel with devil flora betrays, as might be expected, a tenderer folk regard for the former. There are dozens of plants with the "snake" praenomen, but no folk condemnation of the reptile is apparent. There is evident, however, an acute awareness of any snakelike character. Folks are fascinated by snakes; become familiar with their looks and ways, and sensitive to snake resemblances found otherwhere in nature. There are, of course, snakeroots the world over, usually snake-bite cures in which folk faith rests so confidently that any curious depression or irregularity in such a root earns it another name, "devil's bit," or "devil's bite," since the devil, always frustrating man and ever taking sides with the snake, bit a piece out of this beneficent root in rage and spite.

16. The Mockingbird: Character and Disposition

On first acquaintance, especially in fall and winter, the mockingbird is apt to be disappointing. Famed chiefly for his song, he is now silent or simply murmuring a memory of some springtime ecstasy—shadow-singing, it might be called. Aside from a flash of white in his gray wings as he flies, there is little in his dress to attract attention. But he makes up in personality for what he lacks in appearance.

It is his extreme pugnacity and his mannerisms that set him apart. He dashes fearlessly from his perch to snap up an insect almost between your feet; he dives time and again at a cat who slowly yields ground. Scolding, he literally rides a dog out of the way. While he and the cardinal have their differences, they seem to have established a kind of tolerance for each other, but the noisy bluejay must not seek harborage in the mocker's oak, nor may the robin, which he abominates above all other neighbors, come within twenty yards of his lookout.

Some birds are easily remembered because they come tagged with a physical peculiarity. The color pattern of the painted bunting, of the painted redstart, or of an oriole, once seen, is not likely to be forgotten. The bridled titmouse, the magpie, and the shrike have no color but memorable designs. The enormous bill of toucan or pelican, the curiously shaped one of the spoonbill, the posture of the penguin, or the neck of the flamingo ticket these species sufficiently.

Songs or calls of a distinctive nature, especially pleasant ones like the whistle of the bobwhite, tend to make an identification permanent. Very large birds and extremely small ones, tomtits and eagles, are easy; and on a practical level, it must be remembered that some birds are good to eat. The savory ones are generally the best known—game birds, we call them.

But with all these things to remember birds by, most people know surprisingly few. Ask the first person you meet to name the birds he readily identifies: a dozen, perhaps, rarely twenty-five, or at most forty, among the one hundred or more present in the course of the year. Out of all this exuberance of color, variety of song, mysterious ways, magic materializations and vanishings, to say nothing of table qualities, the majority of people select only a few species for attention.

The mockingbird has no color, no peculiarity of form, is of conventional size for the passerine order to which he belongs, never appears in great numbers, can't be eaten, and is not a pest unless there is ripe fruit about the place.

He is a gray bird and at rest seems wholly gray except for two narrow white wing bars. In flight, however, the bars coalesce to form a white patch of considerable size, while the tail outspread shows outer tail feathers white converging toward the rump in V-shape.

Yet inconspicuous as he is in appearance, if a poll were taken throughout his range, he would come forward in the upper five per cent of the birds readily recognized. There are dozens of other birds just as common that we see every day and never think to ask the names of. It is the mockingbird's personality, even more than his song, which distinguishes him. He has qualities we admire and talk about.

He is indomitable. I remember well a pair nesting near my back porch during an extended drought. Except the English sparrows, nearly all the other birds gave up. It was not uncommon that year to find starved nestlings deserted by their parents. Early in the season the male mocker quit his singing and devoted himself throughout the daylight hours to helping his mate feed the little ones. There was no time now for the frivolity of song. Bugs were scarce, earthworms non-existent, and the city's limitation on the use of water dried up many lawns, which are the mocker's favorite urban feeding ground. Both birds worked like beavers. There were no boll weevils or bollworms because there was no cotton. These two birds, so hard put to it, were constantly out of temper, scolding, dashing at other birds and at cats and dogs, furious at any intrusion upon their territory. As a last resort in the late afternoons they visited a large ant bed in the corner of the yard to eke out their slender fare. And these daily doses of formic acid didn't improve their dispositions any. But they fought it out and came through the drought in the withering heat of early July with a brood of four hungrily chirping youngsters who were able, after a few days' coaching, to follow off to a creek bottom where living was somewhat easier.

Mannerisms of the mocker further distinguish him. He runs along the ground, spreading his wings a little at a time by sudden jerks with mechanical precision. I have counted as many as five notches before the extension was complete. Numerous reasons for this action have been assigned. The best explanation is that he does it because he wants to.[1]

He spies out his prey from a perch, as a Cooper's hawk does, or a shrike, and pounces upon it. He can see an insect fifty feet away, or blade of grass or leaf moved by a worm burrowing underneath it. He darts to the spot, secures the morsel, and flies back in a jiffy. He rarely eats on the ground, since it economizes time to eat on a perch while spying out another bug. I have seen one quit singing suddenly, pounce upon his prey, fly back to his perch, swallow, and continue his song just where he left off. I have never seen him fly singing with an insect in his mouth, as other observers have.

[1]An ingenious suggestion is that he does it to scare insects out of hiding, but I have never seen him apprehend an insect in this way.

We think of mockers as more plentiful than they really are. After the brood is reared, each individual shifts for himself, staking out a plot of ground upon which he permits as little encroachment as possible. They tolerate no near neighbors, especially of their own kind, and thus attain an even distribution. Sociability, if any, is sacrificed to better feeding facilities. Although a census in a given area may show comparatively small numbers, the distribution is such that you seem to encounter him everywhere. He is found in the open country wherever trees are available, as well as about urban homes and farmsteads. He is indifferent to man, neither seeking nor avoiding his company.

I have found the mocker possessed of the pioneer spirit, always pushing out and extending his range wherever he can find trees, or even shrubs ten or fifteen feet high. Although there is a record of one nesting within a foot of the ground, he prefers more elevation for his nest. The lowest nest I ever found was two and a half feet up in a hackberry bush growing in a fence and entangled with barbed wire. I found another nest in a coil of old barbed wire lying on top of a low shed. But he likes a tree to nest in, since it furnishes him an elevated perch for spying out his prey while he keeps watch over the nest.

He is rare in the dense woods of the Big Thicket of eastern Texas, but is quite common about the clearings and in towns and villages there. He stayed off the plains of western Texas until that section settled up and the settlers planted trees about their residences. Then the mockingbird was one of the first of the tree-nesting species to leave the ravines and canyons below the cap rock and come up into the open country.[2]

[2]W. G. McMillan, of Lubbock, a competent and reliable observer, gives me, in a letter dated July 5, 1946, the following account of the first appearance of the mockingbird in Lubbock, now a city of 40,000 population, built up in recent years on a treeless area just above the cap rock in the breaks of a tributary of the upper Brazos River:
"The western mockingbird came into Lubbock in noticeable numbers about 1932. I had observed them below the cap rock prior to that time, where the brush and bushes along the small streams in the canyon had long afforded them nesting places. In 1942 . . . I purchased a pine tree which was about ten years old. When the florist

For many years mockers and bluejays have been food rivals as each season my figs begin to ripen. The jay hops joyously from limb to limb, taking here a bite and there a bite, ruining half a dozen luscious "magnolias" in one visit. The mocker, not such a hog, sits by a ripening fig and drills daintly into it. He savors each bit of the fruit, often singing between nibbles. He gobbles up an insect, but fruit he eats after the manner of an epicure. The next day about the same time he returns to the tiny hole in the same fig, and the day after, also. One fig sometimes feeds a mocker for several days.

At first I thought I was being treated with consideration. The jay was a wastrel; the mocker frugal, careful of the interests of his host; but one day I peered into the hole which a mockingbird had left in a fig and found his little well full of small fruit flies of some sort mired down in the sticky juice. When I found other similar holes with insects in them, my suspicions were aroused. Was the bird merely trapping insects in my figs? I concluded that the difference between him and the jay was that the mocker liked fruit flies in his fruit juice while the jay preferred his figs straight, and that each bird was equally indifferent to my interests.

Out of temper with other birds generally and testy at every trespass, the mockingbirds in Austin become utterly infuriated as January brings into the city the annual invading hordes of robins. By this time the leaves have all fallen away from the hackberry trees, leaving the red, hard, little fruit exposed; and in from the cedar-covered hills where they have spent the fall and early winter gorging on cedar berries come robins by the thousand.

---

moved the tree to my new home four miles out of town, I noticed an old mockingbird nest in the tree and tore it down. In the spring of 1943 a pair of mockingbirds took up abode in my yard and, oddly enough, they selected the very same tree and the very same crotch in the pine tree from which I had torn the old nest away. They used it again in 1944. By that time other shrubbery about the place had developed and offered a larger selection for nest sites."

Chirruping, flitting noisily from tree to tree, trotting and hopping along the ground, scratching among the dead leaves and plunging their strong beaks into the soft earth for grubs, gobbling up hackberries and making a distressing mess of it on the sidewalks below, they are marauders who know not, or knowing utterly disregard, the laws of bird land. In its Sherman's March to the Sea, this straggling, harum-scarum army runs roughshod over all the usages and customs of polite society.

Other birds tolerate them or move out of their way. The trim titmice, for example, chee-chee their way through the underbrush in select parties, not even noticing the rude aggregations of gaudily outfitted newcomers who chew and chatter and besplatter the sidewalks.

But the mockingbird simply cannot abide this carpet-bagging invasion. Whether it is the peculiar shade of rusty red on the robin's breast that is displeasing, or the ravaging of food supplies, or his attempts at song—whatever the cause, it is a fact that the mockingbird's nerves are all upset from the day that the first robin appears until the last one has gone. Between tantrums he becomes sullen, rarely sings,

sits for hours with his feathers fluffed out and his bill tilted at a wicked angle, emitting now and then an angry chirp. He mercilessly attacks every robin that invades a restricted territory which he has staked out as his own individual claim.

One bright winter morning I noticed that the hackberry trees which line the streets of the northern portion of the city were filled with robins. They were having a gay time, chattering to each other, eating hackberries, and flitting about among the branches and from one tree to another—thousands of them. One large hackberry, and only one in the entire neighborhood, contained no robins. The trees on each side were filled with them. Something is the matter with the berries, I thought. I tasted them to see if they had gone sour, but they were perfect. Soon a robin flitted over and attempted to alight in the apparently deserted tree. Like a silver arrow from the bow of some high-stationed archer, down darted a mockingbird upon the incautious intruder. Several feathers floated from the point in mid-air at which contact was established, and the robin beat a precipitate retreat. The mocker flew up again to his lookout and waited. Another thoughtless one approached the tree and again the mocker descended upon him like a hawk. For the two hours that I stayed there this lone guardian of the sacred hackberry kept every robin away. A wren visited the tree unmolested, cardinals were permitted to flit about in it, two jays screamed in its branches for a short time, but not once did a robin come near without being severely trounced. Meantime, trees to the right and to the left and across the street and in the adjacent yards were filled with an ever-moving throng of robins.

Two fatalities in the robin-mocker feud were reported to me in the spring of 1943, one by Mrs. Fred Crouch, at 2907 San Gabriel Street; and the other in South Austin by Mrs. Sarah Lee Brooks Martin, Technician in Zoology at the University of Texas.

Mrs. Crouch said she saw a mockingbird strike a robin a blow with his beak on the head, whereupon the robin fell from the tree. She picked up the fallen bird and found him lifeless. Mrs. Martin observed two birds fighting in the air near her home, and one of the birds fell. It proved to be a robin. The mocker followed, mounted his fallen enemy, and moved away only when she approached. As she bent over to pick the bird up, it fluttered about and flew straight up about twenty feet, suddenly collapsed, and fell like a stone over the cliff. Mrs. Martin was sure it was dead. As it lay on the ground, she had noticed that one of its eyes had been pecked out. This occurred, she said, in November or December of 1942.

Professor M. L. Williams of Southwestern University, Georgetown, Texas, writes me, September 7, 1942, the following eyewitness account of a mockingbird's attack upon a rattlesnake, so circumstantial that I give it in his own words and in full:

"In answer to your letter, in the summer of 1893 I was with my father on a ranch in McCulloch County, about ten miles west of Lohn Post Office, on the old Hinton ranch. It was my job, or rather one of my jobs, to ride the fence around the pasture to see that no one had taken it down, or that no cattle had gone out of the pasture.

"One day while on my job, I was nearing a dry branch on the west side of the pasture, when I heard the sound of a rattler ahead. Riding cautiously, I was about thirty yards from the branch, when I saw the large diamond rattler on the opposite bank, up under some bushes. The bushes were oak, with no low underbrush, about twelve feet high. I could see the rattler clearly, his tail up, and singing steadily. I knew there was something wrong, but I could see no cause for his anger. I decided to wait. After some minutes he suddenly stopped, and quickly started to run to the south. He was hardly well-extended before a mockingbird darted from above and, flying down his length, struck at his head, circled above and quickly came down again. Sweeping down the snake's back each time, the bird made some four or five strikes at the head. Then the rattler stopped, coiled and struck several times, and began to rattle. I was fascinated, and rode nearer, up to within some twenty feet of the snake.

"Then I saw that one of his eyes was out and bleeding— my remembrance is that it was the right eye. In a few minutes the rattler made another dash, the mockingbird in the meantime having perched on a limb just above him. Immediately the bird went into action, as before. The snake again stopped. This fight went on for some thirty minutes, the scene of action moving some thirty feet. The snake seemed afraid, trying to escape. The bird gave him no chance. Finally, the bird struck the other eye, held on and flapped vigorously, then darted upward. The blood spurted from the eye.

"The rattler coiled and began striking in all directions, then sank his fangs into his own body, began rolling over, and finally came tumbling down the bank into the rocky branch, where he writhed in pain. The mockingbird flew up into the bushes and began to sing. I put the rattler out of his misery with a large stone. I confess it was one of the most interesting battles I have ever witnessed. The snake, of the large diamond type, was, I guess, about five feet long. Judging from his general appearance and his rattles, he must have been some twelve years old."

The belligerency of the mockingbird can hardly be exaggerated. Walter P. Webb, Professor of History in the University of Texas, tells me that a mocker for the past several mating seasons has waged daily warfare against a north windowpane in Garrison Hall. The darkness inside evidently gives this bird a disagreeable reflection against which he hurls himself.

Mr. Oran V. Luke, Instructor in Chemistry, with a fellow instructor, William Leslie, rescued a young nighthawk from the assaults of a mockingbird just in time to save the nighthawk's life. They interfered also with an attack of three mockers upon a young pigeon which had fallen prematurely from the nest.

In my own observation and reading it is rare that a bird interferes with the mating activities of another species. I remember reading in an outdoor magazine,[3] a report in which the author describes interference of American coots with mating of teal ducks. I have myself seen a mockingbird dash into a cluster of mating sparrows time and again. From one part of my lawn to another the stern censor followed the mating sparrows and scattered them right and left as soon as they assembled. I had time to watch this curious behavior for only ten or fifteen minutes, and I have never seen it repeated. Perhaps he was only indulging his sense of humor.

The late J. E. Pearce, for many years Professor of Anthropology in the University of Texas, came in from his farm one day convinced that the mockingbird has a sense of humor.

"It's a low kind of humor," he admitted, "the practical-joke type, but still it's humor. The farmer on my place," he explained, "feeds his chickens in a large horse lot adjoining a barn. This morning, when several dozen chickens were feeding in close formation, a mockingbird dashed over, barely skimming their backs. Apparently mistaking him for a hawk, they scattered and ran squawking for cover, most of them taking refuge under the barn. Whereupon the mocker assumed a perch near by and waited patiently for them to reassemble, when he repeated the performance. While I was there he did this four times, so it could hardly have been an accident. Certainly it had no utilitarian purpose, since he did not offer to take any of the chickens' food. I mentioned this to the farmer, who assured me that the bird had been doing that every day for a week."

I carried this story around with me for several years and repeated it a number of times, but was too doubtful to publish it. Then one morning I happened to have my binoculars

[3]"The Coot Problem," Allan Brooks, *Field and Stream,* October 1941, pp. 67–68.

focused on the colony house of a large chicken ranch in a suburban area of Austin. White Leghorns were feeding in the middle of their pen. Suddenly they scattered. Hoping to see a hawk, I kept my glasses on the yard. In a few minutes they reassembled and again they scattered. I moved closer and soon I saw that it was a mockingbird skimming over them which caused the disturbance. He had two perches, one on each side of the pen. He would swoop over the chickens and rise to the alternate perch, sit still until the chickens came together again, and repeat, coming up to rest on his original perch. Thus he shuttled back and forth six times in make-believe stoops, while I was looking, and ceased only after the chickens had cleaned up their food.

This incident, coinciding as it does with Professor Pearce's observation, relieved any suspicion of nature-faking, but still I could not accept his interpretation. There will surely be some more rational interpretation of this, I thought.

Shortly afterward I read in Alexander Wetmore's "The Eagle, King of Birds and his Kin,"[4] a statement to the effect that the duck hawk "when not hungry, . . . feeling his superior strength, frequently indulges in harmless play at the expense of his bird neighbors. Often I have seen them flying along river channels, driving ahead of them a motley flock of blackbirds, herons, avocets, and other birds, herding them in disorder like sheep, but without offering to harm them."

Mr. Wetmore further describes a duck hawk tapping a cormorant playfully in mid-air and circling easily away. "Frequently falcons at play," he concludes, "dashed at top speed through milling flocks of flying sandpipers, scattering them like leaves in the wind, but not striking any of them."

All this accords very well with Karl Groos's[5] "surplus-energy theory of play," which I believe accounts for the mockingbird's joking with the chickens. He exhibits a sense of play if not of humor.

The story of the mockingbird's poisoning its captive young

[4]*The National Geographic Magazine,* July 1933, p. 50.
[5]*Play of Animals,* D. Appleton and Co., 1898. Chapter I.

crops up quite frequently. Redbirds, I have been told, will do the same thing. I have seen many cardinals and mockers caged but have never known of one of them being poisoned by the parent. This story has the earmarks of folklore. Arthur Rutledge,[6] however, declares that a young mocker he had caged died the morning following a feeding by the mother bird. "When I recounted this experience to Arthur Wayne, the renowned ornithologist, he said:

" 'A mother mockingbird, finding her young in a cage, will sometimes take it poisoned berries. She thinks it better for one she loves to die rather than to live in captivity!' "

It will be noted that it is the mother who does the poisoning, not the father. I have never been able to tell a male mockingbird from a female, and I think it would be difficult even for Mr. Wayne, without killing the bird, to be sure it is the mother which poisons the young bird. But whether or not Mr. Rutledge's caged bird died of poisoned berries administered by the mother or from some other cause, perhaps his own inexpert feeding, the story is in keeping with the spirit of this most rugged of bird individualists.

Reputed friendly, the mocker is no more so than the cat, who takes from man what he wants and thinks his due, returning, in my opinion, neither service nor affection. The mockingbird associates with man because the activities of human beings increase the natural supply of worms, bugs, and fruit. He haunts man's yards, gardens, orchards but not, I think, for love.

Through a good pair of binoculars in a favorable light his facial expression is hawklike rather than passerine, anything but friendly. Look first at the eye. It is not dark, as many suppose, but a baleful amber, keen, searching, fierce. Contrast his eye with the large, mild eye of the bluebird; his brusque, no-foolin' manner with the engaging approaches of the kinglet; or his dour disposition with the cheerfulness

Reader's Digest, Vol. 37, p. 111, July 1940.

of the chickadee. Most passerine birds look upward at the
sky as often as they do earthward, but not so the mocker. He
looks down constantly which, taken with the slightly decurved bill, gives his physiognomy a predaceous cast. He
seems to be ever resenting an insult. Man delights not him.

Nor is he cheerful. I am not unaware that one of Wordsworth's heroes wandering

> westward tow'rd the unviolated woods
> Failed not to greet the merry mockingbird,

but the great English poet never saw or heard a mockingbird. It is an attractive alliteration, merry mockingbird,
but the observation is secondhand. The mockingbird is anything but merry—even his song is not merry. He is ever too
full of business, too downright, too intense to be merry, or
friendly either. Merry is not the word. Even his humor, if
humor it be, his satisfaction in playing hawk and scattering
the silly hens cackling and squawking about a farmyard in
false alarm, is not a merry prank but a sardonic one.

We call him merry, cheerful, friendly, because we love
him. It is a human failing, or virtue, to give those we love
the benefit of every doubt and to load those we dislike with
evil suspicions. We tend to read into the mockingbird's
character the qualities we most admire, and to assume a
response in kind to the affection we lavish upon him.

Instead of building him into a fictitious character,[7] we

---

[7] American poets have done much with the mockingbird's song, but
little with his character. Perhaps we shall have to await an American
Nietzsche to do him justice in blazing paragraphs of poetical prose.

Sidney Lanier's four sonnets have been quoted to death. They were
never much alive. Excellent as Lanier's nature poems are—"Hymns of
the Marshes," "The Waving of the Corn," "The Song of the Chat-
tahoochie," and others—he is inadequate in his treatment of the
mocker. Aside from a line or two of vivid description of the bird's
technique in taking a grasshopper, the sonnet to "The Mockingbird"
doesn't catch the spirit of the bird, while the concluding couplet containing a query to Science—"Sweet Science," he calls it—

> "How may the death of that dull insect be
> The life of yon trim Shakespeare on the tree?"

written in 1877, is unworthy even of a minor poet. The sonnet sequence
"To Our Mockingbird" is highly overwrought, and the canonization
of the bird the cat killed as a brother to Keats in Paradise is a piece

should instead create for him another morality, as we do for musicians, writers, painters and artists generally whose sins by common consent we hold to be venial. Let us say of him that this king of song can do no wrong and, making a virtue of his arrogance, accept him on his own terms. Friendliness and jollity and other likable qualities of the herd we can find in abundance elsewhere.

Contrast him with his most harmless but most hated enemy, the robin, whose ready cheerfulness is proverbial. How amiable this gossipy winter visitor, how pleasingly gregarious, how friendly and convivial compared with the trim gray aristocrat, sitting apart, consumed with jealousy, burnt-up with a rivalry so intense that it keeps him most of the time poised on his perch ready with a vicious jab at whomever, wherever and whenever he judges its delivery can be made most effective. It is this anti-gregariousness, this intolerance, this general attitude of defiance and splendid isolation, that impart to him that air of superb self-reliance resting, like Youth, "upon earth's native energies." We should look upon this bird as nature's experiment in unrestraint, producing in him a triumph of individualism and in his song *natural* freedom's most authentic voice.

---

of sentimentalizing. Accusing the cat of wrong, imposing upon the feline instinct a human morality, doesn't help any, either:

" 'Twas wrong! 'twas wrong! I care not, *wrong's* the word—
To munch our Keats and crunch our mockingbird."

We like our poets childlike but not childish.

The word "mockingbird" is difficult to handle in serious poetry anyway. It deadens if it does not kill a line. If any of the names given the mocker by early French settlers in Louisiana had stuck, *rossignol,* or *moqueur,* or *grand moqueur,* or *voix d' amour,* what a boon it would have been to poets!

17. Mockingbird: Singer

When I was a boy, a favorite formula among literary smart alecks for disposing of Walt Whitman was simply to repeat a characterization then popular in academic circles, "The most contemptible old hog that ever rooted in the mire of his own imagination." Of course, the ultrawitty threw in an apology to the hog. Whitman then had few defenders even in English faculties.

A fondness for the mire or a disposition to be different induced me to buy at a secondhand bookstore for twenty-five cents a copy of *Leaves of Grass,* Boston, Thayer and Eldridge, "Year 85 of The States." One of the first poems to strike my attention was "A Word out of the Sea," beginning "Out of the Rocked Cradle." It so pleased me that I read it over and over until finally I could repeat sections of it by heart. It is in large part an interpretation of the mockingbird's song. I had a habit of reading this poem aloud to myself out in the hills, now and then pausing to listen to an actual, flesh-and-blood mockingbird sing. I found out years later that the poet, according to his statement, had himself tested every line of his poetry in exactly this way, by reading it aloud out in the open air. That may be the reason why I found the fragments I had memorized so suitable to out-of-door declamation. Any poetry, but especially nature poetry, improves in natural solitudes.

I tried time and again to identify parts of the bird's song

with parts of the poem and gradually I came to know both song and poem very well.

It was not long before I found another bird singing "in the mire"—the hermit thrush—but could not find him singing in the woods, since this bird does not sing in winter in central Texas. He simply sits, chirps a little now and then, moves his tail slowly up and down, and then slyly makes off through the underbrush, the quietest bird I know, almost mouselike. Until I heard him years later, I could hardly believe that the song of this drab little creature was really and truly the song which moved the poet to such rapture in "When Lilacs Last in the Dooryard Bloom'd."

The two most distinguished families of singing birds in North America are the Turdidae and Mimidae, the former including the thrushes, robins, and bluebirds, and the latter a dozen thrashers, the catbird, and the mockingbird. Outstanding among the Turdidae as sweet-voiced singers are the thrushes, and among the thrushes first place is usually accorded the hermit, called the American nightingale. Thrashers are great singers, and the catbird also, but the mocker certainly takes first place in this group. As for the hermit thrush and the mockingbird, each is a distinguished representative of his respective family, both families being notable for the number, the excellence, and the variety of individual singers.

Naturally, therefore, there is a rivalry between these two birds in that portion of the public mind which pays any attention to bird songs. Both are solitary singers and can be judged competitively only in that narrow strip of country running east and west in which their breeding ranges overlap. The hermit doesn't sing while wintering in the Deep South, and the mocker rarely goes north of New Jersey. Comparatively few people hear both birds: one sings north, the other south.

Poets are more concerned with bird songs than with any other natural sound, and I have found it interesting to examine the testimony of Whitman, a great national poet, competent and impartial, as he renders judgment concern-

ing the songs of these two birds. As in England Shelley cele-
brates the skylark and Keats the nightingale, so in America
there is Whitman with his careful evaluation of the song of
the hermit thrush and of the mockingbird. His judgment is
not a decision but an appraisal, and is recorded in two of
his most poular poems. The theme of one of these poems he
takes out of the "mock-bird's throat, the musical shuttle,"
and the other from the hermit's "song of a bleeding heart."

The evangel song of comrades had already been published before the war came on to absorb all of the poet's
energies. The war years, including his ghastly hospital experiences climaxed by the tragic death of Lincoln, produced
"When Lilacs Last in the Dooryard Bloom'd," the hermit-
thrush poem, which is the crown and completion of the
prewar series devoted to brotherhood, comradeship, man's
love for mankind.

The series celebrating romantic love, poems of rapture
and abandon, had been completed and published in the ante-
bellum period. Now, with the heavy shadow of a great war
falling across the land, and as if in anticipation of war's multitudinous frustrations, he weaves into a poem of romantic
love, the mockingbird's song, the theme of death, "the sure
enwinding arms of all-enfolding death." Thus "Out of the
Cradle Endlessly Rocking," seems to come as a spiritualiz-
ing epilogue to "Infants of Adam" as perfectly as the
Lincoln poem crowns the "Calamus" series. The former is
concerned with youth and love; the latter with a more permanent but not more important affection of the heart—
obverse and reverse, respectively, of the human coin.

The poet's ear is extremely delicate. In the song of the
hermit thrush Whitman hears a lament for the death of a
great comrade; in the mockingbird's song, death's frustration of romantic love. Keynote of the one is spirituality; of
the other, lovesickness, longing "wild with all regret."

The hermit's song is first of all a "warble"; the bird "sings
by himself." Listening in the twilight, the poet finds the
utterance so freighted with feeling that he names it "death's
outlet song of life," implying that the singer must surely

die but for the song's serving as an outlet for the emotion. Again, it is "reedy," "a loud human song with voice of uttermost woe." It is

"liquid and free and tender
O wild and loose to my soul."

The singer is "shy . . . bashful and tender," singing his "carol of death . . . from deep secluded recesses . . . with pure deliberate notes, spreading, filling the night . . . tallying song of my soul . . . low and wailing, yet clear the notes rising and falling . . . sadly sinking and fainting, as warning and warning and yet again bursting with joy." So Whitman describes "the wondrous chant of the gray-brown bird," serving him as a voice for his own grief at the loss of a comrade, a great man greatly loved.

In "Out of the Cradle Endlessly Rocking," the poet recalls that as a boy down by the seashore in midnight he listened to "beginning notes of yearning and love." The "two guests from Alabama," doubtless eloping lovers, had built their nest,[1] and all the time brooding activities were in progress the song maintained its burden of yearning and love. But the female disappears and does not return. Then

Loud! loud! loud!
Loud I call to you my love, my love,
High and clear I shoot my voice over the waves.

Those who have seen the mockingbird singing are not surprised at the repeated references to the vibrations of the bird's throat, more conspicuous in the mocker, it seems to me, than in any other songster. Whitman observes that the mockingbird, like the thrush, is a solitary singer. But unlike the thrush, the mockingbird vents "cries of unsatisfied

[1]The author of *Birds of New York,* issued by the New York State Museum, Albany, 1914, p. 471, says relative to the mockingbird's nesting in the state, "There seems to be some evidence that it has bred near Rockaway, Long Island, and possibly in other portions of southeastern New York." I would consider Whitman's observation overwhelming testimony of the mockingbird's nesting on Long Island. Do the State Museum ornithologists think so lightly of the eyewitness account of the state's greatest poet, as to say, "There seems to be some evidence"?

love"; and he greets the bird as "my dusky demon and brother" who "carols of lonesome love."

In all this there is no partisanship, but appraisal purely: a comparison, almost item for item, of the songs of the two great singing families of North American birds as represented by the protagonist of each group. One is the song of the body, the other of the soul; one is a "carol of lonesome love," the other "a song from a bleeding throat"; and I know of no more valid distinction.

Here, a curious conjuncture—poetry, natural history, national development: America's greatest poet, greatest political leader, and greatest bird songs—one of the North, one of the South, joined in companion threnodies, each concerned respectively with the poet's master themes, climaxing the poet's career, the political leader's martyrdom, and the terrific struggle for national unity. The web of coincidence is neatly woven.

Whitman commits the error of making the "whisper" song of the mockingbird intercalary, which it is not.

> Soft, let me just murmur so faint
> With this just-sustained note . . .

This "murmur" or "just-sustained note," with the beak closed or nearly closed, does not come in between the musical outbursts of a spring passion violently frustrated. It is heard at a different season, in another mood, from a lower perch. The three phases of mockingbird singing are caught in a little poem by Dorothy Grace Beck.[2] The first stanza describes the song of true love before mating; the second, a song of mated love; the third, the autumn or "whisper" song:

> Stand still
> And listen now,
> While one small bird-throat pours
> Cascades of silver down the slope
> of night.

[2] *The Christian Science Monitor*, July 15, 1946. "Mocking Bird at Night: Three Moods." Published by permission of *The Christian Science Monitor* and the author.

Sing high,
Gray mocker, sing!
Sing silver to the stars—
Sing summer moonlight! Pierce the night
With song!

Once more,
Leaf-hidden one,
Dark minstrel of the heart
Of summer, weave once more a dream
Of song.

I cannot recall a single instance of hearing the mocker sandwich in this "dream of song" between the more or less intoxicated outbursts of the premating or mating period.

Before the male mates in the spring or when, after mating, he loses his mate, his song increases in vehemence. He pours forth a torrent, seeks a higher and higher perch until he sits upon the topmost twig of the highest tree from which now and then he darts toward the zenith fifteen or twenty feet, singing as he rises and, falling, sings. It is a loud, challenging, mate-seeking song. Some say that, having lost one mate, he is readily consoled when this far-heard musical invitation is accepted by another female. I have observed his actions after he has secured another mate in place of the one the cat got, and will go only so far as to say that he is *apparently* consoled.

The attributing of human emotions to animals is frowned upon. It is the basis of much sentimentality. The great poet, however, is permitted to be as pathetic in his fallacies or as fallacious in his pathos as he chooses;

The poets in their elegies and songs
Lamenting the departed, call the groves
They call upon the hills and streams, to mourn,
And senseless rocks; nor idly; for they speak,
In these their invocations, *with a voice*
Obedient to the strong creative power
Of human passion. (Italics supplied)

It is a function of poetry to deal creatively with myths. "The nightingale cries to the rose," is myth in the mouth of the poet trying to temper truth or clothe its austerity. It is easy for Whitman to believe that this superb vocalizing actually relieves the pain and reduces the fever in the singer's heart. The facts of science—indispensable, surely—are but the front yard or approach to the poet's dwelling, as this particular poet himself declares in another connection.

The low, "just-sustained note" to which Whitman refers comes after the mockingbird's molt in the dreamy days of autumn, still and cool but sunshiny. It is then that, content with a low perch, he mutes his strings not in pleading, but in a mood of musing or retrospection. It is a "dream of song." It accords with the autumn reverie induced by stillness, haze, and falling leaves. Often this quiet song issues from a young bird just learning to sing, for the young mocker does not risk cracking his voice, as the young of the oriole does, or the second-year summer tanager, or the cockerel for that matter. The young mocker first goes over the notes carefully, tentatively, "sweet and low," permitting strength and volume to come naturally with time and frequent rehearsals. His song ripens gradually.

It will be observed that throughout the poem which seeks to analyze and interpret the mockingbird's song, there is not a single hint that any strain or phrase in it is borrowed from another singer. The song is treated as an original production from beginning to end. That the poet's ear does not detect in it imitation or mockery must be considered curious since the popular ear hears in it little else. The bird is named from his supposed power of mimicry. His scientific name means literally "a many-voiced mimic." But Linnaeus named him on hearsay. Whitman listened to the migrant in New York long and attentively; and while he was himself a "migrant" in the homeland of the bird, he doubtless heard many mockingbirds sing. He records hearing many notes, phrases, and themes, but not one of mockery.

18. Mockingbird: Does He Mock?

Does the North American mockingbird mock?

No poll has been taken, but I estimate that ninety per cent of the people in the mockingbird's homeland believe that he does. Much has been said on both sides, or rather upon three sides, since there is a *tertium quid* saying he mocks a little, sometimes, always doubtfully, or that only certain individuals mock while others are possessed of a wholly original repertory. I find myself among the less than five per cent of the population who believe that he mocks not at all.

Sensory impressions are notoriously unreliable. Court testimony has proved frequently that no two eye- and ear-witnesses ever see and hear the same occurrence exactly alike, and laboratory tests confirm the finding. Messages from the objective world come to us gummed-up with prejudices, colored by suggestions, and confused with associated memories.

From earliest childhood we are told that the mockingbird mocks, else why is he called a mockingbird? Early associations are tenacious and influence adult belief in subterranean ways that escape detection. The odor of decaying vegetables is pleasant to me, because during my sixteenth and seventeenth years I passed on my way to lunch a large produce house which breathed forth from its immense doors the fumes of vegetables past their prime. Two years of this odor, daily administered along with sensations of relief from a disagreeable office routine and with my mouth watering at prospect of an excellent meal, formed so pleasing a complex in my consciousness that to this day I enjoy sniffing the air of a second-class vegetable market.

Although untrustworthy, our sensory organs are the sole advisers of what is going on "out there." Science extends the range of our senses by mechanical means, refining and rendering their messages more authentic, but still these carefully processed data must be presented to us through the same old senses or not at all. By checking one sense against another, sight against hearing and vice versa, the laboratory shows how far astray one sense or another is apt to go. But we can't carry laboratory paraphernalia around with us and momently check on the flood of impressions which pour in throughout the waking period. And no matter what the laboratory might tell me, the odor of decaying vegetables would still be pleasant.

The senses are easily the dupes of suggestion. In mountainous regions all over the world there is many a Great Stone Face. In a southwestern spur of the Rockies, all within a compass of forty miles, I know a Ben Franklin profile, a kneeling nun, and a man and a woman in an indecent embrace, the last-mentioned being the creation of Mexican wood-haulers and sheepherders. It became so popular under a folk name, especially with tourists, that the better element of the community, scandalized, endeavored to persuade the poor peons that what they saw was an illusion, and supplied them with a lovely Spanish name for the mountain. The peon element persisted in its error and rejected the new name, but changed the offensive one to *Mal Nombre*—Bad Name Mountain—and so it remains to this day, universally accepted.

A country-store amusement handed down from pioneers and still practiced in some sections of the country is based upon this same fallibility of the senses, recipe for which follows:

Blow out the contents of a hen's egg, wash out the shell, fill partially with clean water, and then tell your victim to listen and say whether or not it "shakes." The more it sloshes, of course, the rottener it is. Let the person upon whom this experiment is being performed be convinced that the egg is rotten. Then suddenly burst it on his forehead. It is only clean, odorless water that trickles down over his face, but he will probably smell the odor of a rotten egg.

Sounds also have their confusing similarities. The witch in "Goldilocks" speaks "in a voice like an unoiled wheel at work." The rumble of a truck is taken for thunder, the flap of a curtain for someone knocking, the cry of a panther for a woman's scream. Indeed the ear is generally more untrustworthy than the eye, as arrangers of radio programs have found out.

Except touch, taste is earliest and most fundamental of the senses. Hence, if there is logic in evolution, taste should be the next most difficult sense to deceive. But is not the housewife at pains to tint a vegetable grease to the shade of a certain animal grease? And is not her success in making it go down without protest proof that the eye can fool the taste buds with all their eons of experience in guarding and preserving life long before the appearance of sight, smell, or hearing. Pale-green oranges are unsalable until colored a golden yellow, and then they go very well in spite of the plainly stamped "color added" which in all reason should break the spell. But we are not dealing with reason.

The southern Negro is adept at making something of the more featurable bird songs. He has the ear for music, an urge to impersonation, an inheritance of sentimentalism, and a naïve welcome for all sensuous delights.

Ben King puts into the mouth of an aged Negro sitting by a deserted cabin listening to a mockingbird, the words

> Jes a mockin'bird a-singin' to de
> lonesomeness, dat's all.

To the Negro there is a lonesomeness possessed of personality, toward which the bird is directing an appropriate song. The poet here gets quite inside the Negro's mind. To him a bird song says something concrete, and he builds the stresses, inflections, and tempo of it into a statement which accords with his experience, his philosophy, or with the emotional tension of the moment.

Long ago a Negro with whom I was chopping cotton ruined the western meadow lark's song for me. It was late in the afternoon, and I had fallen behind the other choppers. I stood, my right leg thrown over the hoe handle, pressing the upper end of it hard against my left shoulder. A meadow lark on a post briskly twerping his tail sang his limited but lovely song. He spoke to me of holiday freedom, of roaming at will across a pasture and down winding creek bottoms with a wise old coon dog at my heels. My reverie was broken by the voice of the Negro who came up chopping both his row and mine.

"Does yuh know," he inquired in a voice of velvet, "what dat fee'lark is a-singing to yuh?"

"No, what is he saying?"

"Why he's a-sayin', plain as kin be, 'Laz-ness *kill* you—*kill* you—*kill* you.' "

He repeated these words after each outburst of singing from the bird. The old fellow drew out the *la-azz'ness* and pronounced the *kill-you's* rapidly in falsetto. I felt a deep twinge of conscience. I still hear with irritation those very syllables in the song of the western meadowlark.

Chaucer attributes to the nightingale, *"Beshrew all them that are in love untrue"*; also, *"For term of life Love shall have hold on me."* My wife, whose ear is supersensitive from years of language-teaching, insists that the white-eyed vireo says, *"Hello, Mr. Robinson; Hello, Mr. Robinson."* Bradford Torrey credits the song of the olive-backed thrush with *"I love you, I love you, I love you truly."*

Naming birds from their calls is almost universal. In winter on the Mexican border, birds with English names for their calls mix and mingle with the caracara and the chachalaca and other birds the Mexicans have named from their calls.

A country Negro told J. Frank Dobie, southwestern folk-lorist, that the mockingbird says to him:

Niggah, niggah, niggah (said very quickly)
Worl' o' trouble, worl' o' trouble
(this long-drawn-out, especially *worl'*)
Thief, thief, thief, thief (make it snappy)
Lie, lie, lie (sharply, spitefully, keeping syllables distinct)
Put 'im in jail, put 'im in jail
(drawn out mournfully to balance "worl' o' trouble")

I have been able to fit these words fairly well into certain portions of the mockingbird's song.

George Finley Simmons credits the following interpretation of the barred owl's hoot to Stanley Clisby Arthur, "*Oo-hoo-hoo-hoo-You cook for me, I'll cook for you—Oh-hoo-hoo.*" But Mr. Dobie furnished me a still better rendition coming from his father:

> I cook for *my*se'f
> I cook for *my*se'f
> Who cooks fo' you *all?*
> Who cooks fo' you *all?*

A little experimentation in the field—that is, in a moonlit river bottom with the owl as prompter—will convince any-one that these words and stresses lend themselves readily to a representation of what the barred owl is really trying to say.

It was a Negro who purloined from the mocker's song the melody which became the basis of "Listen to the Mocking-bird." A review in *Time* (May 24, 1937) gives credit for the words of the song to Septimus Winner, but it fails to say that Winner got the melody for his most famous song from the Negro barber, Whistling Dick.[1]

---

[1]James Weldon Johnson, Professor of English in Fisk University, naturally jealous of the artistic accomplishments of his race, takes the re-viewer of Claghorn's *The Mocking Bird* sharply to task for the omission. His letter, published in *Time* (June 14, pp. 6–7, 1937), follows:

"The issue of *Time*, May 24, contains a review of Charles Eugene Claghorn's *The Mocking Bird* in which credit for writing the song,

The point is we are always alert to hear something that is not there in any bird song. In Great Britain the bird is made to talk English or one of the dialects; here also he speaks a various language, seeming to prefer, in the South at least, Negro dialect. In Germany he talks German; in Arabia, Arabic; in India one or another of the one hundred forty-seven distinct languages recorded as vernacular there. This habit of mind is universal. The more primitive the people, the more firmly rooted is the desire for this commerce. It is due to this tendency, in part, that the popular mind converts the mocker, a truly original composer, into a copyist taking snatches of song here and there, wherever he can find them. For a thousand or more years the Romans believed that nighthawks, or bullbats, sucked goats, and they called them goatsuckers just as confidently as we call the gray and white singer a mockingbird.

The mockingbird is a general favorite throughout his range. Four states have officially designated him as the state bird, and another is now hesitating between him and the meadow lark. The fact that he is universally loved and ad-

---

Listen to the Mocking Bird, is given to the late Septimus Winner. The review does go on to state that "Sep" got the idea for his most famous song from "Whistling Dick," a Negro beggar who used to strum his guitar and whistle like a bird.

"This statement about "Whistling Dick" (Richard Milburn) is very much less than adequate. Milburn was a barber who worked in his father's shop on Lombard Street in Philadelphia. He was a guitar player and a marvelous whistler, and it was he who originated the melody and at least the title of *Listen to the Mocking Bird.* Winner only set down the melody and arranged it after it had been played and whistled and sung over to him by Milburn. Winner may have furnished most or all of the words as published, but the life of the song springs from the melody.

"Before the song was ever published Milburn used to play and whistle it at church concerts and other occasions. There is a record of his having done so at St. Thomas' Church, the colored Episcopal church in Philadelphia. But the incontrovertible proof of Milburn's part in the making of the song is shown by its title page as originally published by Winner and Shuster, under the copyright date of 1855, which reads: "Sentimental Ethiopian Ballad—*Listen To The Mocking Bird*—Melody by Richard Milburn—Written and arranged by Alice Hawthorne." Winner used "Alice Hawthorne" in publishing a number of his songs. The title page of the song as published by Lee and Walker, under the copyright date of 1856, reads: *"Listen to the Mocking Bird*—As sung by Rose Merrifield—Written and arranged by Alice Hawthorne."—Courtesy of *Time.* Copyright, Time, Inc., 1937.

mired is responsible for many tales of his prowess and cleverness and especially for his powers of mimicry.

Mimicry, one of the tools of ridicule, always looks down, maintains distance, condescends. It has no mercy and droppeth not "as the gentle rain," but blightingly; vaunteth itself, is puffed up, and from a superior perch behaves unseemly. This flaunting, devil-may-care arrogance of the mimic fits the popular conception of the general superiority of the mockingbird and does much to uphold the belief that this bird, who generally assumes the highest perch available, is looking down with contempt upon lesser orders and expressing himself in mockery.

From Audubon in the woods of Louisiana where he first heard the mockingbird's song on down to T. Gilbert Pearson, I think most naturalists credit—or discredit—the mockingbird with mimesis. They put into his throat involved and difficult songs of other birds as well as the cheeps of the immature, and throw in for good measure mechanical noises that occur around the homestead—a rusty hinge, simmer of the teakettle, and the like.

This is the general verdict, but it is not unanimous. Dr. Witmer Stone says, "We should have welcomed more attention to imitations, as we have always thought that many so-called imitations recorded in print are really not imitations at all."[2] Mrs. Laskey also cites D. R. Dickey (1922) and J. Paul Visscher (1928) who consider the mockingbird's repertoire inherited rather than mimetic. She quotes Dr. George R. Mayfield (1934) as crediting the mockingbird with imitations of thirty to thirty-five different species and, adding in several different songs or calls from one or another species, arrives at the impressive total of fifty imitations. Dr. Loye Miller, of California, uses the term "fortuitous similarity" to cover most cases of mocking, and says only two to eleven percent is true mimesis. The sparrow hawk's *killy-killy*, which Mrs. Merriam Bailey is quite sure the bird imitates, he calls *klee-klee* and declares "too highly pitched" to

[2]*Auk* 52:344. 1935. Quoted by Amelia Laskey "A Mockingbird Acquires His Repertory," *Auk*, Vol. 61, April 1944, p. 211.

accord with the mockingbird's so-called imitation of it. One writer quoted in the same connection uses the phrase "adventitious similarity" to describe the mimicry popularly attributed to the mockingbird. Mrs. Margaret Nice, widely known for minute and accurate bird studies, says "not all mockingbirds mock, and those that do have only a limited repertoire." "A mockingbird from the end of the Panhandle (Okla.) mocked six western species that nest in that area."[3]

Having reviewed the controversy, Mrs. Laskey tells a remarkable story of a pet mockingbird which acquired his songs by mocking one species after another from day to day. During her experiment, Dr. G. R. Mayfield listened to her pet sixteen minutes and "listed one hundred forty-three calls or songs of other species, averaging nine imitations per minute interspersed among the mocker's own songs." This remarkable bird called *wicka-wicka* every time he saw a flicker whether or not the flicker uttered his call, thus practically naming and identifying another species! She concludes:

> When nine months old he [the pet mocker] started answering outdoor birds in the same call or song each had just uttered and . . . twice greeted visiting flickers with the flicker call although the flickers were silent.

Early settlers of Louisiana found Indians calling the bird by names suggestive of his power of imitation: the Ofo's name was *teska iyonaki* ("bird" and "to mock"); the Biloxi Indians said of the mocker *ade kdakayi* (it mocks one's words); but the Choctaws took exactly the opposite view, calling him *hushi balbaha* (the bird that speaks a foreign language.)[4] Dr. Harry C. Oberholser, careful scientist, emphasizes the richness of the bird's song rather than its imitative nature, and warns that the mockingbird's reputation for mimicry is so great "that it often is *not sufficiently*

[3]Birds of Oklahoma (1931), quoted by Laskey.

[4]*The Birds of Louisiana,* State of Louisiana, Department of Conservation, Bulletin No. 20, p. 448, New Orleans, 1931.

credited with original compositions." (italics supplied)[5]
"There is no sound, whether made by bird or beast about
him, that he cannot imitate so clearly as to deceive everyone
but himself," says Neltje Blanchan (*Bird Neighbors,* p. 82)
and further credits the bird with self-conscious ventriloquism! George Finley Simmons declares that the mocker
imitates nearly all the local birds and many of the migrants.
Since, in the area covered by Mr. Simmons' study, there are
at least a hundred resident species which have some kind of
call or song, these, taken together with the songs and calls
of many migrants, give the mocker a considerable repertoire.
The weight of authority favoring the affirmative increases
the deeper you delve into the literature of the mockingbird,
which has been accumulating for a hundred years.

The latest comer, Elmer Ransom,[6] after according a word
of pity to poor Keats and his nightingale, declares that

> . . . he [the mocker] can mimic anything from the
> squeak of your rusty brakes to the crowing of a
> rooster. He will whistle your favorite record two
> weeks after he hears it, or fool you with the *pretty-
> pretty-pretty* of a cardinal. . . . .

"The imitative ability of the mocker," says Richard H.
Pough[7] "extends beyond birds and often seems to include all
common sounds of their environment, from the squeak of a
wheel to the bark of a dog."

But cautious Florence Merriam Bailey[8] reports: "One
of the Cuervo mockers was the best mimic I have ever heard,

---

[5]*The Bird Life of Louisiana,* by Harry C. Oberholser, State of
Louisiana, Department of Conservation, Bulletin No. 28, p. 450, New
Orleans, 1938.

We have the evidence of another primitive ear in that of the border
Mexicans who call the mockingbird *sinsonte,* also spelled *censonte* or
censontle (Aztec) meaning "senseless chatter," as in the popular phrase
sin son ni ton, without rhyme or reason. There is no suggestion of
imitation or mockery in the name, but a curious agreement with the
Choctaws' estimate of his song.

[6]The Woodland Book, Howell, Soskin. New York, 1945.

[7]*Audubon Bird Guide,* Doubleday and Company, Inc., Garden City,
New York, 1946, pp. 107–8.

[8]*Birds of New Mexico,* p. 553.

if none of the notes attributed to the others were part of his personal repertoire." (italics supplied). She hears in his song the songs of other birds not in the mocker's present range and calls it "reminiscent mimicry," but guards again with a subjunctive "if"—*"if it were such."* (italics supplied).

The scientist is no happier meeting head-on a popular superstition than a politician is, although much more courageous in issues that really count. In little things like bird songs, however, he is inclined to lift an eyebrow and let harmless belief alone.

But I take my stand with the Choctaws. Having listened to other birds and then to the mockingbird, I say, far from imitating, he speaks a foreign language. Only the briefest snatches from other songs do I hear in his. Maybe a *peter* or two, reminding me of the titmouse, and then instead of a five- or six-time repetition he is off to the other side of the world. I hear occasionally in his call cheeps of a baby chick, but they are immediately scrambled with something else; and I hear now and then from him a quarrel note like that of a blue jay in an evil mood, or of a wren scolding, but he doesn't hold on to either one. If one wants to call a single note, or a phrase uttered here and there entirely out of context, the imitation of a song—that is, if he doesn't care how loosely he uses the word "imitation"—he may say the mocker imitates. But when I hear it said that he can fool anybody, I dissent. I have never been fooled more than momentarily by the so-called mimicry of the mockingbird.

Consider how different the evidence which comes to us of a mocker who really mocks, the white mocker of South America. We have it from W. H. Hudson,[9] poet and naturalist, that the white mocker returns from his migrations to La Plata with a pokeful of songs he has picked up travelling about, which he delights to rehearse upon his return. Hudson reports that he has been fooled for as long as five minutes when the mocker is singing concealed in a bush. We have here a witness who held ninety-six different bird songs

[9]*Birds of LaPlata,* E. P. Dutton & Co., New York, 1923, p. 12.

in mind for fifty years and could give a fair imitation of each one. We have a witness so conscientious that he told his English readers that the white mocker's song was far superior to that of the nightingale.[10]

Now if one of the migrating mockers of central Texas should return from the East with the song of the bobolink, or one should drift in from the cactus and mesquite country with the song, call, or scold of the cactus wren and, concealed in a bush, fool me with either of these songs for as long as one minute, I would be convinced. But he does no such thing. Out in the mesquite and cactus country I have listened to him day after day and night after night without ever detecting in his desert repertoire anything resembling the call of a cactus wren more closely than the notes I hear every day from mockers who have never heard the cactus wren. I have heard an occasional *peter* out of him also in areas where there are no titmice. In southern New Mexico where the song of Cassin's sparrow rings constantly over the desert wastes, I have never heard out of a mocker a simple phrase from this little sparrow's song. In the mesquite pastures between Hebronville and the Rio Grande I have heard dozens of mockers singing in the moonlight all at once like competitive prima donnas, but it is the selfsame song that is heard, so far as my ear can tell, from his congeners of central Texas or southern New Mexico.

The Harris sparrow arrives in central Texas in latter November. In warm weather, especially about sun-up, the second-year birds sing a jumbled warble followed by a squeak. Nothing else like it is heard here. I am particularly fond of this handsome sparrow and listen and look for him

---

[10]The white mocker surely mocks, but *all* South American mockers do not mock. Both Hudson and Azara say the Calandria mocker (*Mimus modulator*) does not; neither does the Patagonian mocker (*Mimus patachonicus*). The Calandria mockingbird has an eye color similar to that of our own species and has the same habit of darting upward while singing.

It is true that Hudson says the North American mocker mocks, but he says so incidentally, in an aside. He never visited the United States and was therefore speaking from report and not from observation.

every fall. Sometimes I see him before hearing his song; sometimes I hear him first. I have never been fooled by a mocker's imitation of this distinctive song. It is true the young birds often sing together, and no one claims for the mocker the power of reproducing a concert, but often the Harris sparrow sings solo.

The test of imitation is deception—the criterion which Hudson applies. It is no proof of the mimetic power of the mocker to sit by listening to his various songs and see how many fragments of the mosaic can be identified which resemble chips from other bird songs, while ignoring design which is all there is to a mosaic.

It is said that the mocker imitates the yellow-breasted chat, himself accused of various imitations, also of ventriloquism. If he mocks the chat, he is a mocker of a mocker, plagiarizing another's plagiarisms. I have had an excellent opportunity of judging the validity of this claim. The chat arrives in my neighborhood each year about the middle of April, and he arrives singing and cavorting. He sings, calls, chatters from thick vines or underbrush. I have waited as long as half an hour for him to come out, and eventually he does to display himself, for which he may be forgiven since the brilliant yellow beneath contrasted with the dark olive-brown of upper parts is something to look at against a rich foliage brightened by April showers. He's worth waiting for. If at the end of any of my periods of waiting for this songster to emerge in his fine spring clothes a mockingbird had come out instead, my doubts would all be resolved. But in twenty-five Aprils this has never happened. The chat's voice consistently materializes a chat.

It is said that the mocker mocks the robin. I rarely hear a robin's song and cannot be confident on that score, but the robin's winter call I hear out in the cedar brake from October to January each year. Robins arrive in numbers there long before they appear in the cities of the cedar-brake country, for they are hungry for cedar berries. The mockers are not in full song, but on warm days they frequently sing and do a lot of calling and scolding. The robin's note or call as he leaves his perch is distinctive. If only once a mockingbird had made me believe that the robins had arrived before they were actually here, I would submit. But this alleged mimic has never once deceived me with the robin's startled call.

The scissor-tailed flycatcher is another bird whose distinctive twitterings the imitationist school assures us often issue from the mockingbird. This bird leaves central Texas in the latter part of October, having associated intimately with mockers for five months; but after the scissortails leave, I never hear anything resembling their excited twittering.

Following closely the departure of the scissortail comes the fall flood of meadow larks, silent at this season but as spring approaches very vocal, filling woods, fields, and meadows with their lively and distinctive songs. Although I have listened attentively, I have never mistaken any song of the mocker for that of the meadow lark.

I have not depended on my own ear exclusively. Whenever I have a companion whose ear seems to be as good as or better than mine, I usually raise the question, "Does the mockingbird mock?" Those who have assured me he does, endeavor to identify in the mocker's song strains from other birds. They say, "Listen to him, he is now mocking a thusand-so." But when they say "listen to him" they have already identified the mocker. If one had said, "Listen to the titmouse," and upon investigation we had found no titmouse there but instead a mockingbird calling, the evidence would be favorable but still not conclusive, for even the best listeners sometimes mistake one bird's song for another's.

I am not attacking any listener's integrity or accusing anyone of nature-faking. I believe that the continual current of suggestion triumphs over the critical faculty in default of a more accurate instrument than the human ear for comparing the elusive music of bird songs. Besides, nearly everyone *wants* to believe that this wonderful bird is clever enough and disdainful enough to make fun of his presumptuous rivals.

There is a wide expanse of cactus-and-mesquite country, typical of the Southwest, lying between Hebronville, Texas, and the Rio Grande. Mixed in with cactus and mesquite are many other scrubby, semiarid bushes. Lignum vitae or guayacan (*Porliera angustifolia*), evergreen and head-high when you are on horseback, stands stiff and sturdy on many of the slopes. The leaves of this plant are pinnate with tiny leaflets and have a peculiar way of growing along the trunk and branches without bothering to put out twigs to hold them up as the more conventional plants do. The leaves come out thick as hair on a dog's back, appearing at a little distance as a fuzz of deepest green. For contrast the leucophyllum interspersed here and there is ashy gray. Also there are many droop- or berry-producing shrubs, especially the thorny-leaved agarita.

This kind of country in the Southwest supports more mockingbirds to the acre than any other, I believe. They seem to be happier here than anywhere else, for here they tyrannize over other bird life by weight of numbers as well as by individual prowess.

I made camp for the night a few years ago in this thorny area near a Mexican village quite as primitive as may be found anywhere in Mexico itself. A full moon, ghostly pale, had just cleared the horizon. As the western sky darkened and the moon assumed her normal color, a solitary mockingbird not more than twenty feet away from my campfire began singing, tentatively at first, but gathering strength and continuity as his voice awakened other singers.

Soon the rivalry was going full blast, and the melodious contagion spread far over flat-bottomed valleys and gradual hillsides—those thorny-thicketed undulations known as the Plains of the Rio Grande. Some of the songs came faintly through the moonlight from a mile or more away, others nearer, and, of the many close by, each singer seemed set upon drowning out all the other voices to the end that he might dominate the moonlit night alone. There is never any concert or choral suggestion in the singing of many mockers at once. They do not supplement and support each other as a singing treeful of blackbirds, grackles, meadow larks, or other Icteridae do. Nor is there any such courtesy or sportsmanship as is noted among thrushes in the northern twilight when one thrush seems to wait for a neighbor to finish before he begins his own song. On the other hand, in this melodic melee of rival mockers each singer is singing for himself alone with all his might and main, determined, if he can, to sing all the others down.

Stretched out on my cot, listening intently, I tried to disentangle from the festival the mimicry which I have been assured many times is the chief characteristic of the mockingbird's song.

But my attention was soon diverted. I drifted off into imagining a world-wide bird-singing contest by radio with ambitious entries of the most famous singers of all continents and of all the islands of the seven seas. I imagined receiving sets strung up here in the scantily leaved mesquite to sweep this music over the world. If the transmission were but faithful, I thought, how the great audience would be amazed at this epic performance, even as I doubtless would be if I could reach out a hand and dial in the song of the nightingale uttered at that moment in some valley-glade of Sussex. To those listeners in a remote corner of the earth who had never before heard a bird song, the radio concert would burst upon them as a revelation from another world; and forthwith the suggestion invested the present singing with an other-worldliness in my ears. Maybe those extremely strange and puzzling phrases are transcribed sound-recordings, fossil songs sung originally in dark fern-forests of another geologic age.

If this bird is only a mimic, I argued, how account for those bits of vocal ecstasy heard nowhere else on land or sea? Whence come they? Is it not possible that the mockingbird's ancient progenitors, also mimetic and equipped with the same miraculous syrinx, caught up, conserved, and transmitted fragments of songs long since silenced as one singing species after another declined and finally perished from the earth? Nature's thrift, perhaps. Maybe the amazing variety of the mocker's repertoire is due to cumulative enrichment, to those bright residues gathered funnelwise over wide areas of time and space, now to be melodiously mingled and poured forth through one small, perfect throat?

Even for such moonlight musings "Nature fails not to provide impulse and utterance," and here in this weird landscape she provided also a setting which made them seem almost plausible.

We are indebted to modern developments in the camera for solution of many nature mysteries and for quieting many contentious issues. The motion picture caught the European cuckoo in the act of carrying her egg in her mouth to deposit in the host's nest. It settled only recently a two-hundred-year argument about how the drumming grouse produces the drumming sound by showing the wings beating upon thin air and upon nothing else. Fifty years ago there was a spirited dispute among naturalists concerning the flight of the hummingbird, some contending that he actually flew backward. Bradford Torrey, not a naturalist but a poetic essayist with a keen and sympathetic eye, declared that he could see the bird fly backward. Motion photography forty-four years later proved him right. "That the hummingbird does fly backward," says A. C. Bent, "has been definitely proved . . . by a new application of photography."[11]

Similarly, it is predicted, mechanical recordings of bird voices will enable the technician to analyze and compare two songs in such detail that a copyist can no longer claim originality. The technique suggested is quoted by Laskey[12]

[11]"In 1936 . . . Dr. Harold E. Edgerton took advantage of the intermittent flashes in a low-pressure tube in which the flashes occur for one one-hundred-thousandth of a second with a period of darkness between them lasting one five-hundredth of a second. He uses a constantly moving film, geared so that a new bit of film came opposite the lens of the camera at each flash, and thus secured about 540 pictures per second."—A. C. Bent, ibid. Bulletin 176, p. 344-5.

[12]Op. cit. *supra*.

from A. R. Brand,[13] as follows: "In many instances it is quite impossible to evaluate what a bird's sound production is by relying on the ear, for the ear is incapable of telling the whole story. Until another medium was found it was quite impossible to make objective studies of bird songs. The medium has now arrived. By adapting the machinery of the sound motion picture, it is possible to photograph bird songs. We can record the bird song on sensitized film, and, after development, have an objective medium of study."

But when all is said and done, should such an objective study be made and its results show that the mere similarities which my ear recognizes are too faithful, too accurate, too long sustained to be accounted for on any other theory than that of deliberate mockery, then I shall repeat the story I read somewhere or someone told me—maybe I dreamed it. It has to do with something resembling the classic Parliament of Birds. It comes in an Indian legend from the white mocker's range in South America. The story runneth thus:

There was a great jealousy among all the birds because the white mocker was the only bird who had been given a voice. All the rest were dumb and they didn't like it. To quiet the revolt, Waki-waki, the Great Spirit, sent out his chief minister to summon all birds to a great convention in the forest. Waki-waki's messenger had to talk to them by signs, for none could express himself vocally except the white mocker who sat sullenly apart refusing to take any part in the proceedings. There ensued a great puffing out of feathers, straining open of bills—the cowbird gaped so widely that it gagged him—and there was a unanimous pointing of envious wings toward the white mocker sitting sullenly apart.

Waki-waki's messenger saw that something had to be done. He forthwith demanded that the white mocker teach the complainants his song, whereupon the white mocker sprang upward twenty or thirty feet, uttering such a complicated and melodious shriek that the Great Spirit's messenger

[13]"Bird Song Study Problems" *Bird-lore,* Vol. 38, May, 1936, pp. 187–94.

gulped in surprise and commanded him to be still. The whole silly concourse was also taken by surprise and goggled at the white mocker, inflated their futile throats, but uttered no sound. Then the white mocker began a low, hardly audible, drowsy song and behold, the audience nodded and the messenger himself had to rub his eyes to keep awake. The yellow-billed cuckoo or one of his kinsmen, fell off his perch but caught himself in some vines.

Then the wise messenger realized that some sort of compromise was necessary. Negotiations were long and difficult, and the messenger had to resort to threats and cajoleries to keep the white mocker mollified, but finally managed to wangle from the temperamental one a promise to teach each species that could be taught anything at all a little simple piece, sometimes a single note, of his own song. Each bird was then called to a perch just in front of the white mocker who simplified, analyzed, and split his song up, selecting a fragment best suited to the limited capabilities of each species. They finally learned after a fashion, not very well, each one his little fraction and went away repeating it.

But as soon as they got out from under the dominating personality of the teacher and the spell of the Great Spirit's messenger, their rehearsals became lax; they let anything do; and so most of the songs degenerated and lost whatever resemblance they had to the source from which they sprang. The vultures and sea birds generally practiced their pieces hardly at all. A few of the species, having acquired the knack of vocalizing, by dint of continual practice developed creditable songs of their own.

Still there are echoes here and there of the great singer's voice in nearly every bird song; and that's the reason, children, why so many people think they hear in the mockingbird's divine and inimitable song certain notes and phrases from other birds. The plagiarism, if any, is the other way around.

19. Heronry on Keller's Creek

It was early spring in 1943 when I received a card from George Skoberg, dated at Olivia, Texas, telling me of a colony of birds preparing to nest near there. I got a map and with the aid of a magnifying glass located the right spot on Lavaca Bay, an arm of Matagorda Bay. At the State Land Office, I found a map of larger scale which shows that the upper reaches of Lavaca Bay form the estuary of Keller's Creek. I kept up correspondence with Skoberg, but there were wartime shortages of color film and gasoline, so the spring passed without my being able to visit the colony.

March 1, 1944, another note came saying the birds were reassembling. Dean T. H. Shelby, D. W. McCavick, and I chose middle May for the excursion. Luck favored us. Following a protracted rainy spell, we arrived at Olivia May 13 in clearing weather. Skogberg, a delightful Michigan Swede with a strong interest in nature, had built a platform overlooking the colony to accommodate the camera, well above the masses of small shrubs, cactus, and stunted trees, all sewn together with a tangle of tough vines—a dense mass of subtropical vegetation, in the tops of and on top of which the herons and their kin had built their nests.

The country around Olivia is flat as a pancake. The elevation is only a few feet above sea level. Scattered over the mile of pasture land we traversed in getting to the site were clumps of scrub mesquite and a few bunches of cactus. As we approached the shore, however, the vegetation thickened, and the few acres on which the 2,000[1] or more birds were nesting was genuine jungle, nothing else.

Skulking on the outskirts was a pair of caracara, a degenerate eagle called locally the Mexican eagle, a bird which will take live prey or feed on carrion, whichever is the more convenient. I have seen caracara on terms of disgusting intimacy associating with the black vultures around the most putrid of carcasses, and again, like a hawk, pursuing a lizard or field mouse. Although dressed like an Elizabethan dandy in black and red, not forgetting an enormous ruff of white, he is a porch-climber and a thief, and the name "eagle" is a misnomer. He was there for no good purpose, nor were the black vultures. The grackles (*Cassidex mexicanus*) both boat-tailed and great-tailed, were buzzing around over the colony like gigantic flies, black and pestiferous. Excluding the two vultures who lived not with but on the colony, and counting the grackle, a parasite scavenger nesting therein, there were two different orders of birds and four families, comprising eight genuses and as many different species, all living together within the compass of a few acres.

The annual association of these diverse forms of bird life justifies itself with an end result of so many young—feathered out, equipped, taught the rudiments of making a living, and forthwith launched into a wholesomely hazardous existence —all within the space of a few months. For this the long migration, the tireless seeking and the finding, dangers and disasters; for this the strange tolerances, tedium, and confinement, and for this "the passion to excess was driven." In August these birds, old and young, will scatter to the four winds. The knot is untied, the pod bursts, and the colony home deserted. The principle of mutual aid weakens, and a period of competitive struggle ensues in which each individual must prove himself fit or perish. But even while the struggle is on and while the fiercest rivalries flourish, seed

[1]This figure includes nesting grackles. We estimated the seabird nesting population at 1,500, bulk of which were herons and egrets. There were not more than 40 spoonbills and half as many white ibis. We attempted no actual count of nests for fear of disturbing the birds.

germinate which in due time will flower in another period of co-operation and fruit in another dispersal. We caught the colony at the peak of its activities: we were brought face to face with a climax. The curtain had risen on the third act before we had got to the theater and were well settled in our seats.

From time to time, during the past twenty years, I have visited similar rookeries along the Texas coast from Vingt'-une Islands at the mouth of the Trinity River to Green Island, away down in the lower reaches of the Laguna Madre near Port Isabel. I have been out on the open salt flats in late February and early March when the birds begin to gather, and have watched them gradually become possessed with the procreative drive. I have seen the first tentative advances of prospective mates increase in boldness and mount in intensity day by day until, with the parades and display, the curious dances, the sudden and violent rivalries, the whole scene assumes the character of an orgy; and still there is maintained a certain nobleness and dignity which distinguish it from the sometimes abandoned debauches of our own species moved by similar impulses.

The herons are delicate courters. Approaches are elaborate, patient, and dignified. Nature has adorned them for the ceremony, particularly the egrets, with filmy, flowing plumes, lacelike, dazzlingly white and of nuptial suggestiveness. There is a kind of code rarely breached. I think one might study them in this association long enough and carefully enough to compile a book of their etiquette, or formulation of rules by which they are guided. As the mating and nesting instincts proceed toward their seasonable climax, however, these creatures perform in a way which comes nearer materializing like magic the Spirit of Life struggling to express itself against the passive opposition of the material world, than any other sight in nature.[2]

[2] I am not unaware of the present tendency, especially among the more scientific nature-writers, to reduce all this to automatism. I have

In the presence of this smoothly functioning colony, I feel the massive opposition offered it by blind material forces, and as a partisan I witness with some elation the ingenious and finally triumphant warfare waged against them as they are bent to the creative will. I come to the conviction that some eighteen-million centuries after the nebula cohered into an orb, something new entered, not at all controlled but destined eventually to dominate physical laws or at least to adapt and use them for its own purposes. Under this seaside spell I repudiate mechanism and all its thin and shivering conceptions. In this demonstration "There is more in the result than we abstract in the causal conditions." Here's an arithmetic in which two and two make five. I cannot accept such a creation, or the thousand and one other creative manifestations all about us, as something thrown up by chance after the long lapse of ages, "a fortuitous concourse of atoms," in the play and interplay of mechanical forces. If chance creates, why call it "chance"? The very conception of chance, of course, has no validity. It is a scaffolding the human mind tears down and junks as soon as its temporary purpose is served. It is already defined away and no philosopher uses the term except to expose its unreality.

I was particularly interested in this colony site, for it was a new one. The birds chose it for the first time in 1943. Why did they choose this and not another location along the coast?

---

even read detailed reports of sexual manifestations induced by presenting stuffed specimens to imprisoned birds. Captivity, segregation, unaccustomed food, nervous tensions, frights, all inseparable from imprisonment, produce in man as well as in other animals unnatural behavior. Such experiments seem to fall within the field of abnormal psychology and proved nothing to me except that "the charm of Nature is that everything is with the rest," and that "a robin redbreast in a cage sets all Heaven in a rage." Segregate hens for a couple of months, and you don't need even a stuffed rooster to get such reactions. A human being, a dog, a cat, or almost any moving animal will induce them. If one might go out into the woods with a sackful of stuffed specimens and secure the reactions described by tossing them out to healthy birds in their natural environment, I would follow such experiments with more patience.

The country lying shoreward from the colony comprises what the topographers of that region call the low flats, only six to twelve feet above sea level. The base of the ten-foot bluff on which the colony is situated is washed by high tide. That portion of the beach lying between high tide and low, called the strand, furnishes rich and constantly replenished feeding grounds. Inland there is a flat stretch of fifty miles of coastal prairie before anything resembling a hill or knoll can be found. Across this prairie on their way to the Gulf, the streams from the uplands become thick and sluggish, developing swamps here and there and marshy banks; and the water level of each stream, as it approaches the coast, comes within the domination of the tides. This is where marine life meets and commingles with fresh-water life and where a alternate lift and subsidence of the water level exposes both to the sharp eyes of the hungry colonists.

Shallow bays abound, feeding grounds for the waders. But the presence of food is not sufficient reason for the selection of this particular site. There are many other sites within wing reach of ample food in the more than five hundred miles of coastal bays and fresh- and semi-fresh-water estuaries stretching from Sabine Lake to the mouth of the Rio Grande.

The same problem of transport, quartering, and supply confronts this colony of birds as the commander of a military expedition faces when it becomes necessary to move his base into an enemy country. It is the problem the scouts of the pioneer wagon train always had to solve as it moved to advance the frontier, and the same imposed long ago by Moses when he sent forward a small party to spy out the land.

There must be food, there must be building materials for whatever structures are necessary, and there must be natural conditions which lend themselves to an adequate defense of whatever unit is thrust forward.

The time element has also to be considered. Nature does not give the colony the whole year to accomplish her purpose. She sets definite limits. For all the species represented here except the Ward heron the period assigned is from middle March until mid-July. There is not a moment to lose. Courtship must be consummated, site selected, nest built, eggs laid; brooding takes a couple or three weeks; nourishing, sheltering, protecting the young require enormous labor and constant vigilance; and finally the young must be taught to fly, to find and capture their own food so as to be self-sustaining. All this must be accomplished in the short space of three or four months.

With these birds, building material is a problem of first importance, because they are dependent upon dead sticks with which to lay the foundations of their huge nests, and it takes a lot of sticks. They must find light, loose sticks of suitable size or a dead branch of tree or shrub that is easily broken off. They gather this material and fashion it into nests only with their bills. I found at this colony a building-material shortage already apparent. Every dead branch and twig had been stripped from trees, shrubs, and bushes for a mile around the place. They can't manage green stems. They have to search until they find dead limbs sufficiently small, or large ones sufficiently rotten, to break easily. The beaks, long and slender in herons for spearing fish, or in the spoonbills grotesquely distorted for seining and grabbling, or in the ibis decurved for probing crayfish and sand-crab holes, are specialized instruments and cannot be turned readily to such crude uses as gathering nesting material. Nor are the feet any help in this matter. They are not taloned, as are those of the vulture tribe, and designed for grasping. They are made for wading knee-deep or for walking on soft, oozy ground. They have difficulty in perching and often lose balance. They must therefore do all their nest-building with their bills which are ill-adapted to this work.

Defense is the next problem. They are subject to both land and air attack. These comparatively huge creatures cannot dart through underbrush like a warbler: they must

have free access to the upper air without danger of en-
tangling themselves in limbs and branches. They must build
on or near the top of something and yet on top of something
that is protected from below, for small prowlers abound—
coons, coyotes, skunks, bobcats, stray house cats, and the
clumsy opossum—all avid for eggs, for young, or for a taste
of the adult birds themselves. They choose this mass of jungle
growth, all interlaced with stringy, tenacious vines and
plants armed with sharp thorns, in order to be as secure as
possible against ground enemies.

Snakes also take their toll, particularly rattlesnakes. However, even snakes are handicapped by the matted vegetation
woven across their trails. The Mexicans say the rattlesnake
hesitates to crawl through cactus, because the spines "tickle
his nose"; and a story is told of a cowboy who, withdrawing
himself from one of these coastal thickets, explained his retreat before accomplishing his mission by observing that the
brush was so thick he had met a rattlesnake backing out.

Defense from air attack is another matter. They must
build exposed nests, and very soon these nests, painted white
with excrement, are visible for miles to keen-sighted predators of the upper air. Here is the danger which imposes
upon them a kind of social organization. An isolated white
nest containing four fat and downy young would be quickly
ravaged, for the parents are necessarily away much of the
time on food-getting expeditions. Co-operation in guarding
each other's nests is thus forced upon them. The larger the
colony, and the more compact the nest arrangement, the
better they are guarded, since a greater number of adults
are present continually. Hence the larger the colony, other
things being equal, the more stable it is.

The spyers-out for this colony chose the site first, of
course, for its accessibility to feeding grounds. They liked
the great stretches of shallow water within influence of the
tides and therefore constantly replenished with small fish,
crustaceans, water insects and so on. They had an eye also
to the wide flats perforated in many swampy areas with crayfish holes, especially attractive to the white ibis, and furnish-

ing all the birds hunting grounds for grasshoppers and other land insects, as well as for snakes which the herons snap up with avidity.[8] It is food of this kind that these birds swallow, partially digest, and regurgitate into the throats of their young.

The strength inherent in mere numbers would tend to increase the size of a colony indefinitely but for the shortages

which quickly develop in building material and in the food supply. Food within effective flight range is always limited. The slow, heavy-flying herons must have food near by; those of lighter wing, spoonbills and the strong-winged, swift-flying white ibis, can make the round trip for food to comparatively distant feeding grounds. It is the competition for food and sticks that tends to disperse a colony, while the

[8]One reliable observer records that a Ward heron, frightened by a too-sudden approach to his nest, disgorged an eighteen-inch moccasin.

protective value of large numbers tends to hold it together. These forces, centripetal and centrifugal, operating in every such unit reach an equilibrium and determine its size.

An ibis colony on Karankawa Bay less than ten miles as the crow flies from the Keller's Creek site numbers not less than 15,000 birds. It supports this immense population because the ibis are fast, long-distance fliers and range for their food far and wide, up and down the coast and inland, wherever sand crabs or crayfish may be found. The numbers of associating species here are inconsiderable.

It has been a matter of some curiosity to me why a dozen pair of white ibis should choose to nest in the Keller's Creek colony along with an assortment of herons and egrets when the ibis metropolis of the whole Texas coast lies only ten minutes by wing away. Are there outcasts and pariahs in the bird world? Or is something corresponding to the human penal colony out of the question? Or do certain individuals simply prefer rural or village life?

From behind the brush blind atop the camera platform it is quite evident that the population of the colony may be roughly divided into neck-stretchers and neck-folders. At any rate, in flight it is easy to see that the ibises and the spoonbills belong in the former category and the herons and egrets in the latter. All have long legs. Legs and necks are more in evidence than any other anatomical feature.

Much of the length of the leg is contributed by that portion lying between the so-called knee and the foot. What we commonly call the knee of a bird's leg is not comparable to the human knee at all, as most of us learned in our comparative anatomy courses in high school. This so-called knee of the bird's leg corresponds to the human ankle or wrist. The tarsometatarsus, or shank—that is, the part of the bird's leg between the so-called knee and foot—in these birds is an elongation which lifts the body as upon stilts. Noting this extraordinary length of leg and the wide base given the stilts by four long, unwebbed toes, three spread in front and one behind, you conclude at once that the heron is a wader, procuring his food from shallow water with a smooth bottom.

If the legs of herons and egrets are something to excite wonder, what must we say of their necks? For example, consider the neck of the largest heron, the great blue or, as the subspecies here is called, the Ward heron. Fully one-third of the length of this fifty-two-inch bird is neck and bill. He is the giraffe of the bird world. And how ingeniously is this neck constructed for the work it has to do!

Extended straight up, it serves as a lookout upon which to place the eyes, thus giving the bird a view of the surrounding country and enabling him to detect the approach of land enemies. Moreover it is a revolving lookout that is placed upon the slender tower, for the vertebrae thereof are so articulated that the head may be turned and the eyes sweep an angle of three hundred and sixty degrees with as little effort as we human beings, with our stiff and dumpy necks, can command an angle of thirty degrees. Besides, the heron can tilt his head so as at once to spot his own prey and take instant glances into the upper air which sometimes contains death in the form of an eagle or other powerful hawk.

The suppleness of this neck is a triumph in mechanical construction. The vertebrae are coupled to permit swiveling upon each other at almost any angle, and the whole neck is muscled either to carry the spearlike bill forward with terrific force, or to let it lie along the back at complete rest, or to fold it S-shape for flight, as circumstances may require or as the will of its manipulator may dictate.

This heron often chooses to stand in the midst of tall grass or in the edge of water on a shore lined with reeds. In such a place with his neck extended straight up, standing on guard or resting, he blends into his background. It is clever camouflaging. I have stood for ten minutes with a good pair of binoculars trying without success to locate a Ward heron against such a backdrop. A fisherman I met on the coast added a touch of human fancy to the bird's ability to conceal himself. With all seriousness he assured me that on a windy day a heron thus camouflaged moved his upstretched neck back and forth through exactly the same arc as that described by the wind-swayed reeds.

Besides serving as a lookout and assisting in camouflage, the neck enables the heron to perform an elaborate toilet. Each feather, except those of the head and upper neck, is oiled and preened with the tip of the bill. It is not vanity alone which dictates the time-consuming toilet. The bird's life is constantly dependent upon the condition of his feathers. They must be oiled, straightened, smoothed out, cleaned, dried, and put in place after each flight and fishing trip. This can be done only with the bill, and it is the neck which manipulates the bill. Here is a structure which permits the bird to use the point of his bill to tap the source of oil and distribute it over the feathers; to remove the tiniest, stickiest weed seed; to dry the too-wet feathers. But for this constant activity the bird would not last a week.

The neck implements the sharp, hard bill as a weapon of defense. A strike with it amounts to death to some of his weaker enemies, and is often effective in warding off more powerful ones. Even the half-grown heron has learned to use this, the only weapon with which nature has supplied him.

The neck serves as a springe for snatching up the unwary fish idling along in the clear, shallow waters of the coastal bays. Coiled for a strike, or rather folded or doubled up, it darts the spearlike bill down upon its prey. It is also used to implement the bill in breaking off the twigs and small limbs of trees or shrubs with which the nests are constructed. It tucks them around, pulls and straightens, and finally fashions a platform nest to serve as a receptacle for the eggs and later as a kind of basket for keeping the young huddled together.

The neck supports the channel down which the food is conducted to the organ at its base where a partial digestion takes place. This processing completed, the neck with its bill is slanted downward to funnel the regurgitated food into the throats of the young.

It is when the bird takes off for flight, however, that the convertibility of neck and legs is seen in their most surprising action. Many large birds have to take a running start against the wind to get away from the earth at all. Not so the heron. He is catapulted into the air by the powerful springing action of his legs. Snapped at the moment he leaves the earth, a photograph of a heron shows an approximately straight line from the bill to the toes, extended at an angle of about forty-five degrees from the flat surface of the ground. The moment he gets into the air, the neck begins folding. As flight proceeds, the folding action continues until almost in the twinkling of an eye this delicate member is converted into the keel of a flying ship, streamlined to conform to the long, sharp bill which sticks straight out in front, level in the plane of the bird's body. The heron is flat-chested, and without the convertible keel of folded neck and protruding bill he would be a poor flier if indeed he could fly at all.

Now while the neck is being folded to keel the ship, the legs, having done their catapulting, are assuming a new position. They are acting in quite as remarkable a manner as the neck is, and taking on a function just as useful in flight. They are not tucked up, like the retracting landing gear of an airplane, or as the land bird's legs are put away in flight, but are thrust straight back to serve as a rudder. Here is an economy which uses one instrument to walk and wade, as a spring whose recoil hurls the whole body of the bird into the air, and then converts it into a rudder to supply the deficiency of tail which handicaps the flight of all wading birds. So when you see one of these majestic birds cruising along at the rate of about thirty miles per hour in perfect balance, streamlined, keeled and ruddered, remember the other uses of the keel and the rudder. As the bird alights, the neck unfolds, the legs come down widely spread, the body tilts at an angle which gradually slows the rate of motion, and in a moment the reconversion is complete.

Finally, the bird expresses affection with its neck. Herons, egrets, and other species so equipped twine their long, graceful necks and stand thus for hours at a time during the mating season. I have seen a pair of Louisiana herons stand motionless as statuary for extended periods thus embraced, head resting each on the other's flank, rousing themselves now and then from this loving torpor only long enough to nibble a little, time about, at the roots of each other's mating plumes, and apparently experiencing "the depth but not the tumult of the soul."

Shelley was not insensible to this romantic use of the neck.

> A swan was there,
> Beside a sluggish stream among the reeds,
> It rose as he approached, with strong wings
> Scaling the upward sky, bent its bright course
> High over the immeasurable main.
> His eyes pursued its flight—"Thou hast a home,
> Beautiful bird; thou voyagest to thine home,
> Where thy sweet mate will twine her downy neck
> With thine, and welcome thy return with eyes
> Bright in the lustre of their own fond joy."

Lying behind the blind on top of the camera platform, looking through peepholes at the domestic life of the birds, kept me prostrate and physically uncomfortable for protracted periods each day. Within twenty feet were a pair of Louisiana herons busy either building or repairing a nest. During the whole of one morning the female seemed enamoured of a stick. In this ceremony of the stick, the male uses the stick as a symbol of love, presenting it with great decorum to the female. She receives the token with affection, pulls it and hauls it around, tussles with it, and tries awkwardly to weave it into her nest. She is not an architect; she has no plan, no notion of symmetry or of what makes for a stable structure. She improvises. She fights to the death with any other bird which threatens to pilfer this precious object. This all strikes the observer as rather funny, for there is such an elaborate to-do made over what seems to be a matter of trifling importance. The male presents the stick with the air of a knight bestowing a rose upon the lady of his choice. She receives it with submission and handles it as if it were some priceless and symbolic award. With great seriousness she attempts to weave it into her nest. To one who has watched the deft touches with which the oriole or the tiny vireo does this trick, her bungling, fumbling trials and stupid errors are pitiable. She seems in such deadly earnest, she is ambitious, she tries so hard, she never learns. Nevertheless, the male, her faithful hod carrier, looks on with serene approval while this nightmarish nidification is under way.

Turning away from comedy, I begin focusing my glasses on grackles, and the protective value of colony-nesting becomes at once apparent. A grackle of funereal aspect is found perching near every nest. Indeed, for greater convenience he builds his own nest right under the nest of one of his hosts. Now I see one, catching the owners off guard, get possession for a moment, and before the infuriated heron can plunge upon him, he has dislodged a beautiful blue egg and hops down through the underbrush to enjoy the loot at his leisure. Although the grackle is parasitical and predacious, he serves as a scavenger and is a voracious destroyer of grasshoppers when they happen to be plentiful. He will eat eggs or the young of other birds but I have seen him, in possession of a nest of young herons, picking up the leavings and spillings of the regurgitations. In this he is undoubtedly of service, as his hosts are liberal and careless feeders and the accumulation of putrid food around their nests would be much greater but for the grackle's cleaning-up.

Readjusting my glasses for greater distance, I see now the sight I have been waiting for. An American egret approaches the nest to relieve his mate of the care of the eggs and take his turn at keeping them warm. With slow and dignified movements he comes forward toward the sacred spot as toward a shrine. The long necks come into action: hers comes up as his leans down to form loving contact. Then I see the long plumes at their best, the very moment when the old plumers, economizing ammunition, shot to kill both birds at once, since the bloom then on the aigrettes increased the market price. What plumes! The lacemakers of Belgium never produced anything half so airy, dainty, and altogether exquisite, and a bird without them would be scorned by his mate. At the beginning of the season fifty of these gorgeous appendages sprout right out of the bird's back and grow to a length of eighteen inches, sometimes two feet. The egret has the power of raising them upright until the whole body seems engulfed in a filmy cloud of snow which quivers and seems alive. This is the salute of love as one mate relieves the other at the nest. Each movement of the leg, neck, plumes in this ceremony is gradual, and as the occupant of the nest slowly withdraws, the relief brooder carefully puts his feet in place, disturbing the eggs as little as possible, and stands a moment with plumes erect. Then after a farewell rub of necks, quite deliberate, the great bird settles down, plumes subsiding gently as the legs, relaxing, lower the body, until the sensitive skin of the under parts rests gently upon the eggs, snug and still warm.

When love finishes with the plume, it drops off dead and dispirited. Life has left it because love is no more. It would be an ornament nowhere, much less on a woman's hat. Hence, in the old days, before Audubon societies and similar organizations called at the time by merchandizing interests "starry-eyed idealists," the bird was shot and the plumes were jerked out of the back while the bloom of affection still glistened upon their delicate filaments.[4] It takes 200 plumes to weigh an ounce. A pound can be spread to cover completely an area of 6,000 square feet.

In 1903 women were bidding the price up to $32 per ounce, which was twice what an ounce of gold would bring in that year. An auction in London in 1902 advertised 1,708 packages of this commodity, average weight per package 30 ounces, or a total of 48,420 ounces. Calculating four dead birds to the ounce of marketable plumes, this auction alone

[4]As public sentiment rose against this commerce, the plumers tried to make out that they gathered for the market only the feathers the egrets shed naturally, but this fiction was too transparent to fool anybody.

required the killing of 196,960 egrets and from two to three times that number of young birds starved or eggs destroyed.[5]

My attention now becomes attracted to another nest of American egrets. There are three half-grown, vigorous nestlings in it, all impatiently awaiting the approach of a parent bird, their throats vibrating with anticipation.[6] The feeding takes place in a normal way, but after the dinner a game ensues. Each nestling is given the privilege of swallowing the parent's head. The head is swallowed past the eyes, and when the old bird with some evidence of impatience pulls loose, the crown feathers are fluffed up giving the face a tousled and disgusted look. Not only is the head thus manhandled, but two nestlings in vigorous rivalry take hold of the parent's bill at once, each struggling for the privilege of swallowing it. I could see no purpose in this activity, which went on for half an hour, except pure sport, which the parent endured for the sake of the pleasure the young seemed to derive from it. Finally the parent tired of having her head swallowed and flew away, but these incorrigible swallowers continued their sport by swallowing each other's heads.

Presently a thieving spoonbill attracts my attention. He has given up trying to find nesting material of his own and pulls sticks from unguarded nests of other birds. The colony seems not to have developed any method of restraining crime. This bird goes unpunished unless he happens to approach a nest while the owner is on guard, and then he gets a terrific trouncing and retires to his perch discomfited but unabashed. He simply awaits another opportunity and resumes his activities. When the foundation of this nest was

[5]These figures are taken from Bent's *Life Histories of North American Birds,* Bulletin No. 135.

[6]Some observers say this vibration of the throat is due to excessive heat and is comparable to the panting of a dog. This may be true, but I saw it occur in the cool of the morning as well as in the heat of the day and am inclined to believe that it is a reaction stimulated by the anticipation of food.

laid, he boldly tore lining material from the nests of the grackles unopposed. Of course, if any considerable percentage of the birds became corrupted and started thieving, the whole colony would rapidly disintegrate. During my stay there, however, it remained for this one spoonbill to add the human touch.

The spoonbill is the most highly colored seabird in the world. Roseate is the proper word for him, since a great proportion of the body is only washed with red. On the wings, however, appears a deep vermilion patch called the drip. The rump is nearly yellow, some call it tawny, and there are black markings on the head. At first the bill seems nothing short of monstrous—enormous, unshapely, distorted. But it strangely beautifies the creature and furnishes one of the best illustrations I have ever seen in nature of the Baconian dictum, "There is no excellent beauty that hath not some strangeness in the proportion."

Thus one passes from detail to detail. The moment a description of any natural object is undertaken, it tends to dissociate itself. The very title of a piece serves notice of focus, which implies exclusions, whereas it is the linkage and interdependence that is central and dominates the consciousness of the observer.

Each natural object, the fixed star or the "unenduring cloud," merges itself in a frame from which it cannot be torn without loss. There is no insulated spot in nature, but each link is linked, and it is through the interminable linkage that the active principle of the ancient philosophers and the modern nature poets circulates. Intelligent observation is not an isolating process, but an unfolding.

Meantime, McCavick was grinding away with the movie camera, and at the time I thought we were bringing back home on those dark reels the atmosphere of the place. But later, on the screen in a darkened room, it was only a reminiscence after all. The essence somehow escapes, as in

Hudson's fable of the old man who gathered sunshine and put it in a sack to empty in a dark cathedral—sack after sack of it all day long—only to find the old church as gloomy after his day's work as it was to begin with. "The charm of nature is that everything is *with* the rest . . . but yet distinct, individual and complete in itself." This colony of sea birds is distinct and individual enough, but how reassociate the parts, animate and put them together again, to recapture if only partially the sharp first impressions and original wonder?

As I look now at this movie which we took in 1944, supplementing and splicing-in additions in 1945, I see but a fraction: our sackful of sunlight doesn't go very far. At best it is a counterfeit presentment. The eye of the camera takes in comparatively little. It does not record odors, which mean so much. In this instance it does not record sounds. Had we had sound-equipment, the spectator would become also an auditor and hear a constant, confused mingling of gurgles, chatters, squawks, flappings of wings, cries of the young indicative of pleading, welcome, protest, fear, satisfaction. But even so, the spectator-auditor could not breathe the air nor be warmed by the sun's rays. He could not see, except by camera glimpses, the vast stretch of the bay, the overarching blue of the sky, and the interminable green of the coastal prairie edging up to the water. In short, neither in this picture, nor in any other nature movie I ever saw, is "everything with the rest"—we do not here behold "nature distinct, individual, complete, each toward all and nothing superseding the rest." The picture has jumped its living frame of fluid edges through which it drew life and sustenance and meaning from the rest.

It no longer seems to have come out of the "dark backward and abysm of Time," it is no longer incredible. The spell is broken, and "these our actors . . . were all spirits, and are melted into air, into thin air."

20. Nest Hunger

Under provisions of the Range Improvement Program, the Federal Government has been paying landowners so much per acre for clearing off cedar (*Juniperus mexicana*) from their farms and ranches on the Edwards Plateau. In ten years or so extensive tracts have been denuded under the stimulus of the government's subsidy. The landscape itself is undergoing radical change as distant hills, once seen as masses of dark cedar-green, now show great slopes laid bare; and bald knobs of chalky soil appear dotted in like so many leprous spots eating into the verdure of rounded hills which have not yet been cropped. It is giving this once picturesque country an unkempt, not to say, diseased appearance. When future studies are made, this clearing off of cedar will be found to have affected wild life of the whole region profoundly.

It has often been pointed out that bird life hovers about the edges of a forested area and grows thinner as one penetrates the forest itself. It follows that as more edges are created, the richer the bird life will become. English ornithologists say that the many hedgerows of the English countryside have been a great boon to birds since protection is thus provided handy to feeding areas. A railroad right-of-way cut through forested sections creates two edges where there was none before. So it is, also, with automobile highways, power lines, and the like. Bird life in these cedar brakes is scanty, but the moment you begin following a power line or a highway through the cedars, business picks up, especially with the seed-eating birds. Grasses and weeds take hold when freed from cedar competition and protected from grazing stock, so there is a spread available for the seed eaters. Not only that, but there is left on each side of the feeding ground welcome cover into which the finch may dodge when hawk-pursued, or threatened by other enemies.

There is in this section one highly specialized species to which these remarks do not apply, the golden-cheeked warbler, whose breeding range is already restricted to a few counties lying east central in the Plateau, from Bexar County north to Bosque, and west—rarely—to Tom Green. So dependent has the golden-cheek become upon cedar that it is difficult to see how he will do without it. He nests among scattering cedars on the flat tops of buttes, on promontories overlooking canyons, and on very gentle declivities, never along watercourses or in extremely rough country. Limbs of mountain cedar branch upward at an angle of about thirty degrees from the trunk, and it is in such crotches of cedar or cedar elm or Spanish oak that his nest is found. This warbler makes generous use of long strips of cedar bark in the construction of his bulky nest. Since his nesting-range is limited and the eventual destruction of practically all cedar thereon seems assured, this lovely species is seriously threatened. It is very doubtful if he can adapt himself to other conditions. He will probably go down as one more instance of the deadly penalty nature assesses against overspecialization. More's the pity, since he is one of the very few nesting warblers found here.

Surprising shifts in nesting range occur among species which require some special facility, martins and certain other swallows, woodpeckers, in fact all hole-nesting birds. The importance of nesting conveniences is not generally recognized. Tree-nesting birds must have trees, but people living in wooded sections take this for granted until in a treeless area they miss their old friends. Along many of the highways crossing treeless plains of Texas the highway department has set out native trees. Hardly have the branches begun to spread and thicken enough to afford any cover at all before they are utilized. On the coastal prairie between Hempstead and Houston I took the trouble to count the number of roadside saplings thus occupied for a stretch of ten miles, and found on the average a nest in every other tree. The same nesting hunger for highway trees newly set out may be observed in the South Plains and in certain parts of the Panhandle.

We have little data on the bird life of the coastal prairies of Texas prior to the introduction there of the Cherokee rose in the Seventies of the last century, but without doubt such effective cover, and such safe harbor for nests as these enormous growths widely and suddenly introduced into the bare coastal prairies afford, produced revolutionary changes there.

If you care to secure a local shift in breeding range from your neighbors' yard to your own, simply provide better nesting facilities than your neighbors do. Any kind of facility is usually snapped up with a precipitation which suggests that there is a chronic housing shortage.

A number of years ago I put up a sixteen-hole martin box. Immediately there began a struggle between three different species for possession of this housing, English sparrows, martins, and the little Hasbrouck screech owl. The owl was finally ejected, and sparrows and martins split the box fifty-fifty. At the same time I put up a box designed to attract the golden-fronted woodpecker, and it did attract him—until the martins drove out the screech owl and the owl in turn evicted the woodpecker and occupied the box himself. The golden-front then attacked the hole of a Bewick wren's box, hammering diligently on the inch-sized entrance and gradually enlarging it although the wood was tough. After some days of this labor, he was finally able to squeeze in and throw out the wren who unfortunately had already completed her nest. The usurper, however, was not satisfied with the size of the box and did not nest there, but sat in it with his head stuck out, viewing the world philosophically for long periods each day. But the battle was not yet finished. During the woodpecker's absences, the English sparrows, ever on the alert for the main chance, discovered that he had enlarged the hole sufficiently to permit their entrance, and they began packing the box with tough, stringy Bermuda grass clippings and other trash. So the golden-fronted woodpecker upon his return from each trip found less and less room. After a few days of half-hearted tugging at sparrow trash, he gave up and left the sparrows in undisputed possession.

A sun helmet left hanging on the wall of the garage last spring was occupied by a Carolina wren, depriving the owner of its use until the brood was off. Meantime a male Bewick wren pre-empted as sleeping quarters my bathing trunks hanging on the clothesline. His mate was brooding in a nearby gourd. I might cite many other instances of nest hunger without getting beyond the borders of my own back yard.

During my short stay in this country place, I have had two examples of hunger for nesting sites. In early February, when the Bewick wrens began singing, I tacked up in a suitable location a hollowed-out gourd, leaving the entrance a mite larger than ordinarily provided for a Bewick, since no English sparrows were hanging around to squeeze in. What was my surprise one morning to notice a canyon wren enter this gourd. In this part of the country we have learned to look for the canyon wren out in the wildest canyons, ducking under balanced boulders, genuflecting in doorways of darksome cavities along the more precipitous bluffs.

This wren is a cavern sprite whose song, beginning in a high pitch, descends like the waterfall he haunts, cascading from ledge to ledge, sparkling as it encounters occasional shafts of sunlight, ever seeking lower and lower levels until at the bottom it is "stripped of its voice and left to dimple down." I was delighted to have attracted a species of such wildwood distinction to nest at my very door.

The second instance of nest hunger I find in this place concerns another gourd which I put up with entrance cut to fit the requirements of the bluebird. But some small bird which I didn't succeed in identifying occupied it at once. I found one morning that bit by bit had been broken out around the opening to admit a bird of considerable size. The nest of the small bird was destroyed; I had merely trapped some small bird for the convenience of owl, jay, squirrel, or other member of a robber breed.

My favorite woodpecker, the redhead, is now rarely found about the streets of Austin, where formerly he was one of the commonest nesting species.

Bird observers over the country are recording a restriction of the redhead's range, and some go so far as to predict the extinction of the species. He has developed the fatal habit of chasing insects, especially grasshoppers. Instead of sticking to his woodpecker last, drilling into tree trunks where his ear detects the gnawing of the woodworm, he now imitates the shrike or the flycatcher and, without the flying equipment of either of these agile species, darts down into a highway upon

insects stricken and struggling in the wake of a car. One automobile spreads the bait of mangled insects and the next speeding car hits him before he can make away. Thus the more miles of paved highway and the swifter the traffic, the more insects are knocked down, the more tempting is the bait, and the more redheads are slain.

The automobile, as deadly to some birds as it is favorable to others, is causing many shifts in range and will continue to do so.

But other corporations besides Ford and General Motors are enemies of the redheaded woodpecker. I refer specifically to municipalities and to the American Telephone and Telegraph Company. Originally these pole-erecting agencies were the greatest friends of hole-nesting birds and extended nesting places right out of the forest and on across plains and prairies. From the standpoint of the naturalist this was all to the good. Woodpeckers came to love poles and flew along from one to another, drilling holes up and down in them until many a pole was almost literally consumed. Meantime bluebirds, wrens, nuthatches, and other birds which cannot drill but need holes found them made to order. In due time both the municipality and the telephone company got tired of furnishing poles to woodpeckers and set about devising a remedy. Some chemical works finally mixed up a deadly concoction in which to soak poles. I remember the resentment I felt when the city light department and the telephone company came along my street, tearing down nice, rotten, spongy poles and erecting new poles which had been dunked in this obnoxious preservative. For years I had had the pleasure each spring of seeing the redhead occupy a hole in a pole just across the street. I saw the more belligerent redbelly appear a little later and oust him. Then he would take up residence in a pole on the other side of the street and proceed to rear his brood. I had the great pleasure of watching him put away his insects to season, a shrikelike habit which I believe no other woodpecker has, although other woodpeckers exercise a hoarding instinct. He would usually find a crack about the width of a man's thumb, in the top of a telephone pole, and pack it full of grasshoppers and other in-sects. He hammered this mash down into the crack as if life depended upon getting every possible milligram of sub-stance into the space available. Later, when the store had had time to season, he returned and consumed it.

Up until the creosoting of poles became common, I was opposed to compelling wire-using corporations to lay wires underground. But now I feel that the last excuse for public toleration of these unsightly things has been taken away and that we, the Public, should pass ordinances requiring all wires to be laid underground, affixing—both as a penalty for so long offending public taste and as a memorial to a discarded system—the requirement that at given intervals a properly seasoned and uncreosoted pole be erected for the convenience and protection of the city-loving woodpecker, especially the redhead, and for the bluebird.

Having thus deprived the redhead of his pole we were not yet satisfied. We took to chinking up every cavity in our oak trees with cement under the pretentious name of tree surgery, or dousing it with some evil-smelling liquid sup-posed to stop decay and kill insects injurious to the life of the tree. Wherever applied, this treatment has effectually evicted bird tenants and closed the doors to them forever.

And it is not because they failed to pay rent. Chickadees, wrens, nuthatches, titmouse, woodpeckers, and bluebirds paid handsomely by destroying insects often more harmful to the life of the tree than were the holes, especially those in the upper limbs. Of course, decaying trunks are another matter and call for tree surgery. Commendable work has been done, especially on the ancient oaks. I know of one giant live oak, probably five hundred years old, just east of the Texas State Capitol, that has been given another few hundred years' lease on life by the most expert piece of tree surgery I have ever seen. The trunk of this great patriarch was found to be a mere shell with cavity extending from the ground up and branching out into one of the larger of the lower limbs. It was patiently excavated to the solid and healthy flesh, refilled with cement, the limbs braced with guy wires to support the added weight; and now, ten years later, its wounds have healed and one after another of the wires is being removed as the limbs gain in strength. Healthy bark is gradually covering over the wide surface of cement at the base, and in all probability our grandchildren will see only a slight scar left by the operation.

But holes in the upper limbs are another matter. They do not threaten the life of the tree; if one limb breaks off, the tree grows another. Indeed in upper limbs the decay resulting in cavities seems to be nature's roundabout way of preserving the tree's life, since insect-eating birds nest therein and search the tree over every day. Especially is this true of post oaks which don't require any trimming. It should be left the picturesque roughneck that it is. The more one tries to make it presentable, the worse it looks. Further than stripping off ball moss, it should be left alone. It sheds rotten limbs as naturally as an animal sheds dead fur, and stays in perfect health while doing so.

"General" Beck, for many years Commander of vegetation on the University of Texas campus, told me that the more you trim a post oak the unhealthier it becomes. Although his tree knowledge was gained empirically, he was quite successful in taking care of the native growths. I agree with his treatment of post oaks. In my opinion it is a mistake to saw off a hollow limb among its upper branches, or chink it up, or treat it with any kind of preservative. Tree surgery of the cut-and-fill kind may save an individual tree now and then, but at the same time it shuts off from a given group of trees, or from an entire post-oak area, the natural protectors, hole-nesting birds. And it is certainly a mistake from an aesthetic point of view to trim and dandy-up this fine yokel, or in any other way attempt to give it a slick, citified appearance. Let it stand in pleasing contrast to gentler breeds, unkempt as it was meant to be, and reminiscent of an era before the city with its gridiron patterns, nursery importations, barbered lawns, hedges precisely clipped, and other formal ornamentations had littered up a stretch of native woodland.

21. Root and Rock

It irritates me to hear someone from another part of the country call our hackberry a sugar berry or nettle tree; or black-eyed peas, black-eyed beans. I had never heard it called anything but a hackberry until I was grown and had begun to notice the curious ways and says of people from other parts of the country. I sympathize with the English villager who described his parson as "a bit queer at first, but settling down nicely now"—after the man had been there twenty years.

Folk-naming is among the most unshakable of our social inheritances. Changing a name once generally accepted is dangerous business. Even dictators don't dare do it very often.

Replenishing my camp larder in the county seat of Chambers County, Texas, a short time ago, I had the poor judgment to question the saleslady's pronunciation of Anahuac, contending that by all the rules one should say *an-a-wak* not *an-u-ak*. She would have none of *ana,* it was *anu;* and none of *wak;* it was *ak*. She had lived there all her life and guessed she knew how to pronounce the name of her own home town. I noted that her hand began trembling as she weighed out my cheese. Counter loafers were gradually drawn into the argument, and presently I felt the atmosphere of the little store grow heavy with hostility. Although right, I gave up my contention, deciding that discretion in permitting the u-sound in Anahuac to wander around in the word at will was the better part of valor. Back on my native heath, I feel my hackles rise every time some intrusive smart aleck tries to tell me that the name of the loveliest, if rockiest, of our rivers, the Pedernales, should be pronounced *ped*-er-nal-es and not *per*-da-nal-es, as every reasonable person knows it should be. Thus my dispute with the grocery clerk in Anahuac resolves itself into whether or not the "r" has more right than the "u" to wander about in a word.

We get so attached to names that we almost fight each other over whether this or that is the correct name for a tree, a flower, a little bubbling spring, or a turn in the road. An old friend quitted my company abruptly a little while ago, angry over a dispute we had drifted into concerning just what plant in Texas is properly called bear grass, and just what grasses are called sacahuistle. I regret to lose a friend, but how tenaciously the spirit clings to a name! I let him go without apology or even an intimation that I might at any time in the future be weak enough to make the slightest concession. Of what avail is dictionary or encyclopedia to the heated exclamation, "Why, I've never heard that thing called anything else in all my life!" I am as uncompromising as Cotton Mather who, when he heard that the name of Cape Cod had been changed by princely edict, declared that Cape Cod it is and Cape Cod it shall ever be until "shoals of codfish be seen swimming on its highest hills."

There is, however, a good reason in Georgia for calling the hackberry a sugar berry. There, during Indian summer, its leaves exude a sticky, sweet substance upon which millions of mealy bugs (genus *Dactylopius*) feed. Stuffed with this exudation the bugs secrete a honeydew which falls as a golden mist sweeter than saccharin. Since the phenomenon occurs only in cloudless weather, it is called a ghost rain.

I conceived an early prejudice against the hackberry, especially in domestication, so much so that in my wood-

ramblings I rarely look with any attention at this ugly duckling with its warty bole, ragged top, and erratic configura-
tion. But raggedness and warts do not of themselves account
for my dislike. I am capable of no such aesthetic prejudices.
My early associations with the tree were unpleasant.

The town of Temple near our home had produced an
apostle of the hackberry,[1] who preached its propagation in
season and out and finally became celebrated the nation
over as Hackberry Jones. As a result of his efforts the Temple
townsite, originally a bald, blackland prairie, is now densely
shaded, as well as littered up, with hackberries. Not only
Temple, where—violating the proverb—the prophet is not
without honor, but farm and hamlet heard and heeded the
gospel, especially the sun-baked villages of the blackland
belt.

My father embraced the hackberrian faith. In the enthusiasm of a recent conversion he set out a row of saplings
on each side of the walk leading from our front gate to the
house, a distance of about two hundred yards. In summer
these trees required water, not to make any growth but
barely to stay alive. It was my job in droughty periods to
supply the moisture from a cistern, since our tap water was
mineralized and injured vegetation of any kind. So in the
blazing sun of July and August I was often wet-nurse to
forty hackberries, supplying bucketful after bucketful to
slake their many-rooted thirst. Occasionally other boys came
by on their way to the old swimming hole, and sometimes
two or three of my chums, mounted and spurred, followed
by greyhounds, paused a little while on their way to the big
sheep pasture to chase jack rabbits. Following such interruptions, I thought of pleasanter employment than thus
serving as a kind of human waterworks. Eventually I re-
belled, saying in my heart that I didn't care if they did die

[1]The native hackberry of the Edwards Plateau and of the blackland
prairies is the rough-leaved hackberry. It is found native, particularly
in the draws and rough country, as far west as a north-south line leaning a little east from the mouth of the Pecos to Lipscomb County in the
northeastern corner of the Texas Panhandle.

—which, by the way, they did before any one of them ever cast a shade as big as a horse blanket. I have slighted this tree ever since. Had my father known then what I know now, that the hackberry demands a constant if tiny water supply such as is furnished by seams in limestone, and that it cannot survive naturally on shallow soil overlaying solid stone like that of our homestead, he would have saved himself expense and me much vexation of spirit.

But the other morning, walking along the second terrace above Bear Creek, I was startled into admiration. I happened to notice from some distance away a rock slab weighing several tons, size for a flagstone of a giant's castle, propped up at an angle of thirty degrees. This huge slice of white stone was in such an artificial position that I looked underneath to see what held it up. A surface root of the hackberry, against the trunk of which the monster stone was pressed, had lifted this great burden into its present position and in so doing had kindly prepared a retreat for armadillos, raccoons, opossums, or any other prowling vermin happening to need a lodging for the night.

I tried to estimate how long it had taken the root to raise and crack this tremendous fragment. The age of a standing tree is, as everyone knows, difficult to estimate. The books say the hackberry is short-lived, but there may be exceptions. The pear tree also usually receives a stingy allotment of years, and yet there is a fairly authentic account of a pear tree on Cape Cod which was two hundred years old and still bearing fruit when blown down by a storm in 1840. Henman Doane, on the spot, commemorated it in a lengthy, circumstantial, and very religious poem which Thoreau quotes except—as one would expect—"the more clerical lines." There are living live oaks around Austin, Texas, more than a thousand years old, according to some authorities, and others of equal size not more than a few hundred years of age. If the eminent English botanist, Henry John Elwes, F.R.S., and Mr. W. R. Mattoon of the Forest Service of the U.S. Department of Agriculture, differ by eight hundred years in estimating the age of a live oak, lesser authorities may well be cautious in offering any opinion at all.

Therefore I hesitate to make a guess at the age of this particular tree. It is large for the species and has had to fight for every inch of its life in an inhospitable environment. Considering its handicaps, I judge it to be not less than forty years of age; if so, the rootlet which raised the rock took off forty years ago to search in a seam of limestone for a little nutriment to bring home to the parent stem.

During periods of excessive rainfall these hills become full of water which is held in the natural seams, the stone itself being impervious. The well on the place where I am staying fills to the surface in wet weather and drops forty, fifty, or a hundred feet as the dry season advances. While used only for domestic purposes, it will, without rain, fall thirty feet in two weeks. This shows how quickly the whole hillside drains. There are places here and there which hold the water longer, but the general level slips away quickly. It takes a fast-growing, tough, tenacious tree with widely exploring roots to take advantage of these pockets of moisture and enlarge opportunities for further growth.

The hackberry fits in here perfectly. It is a surface feeder and its roots range far and wide. They are a pest to our city water departments, for they seek out leaks in water pipes and crowd into them like thirsty cows about a watering trough. They have a nose for sewer pipes also and wreck them. They disrupt a watered lawn: they sprinkle tough sprouts all over the place, some of which take to your oak and to other shade trees, clinging with such a leechlike grasp that you often have to wound your tree to dislodge them.

Even in the act of dying, especially in domestication, the hackberry's habit is unpleasant and inconvenient. It dies by inches and sheds its corpse about piecemeal for several years. When its days are done, I like a tree, like little dog Rover in the nursery rhyme, to die all over.

On its native heath, however, habits which in domestication are abominable have their uses. On the wooded hillsides of this area, the hackberry is more effective than any other tree in check-damming, especially in undrained community roads where, without some such protection, wagon ruts quickly become erosion gullies, widening and deepening indefinitely. So, as your car rolls over one of these natural check dams, do not accuse the root of obstructing the thoroughfare. The jolt given vehicular traffic is a reminder that but for the root there would be no road at all. The tree has thrown an arm across the path of the eroding water. Battered and beaten, chewed by iron tires and ground by a thousand rushing torrents, gashed to the quick in places, this root holds the soil in its steady grip, for across the road there is nourishment necessary to sustain the life of the tree and the root proposes to have it, traffic or no traffic, in torrents of water or in parching summer droughts.

I noted the other morning a hackberry root which the traffic of an old road had cut completely through. As if finding the road traffic too heavy, the stub of the old root sent out a smaller root which turned its back upon the road, crossed clear over the top of another system of roots matted about the base of the tree, and dived into the soil on the other side.

Lately I saw a bulldozer uproot a hackberry tree two feet in diameter and at least fifty feet tall and shove it fifty or sixty feet out of the way. Directly beneath the trunk, as the tree fell over, I saw a great fragment of limestone clutched in a mass of roots. This stone was a foot thick and three feet square. In its natural position the trunk of the tree had stood directly over the stone, and the encompassing roots clung with such tenacity that when the tree was pushed over, the great stone was torn from its bed. The hackberry loves the limestone.

The great limestone slab which I found pushed up and held firmly at an angle of thirty degrees was evidence of long-sustained and monumental labor. The task had its beginning forty years ago when a prospecting rootlet took off from the main stem. Taking advantage of crack and crevice, seam and cavity, of every bit of food it could find washed in and of every minute seep of moisture, this rootlet pushed its tender tip forward to penetrate a luxurious bank of soil ten feet away from its starting point.

The problem now was to channel back the flow of nutriment in sufficient quantities really to count for something. The heavy overburden of tons of limestone barring the passage must in some way be circumvented. A thinking organism would probably have been frustrated completely. But your hackberry root can't think. It is merely an instrument of something else that does the thinking. So the rootlet was unimpressed by the obvious impossibility of lifting tons of stone straight up. Gathering strength in the land of milk and honey which its enterprise had discovered, swelled and toughened, this little Atlas took on the burden of the world.

Now, forty years later, you find the outer edge of the massive slab forced eighteen inches above its original bed and strained into a position which has caused it to crack from one side to the other. At point of contact where the upward pressure is exerted, the root is eight inches in diameter. Thus in nearly half a century the whole mass has been lifted a perpendicular distance of eight inches, a fifth of an inch per year. If arithmetic amuses one, he might calculate what fraction of a millimeter this laborious root elevates its burden every week or day or minute. All such estimates would be averages, however, since the movement over the year is not uniform. Nor is it uniform year by year. I judge that most of this lifting, the great grunting effort, is made in the three spring months of warmth and moisture and that the nine succeeding months are spent in catching breath for next spring's heave-ho.

But do not suppose the rugged old slab of stone has taken all this impertinence lying down—this attempt of a mere tree to raise him to a standing position. He has resisted with every device of his stolid and stubborn nature, and he has taken a stupid revenge by eating into the side of the trunk, causing strange, disease-looking welts to form on either side of his bite, and he has squeezed the bole of the tree into a fantastic shape. Indeed he has inflicted grievous wounds which will doubtless shorten the life of his disturber.

Upon closer inspection, it is evident that this particular root is waging, not a detached engagement, but only one wing of a larger battle in which the whole tree is involved against a still greater mass of limestone. The contest began when a sprout slipped through a crack in the middle of a ledge, the crack having been made for it in all probability by an elder generation of hackberries growing on or near this very spot. There it stood in the days of its sprouthood, wedged between two monster slabs, originally one slab but now cracked down its middle, roughly oblong in shape, fifteen by twenty feet, of varying thickness—two feet here, three feet there—and weighing at least calculation twenty tons.

The engagement began with side thrusts of the trunk itself and steady, upward pressure of the roots. On the side opposite the propped-up slab already described, the upward push of a great root had cracked the other slab into three parts by two fissures radiating from the point of contact like spokes of a wheel. Meantime the trunk of the tree forced the halves of the original slab apart for a distance of two feet, which is the diameter of the trunk measured at right angles to the fissure, while its diameter measured parallel thereto is three and a half feet. The resistance of the stone has thus squeezed the trunk out of shape, giving two diameters differing by eighteen inches.

Of course, compared with the age of the slabs, the tree is an ephemerid flaunting its brief day in the sun. When it dies, as die in a few years it will, woodworms will munch the corpse, wind will blow it down, and its roots including the giant ones upholding the fissured slabs will wither and rot.

Gradually the earth will reabsorb the material contributed to its upbuilding and gently, very gently, but more rapidly than they were raised, the great slabs of stone after fifty years in an uncomfortable position will sink to rest again in their original bed. They are tired. Gravity finally triumphs over this puny attempt of life to violate its order.

But things will never be quite the same here again. Life has left its mark with an epitaph not hard to read, quite clear, in fact, to some future naturalist who likes to puzzle around with why things are thus and so. He will see, for one thing, unnatural cracks in what was once apparently a great, flat mass of solid stone. He paws down into these cracks with his stick and finds a "richer dust concealed." He traces the veins to the old stump, or to fragments or moldy residue of it. He sees other slabs as big as or bigger than this one, lying about curiously cracked. He notices a young hackberry growing up among the slabs, and suddenly over a vast stretch of time he sees the battle of a species against a rock. Ancient and overancient cracks he finds with edges weathered smooth and, punching again with his stick, he sees rootlets of the young hackberry taking off under the slabs, beginning a repetition of the story already told. He sees the push-up that will inevitably occur, the crack, the death of the tree, the sinking back of the broken slabs, the rise of another generation of hackberries to resume the contest, and so on and on—the battle of a species against a rock, like two immortal bulldogs locked in combat but neither yet with a lethal hold upon his adversary.

A few hundred yards away, on another ledge of this same hillside, is another clump with the rubble underneath in a still more advanced state of disintegration. You soon conclude that this tree quarries limestone in no figurative sense. Its thirsting, rapacious roots, avid for nourishment, drive in through the natural seams of the stone. Swelling with what they can find, they thereby enlarge the seam, which then permits more moisture to seep in bringing along with it more plant food from the surface, which produces more root growth, more pressure, wider seams, more room for marauding rootlets, and so on until you suddenly come upon a great slab ending itself up out of shallow soil as if by magic. But scratch away the soil, and there you find the miner or the quarrier busily engaged in tearing the ledge to pieces.

As the rocks are torn from their bases and in the course of centuries cracked, crushed, and reduced to rubble, and as the space is cleared and fertilized by the rotting wood of many generations, the hackberry tends to be replaced by other trees, especially cedar elms and oaks. Thus the hackberry would appear to be a pioneer, a tough, hardy rock-breaker, clearing the way for gentler breeds and then moving on to where the going is rough enough to challenge his enterprising spirit. This is why the tree becomes so unpleasant in domestication, like a wild animal, delightful in his native habitat, whose woodland habits become obnoxious about the house; or like a rough-and-ready country dog, stock-herder and skunk-killer, brought as a pet to a city apartment. It is a mistake to try to domesticate the hackberry except under very special conditions.

And why do the gentler breeds displace the hackberry after the fight against the giant slabs of limestone has been won? Because they are longer-lived, they are calmer and more deliberate. Their roots are more cautious and calculating. Hence, when conditions are created where these more conservative trees can survive at all, their greater length of life gives them an advantage over this John-the-Baptist of a tree who has cleared the way; and we find, in many areas where lately the hackberry served as a pioneer, only a few individuals holding on, thin and tall, struggling for a share of sunshine with the oaks and elms, and destined soon to succumb entirely.

This seems a fairly faithful analogue for the frontiersman. He thrives on the open range and in the virgin forest—the Daniel Boones, the Davy Crocketts, the Wild Bill Hickoks of the pioneering era. But as soon as he and his kind have created conditions for a more civilized and conservative life, his virtues tend to become vices and he is pushed aside, sometimes violently.

As a quarrier who performs the first step in the agelong processing of limestone into soil—"black as your hat," the proud settler used to say as he turned the sod on the great, rolling prairies—the hackberry belongs among the rocks and should be left there.

The issue of this bulldog combat between the particular root and the particular rock is already fairly clear. The latter will surely be pulverized to manageable proportions by succeeding generations of hackberries, as the slabs on a thousand hillsides of the Edwards Plateau have already been. Life is delicate but infinitely inventive and, armed with a feather, crushes stones that happen to be in its way. Life has purpose and generalship. Matter has none. It is torpid, benumbed, inert. Life not only conquers it but compels it to serve her.

My boyhood prejudice against the hackberry has been mitigated somewhat, not only by subsequent observation of its spadework in the limestone ledges, but by my becoming acquainted a number of years ago with the dependence of the robin upon the fruits of this tree, which it retains in perfect preservation until midwinter, the very time when the migrating robin is hard-put to find anything at all to eat here in central Texas. Having foraged in the hills from the time of his arrival in early November until cedar berries, wild hackberries, and the fruits of far stingier shrubs are exhausted, he moves suddenly into the towns and villages about the first of February to harvest the fruit of the domesticated hackberries. Many city folk believe that the first wave of robin migration does not reach here until then. On this harvest supplemented by worms of the watered lawns he subsists until he moves northward.

And then a very little thing happened about ten years ago,

"a glimpse that makes me less forlorn" every time I recall it to memory. Starting one morning for a walk through Oakwood Cemetery, I saw in a small hackberry tree near the west entrance two cedar waxwings cuddled up close and now and then touching the tips of their bills together as if, after a brief period of waiting, both were overcome simultaneously by an excess of affection and turned upon each other kissing like two lovers parked on the roadside.

I thought of this curious exhibition of affection all during my walk. Returning an hour later, I found the pair still touching the tips of their bills together every few minutes. This time I took a look at them through my binoculars. They were not, as I had at first supposed, billing like doves, but were passing back and forth a very small object. Focusing and refocusing my glasses, and aided by an instant of sunshine giving just the right light, I identified this symbol of waxwingian devotion as a ripe hackberry.

22. Cedar Cutter

I was camped for a few days under a live oak of enormous spread crowning a bluff which overlooked the Pedernales River with its little pocket bottoms wedged in between cliff and water, strung along its winding course.

Striking camp is a relief something like that the snake feels in sloughing off his old skin. It saves washing up and disposes of stains no washing will remedy. The soiled page gives place to a fresh one with no fingerprints on it, exhaling a wind-washed odor as of bedclothes just in from a thorough airing and with the cleanliness of sun-dried dew upon them. If gypsies have that supersense of smell with which they are credited, it's no wonder that they are always on the move.

A stationary camp is quickly cluttered up. Stay too long or return to the same camping place too often, and the inevitable encrustation appears. You fix up a cupboard, install a bench between two trees, improvise a table. These and other little conveniences may be nothing more than a few pimples, but they indicate that the disease of civilization is setting in. You had better be on your way again; otherwise, you may build a camp house, then a summer home, then neighbors, and eventually find yourself right back where you started.

Moving camp is a sloughing-off process to be undertaken before there are any adhesions. This is the wisdom of the serpent.

Ill luck had shadowed me on this particular trip. I had tramped the river's narrow bottoms and had explored tributary creeks for three days without finding a new bird or learning anything new about an old one. It was early spring, too—time of all times for new things to be turning up, but they didn't choose to turn.

Nature has spells of reserve like this, or else your own spirit is asleep or preoccupied with something lodged in subconsciousness and fermenting there like the yeast of a neglected duty.

I have a theory that one never goes to nature in proper mood, patient and receptive as an earnest student should be, without learning something treasurable, but on this particular occasion defeat was closing in.

On the morning of the fourth day, I was busy packing up when the sun burst over the rim of a hill across the river, sudden as a revelation. I paused, skillet in hand, to look about. Well, I thought, this is rather pleasant and there's no need to hurry so. Why not stay until noon anyway?

I fell to looking at a shadow cast by the live oak across a glade and up a smooth slope to westward. I tried to recall the name and details of a story I had read once on a time about a man who lost his shadow—a fanciful tale; and I seemed to remember that the man had sold his shadow, and that the purchaser, perhaps the devil himself, kneeled and began rolling it tight up to the point where it joined the man's feet. Then with a quick jerk the buyer disengaged it from where it was hinged to the heels and, carefully placing it in his poke, moved off, sardonically wishing the now shadowless vendor good day. The story was concerned from then on with the embarrassments of being without a shadow.

From this I drifted into a consideration of the shadow of the life oak. For how many hundreds of years had this shadow fallen upon that same slope at sunrise, gradually shortening until midday, and then moved out eastward to the edge of the bluff, leaping the river to the rugged declivities on the other side.

I thought of the oak's laboring not to lose its shadow which swayed with the seasons, a little north returning then to center, then a little south, and back again, a pendulum geared to make only one complete swing in the solar year—a slow clock, but harmonious with the age of this long-lived tree, which, some authorities say, stays green a thousand years. Before Columbus this shadow with its diurnal climb, descent, and leap across the river, and with its yearly swing from north to south and back again, had caricatured the tree on slope and glade in the mornings and resumed its fantastic prank on the irregular ledges across the river in the afternoon.

Daily, for ages, the same routine. The first beams of the sun spread it far up the slope, grotesquely diffused. As the morning advances, it is pulled in, sharpened, contracted, and the caricature gradually subdued until at midday a clear and faithful outline of the great tree appears upon the grass. But all this labor goes for naught, for after a short siesta the truant begins escaping eastward and presently leaps from the bluff, landing light as a feather across the river among the tumbled boulders on the other side. Now it is in for steep and laborious climbing, but it manages to edge farther and farther away, finally to make good its escape into the purple hills.

We say of this oak (*Quercus virginiana*) that it is evergreen, but the word "ever" here means only "a long time and continuously," for even to the live oak the spring will finally come when the browned and yellowed leaves it sheds will not be replaced. It becomes first naked, then fleshless; "only the man of bone remains." Its early-morning shadow becomes a wilder caricature, sprawling, thinned, and sketchy; but, drawn up at midday, it verifies the skeleton which casts it—a skeleton trying to dominate its ghost.

I lingered around the camp until after lunch and then struck out across the hills. Following an abandoned wood

road over the cedar-thicketed slope, I soon heard the wooing
note of a paisano and sat down to look and listen. I have
never decided whether to call this bird's amorous noises a
croak or a moan. It's not dreary enough to be called a moan,
and too melodious for a croak. It is a wandering, uncertain sound, now near, now far away, and fading out until
you doubt whether you are hearing anything at all. I have
heard it, however, only in the wooded hills, never on plains
or prairies where it may have a different quality. Perhaps
in this rough and wooded area it comes to the ear modified
by leafy interferences and by bouncing over boulders and
glancing off cliffs or ledges, leaving a fragment of itself with
each obstruction. Apparently the call is not tempered for
such tough going. Maybe sound experts in their laboratories
can take it to pieces and tell exactly what happens and why;
but until then, I can only say of this love call that it seems to
issue from nowhere in particular and go wandering about,
seeking, but without much hope of finding, "the nothing it
set out from."

On this occasion, I had only a few moments to wait before
the paisano appeared, as I was sure he would, crest flushed
and tail near perpendicular. He stood there in the field of my
binoculars for full five minutes, stock-still except for a slight
rotary motion of the head, as if he were turning his glance
now to the ground, now to the sky, giving each eye a look
up and a look down. Then, lowering his tail and stretching
his long neck forward, he made off, sneaking through low
growths in the direction of his answering mate.

The authorities accuse this bird of being careless about
whose nest she lays her eggs in, and of occasionally cuckold-
ing not only her own kind but individuals of other species as
well. The practice is not habitual, however, as with our
cowbird and with the Old World cuckoos.

Presently, hoping for another glimpse of the paisanos who
were still carrying on their amorous converse, I heard the
sound of an axe, slow and measured—very, very slow. I
thought it must be some Mexican chopping by the day

rather than by the post, the strokes fell with such a mañana tempo.

Keeping my direction for a little while, I saw through an opening in the cedars a sight I shall never forget. My glasses brought him up close—an aged man cutting cedar. It was obviously the weight of years upon the trim, streamlined axe which had slowed it down. After a dozen strokes or so, he leaned heavily on a tree, his chest heaving. As soon as his breathing quieted a little, he resumed his chopping, slow, steady, and accurate to a hair, like the "slow-motion" of a woodchopper to show correct form.

His gigantic frame was stripped to the waist. He was at least six-feet-two, broad-shouldered, tapering to the hips, with an almost wasplike waist accentuated by a belt drawn tightly above the bony hips. In full flesh this frame could carry two hundred pounds without feeling it. He now weighed certainly less than one hundred and fifty. I did not know until then that so much skin could be hung upon the bony framework of a man. As his emaciated arms went up with the rising stroke, there was at least a three-inch movement of skin across the washboard of his ribs. Up and down, the loose skin slipped over those regular furrows enclosing the mighty chest, making a ripple like water running across corrugations.

I now realized what the physiology books mean when they talk of a cushion of flesh—that's exactly what our flesh is, a cushion enclosed in skin. Remove the cushion, and the envelope wrinkles and sags. This man's flesh was gone and he was almost literally skin and bone. When his arms dropped to his sides, long, flapping bags of skin hung down at the juncture of arms with shoulders. Aged obesity is grotesque, but better fat flesh than none at all.

Then, focusing my glasses a little better, I saw something along the arms that gave me an additional start. The veins were as big as lead pencils or whipcords, and in the swinging of the arms these hard, huge, purplish blood vessels stretched and slipped under the skin.

Alas, poor Yorick! The grave-diggers arrived too late. A mere skeleton is unimpressive.

Stooping my way through the brush, I came near him and spoke, but he continued chopping. I raised my voice a bit, and still he paid no attention. I spoke louder, then shouted, and he turned his face slowly toward me. There were two large, ulcerous-looking sores on his face, one near the right temple and one on the cheekbone just below it. They had been dusted over with some medicament through which a trickle of sweat had furrowed its way down toward the point of the chin.

As he laid his axe aside, I noticed his hands—immense, bony, enormously veined over the backs and interiorly curved to fit an ax handle. The fingers looked as though they could never be straightened at all, and were hard and horny enough to crack a seed tick.

His eyes were blue and smiling, with a little clouding around the edges of the iris. Unlike the hardened beach-comber whose face Thoreau describes as "too grave to smile, too tough for tears," this man's countenance radiated good will. The skin of the face, contrasting with that of the torso, was drawn tight as a drum over a massive, bony structure, allowing little mobility, one would think, for emotional expression of any kind. But unmistakably he was smiling.

He began apologizing at once for the pitiful little pile of posts he had hewed out since dinner, saying that, although he was old and not able to do much, still he wanted to do *something* or, he was afraid, he might soon become bedridden like his neighbor.

His voice was firm but he could not control its volume, since he was nearly deaf and had long been accustomed to speaking in wind and weather. He shouted at me and I at him, and the conversation which ensued could have been heard at some distance without benefit of amplifiers.

He told me that he couldn't do anything but cut cedar, since that was all he had ever done except to farm a little. I found that he was eighty-six years old and that here in this locality his father had put him to cutting cedar when he was only ten.

Seventy-six years cutting cedar!

I later learned that this man is wealthy. It was not economic necessity that forced him to this dismal labor, but a grim, determined fight against the helplessness which he feared old age would force upon him.

He thought he might die soon anyway and that it was better to keep doing something. His neighbor, eighty-nine, was now in the hospital, had been in there four months, didn't know if he would ever get out—alive.

There was a reproach in the way he told me that this man "stopped doing something" at eighty-eight, and a suggestion that he was now being punished for his dereliction by confinement in the hospital and loss of his voice. "He can't talk any more, you know," he said.

This is the pioneer philosophy of being up and doing, of marching on to the end of the row, of never quitting. It is the gospel of salvation by work.

But the old fellow finally shook his head sadly. "I 'low," he said, "when a man is old there ain't much pleasure left for him; and when he's young, he ain't got sense enough to take care of himself,"—which observation George Bernard Shaw polished up into an epigram. Or maybe Mark Twain said this before Shaw did.

I asked the old man for the time. Glancing at the sun, he said "It's about four: I'd say the sun is two hours high."

"Well," I objected, "if it's only two hours high it must be five, as the sun sets at seven or thereabouts."

"Oh," he grunted, showing irritation, "that's by that fast time."

I sensed here the resentment out-of-door people feel toward artificial time—as if all measuring of time were not artificial—*fast* time, they call it. Tampering with sun time seems to them a sacrilege. Perhaps there's a survival of sun worship hidden deep down from long ago; and this city-folk presumption of telling the sun when to come up and when to go down is a blasphemy. Roosevelt lost more rural votes by tampering with time than he did by trying to modernize the Supreme Court.

All the way through his long novel, *The Magic Mountain,* Thomas Mann is continually tampering with time. He insists on divisions of time into occasions, such as Christmas and Easter; into routine, or the regular daily grind; or into periodical discomforts, such as holding a thermometer in your mouth seven minutes. He emphasizes the essential emptiness of the time concept. It is content of time that matters—all else: illusion. An attempt to divide the flow of time into watertight compartments, irrespective of content, introduces artificiality into our lives. Clocks, calendars, gongs may be a convenience for running a factory or a train, but they are in opposition to the spirit of life. Poets occasionally enlarge upon this point of view. Slipping into a featureless routine, clock-and-calendar governed, is slipping into something really worse than death, because you still remain conscious.

Routine machines our lives to conform to industrialization. Life is its opposite: dawn, stars, storms, calm, the witchery of twilight, the whimsicality of the seasons, and the vast and ample variety of the natural day—all proclaim an antagonism to routine.

I doubt the truth of the oft-told tale of the calendar-governed migrations of the swallows of Capistrano, because the whole of nature leans the other way. I tried for a number of years to make the purple martin arrive in the Texas state capital on March 2, Texas Independence Day. And they did arrive at my box for four consecutive years exactly on that date. Then, not wanting to spoil a good story, I began to fudge a little by not looking very hard until March 2, on which date I looked my eyes out and even called my friends by phone to find out if their martins had arrived. I accumulated six "straights" in this way and was about to offer my research for publication, when a group of four noisy martins awakened me on the morning of a February 15 and stayed around the box the whole day, uttering their cool hello calls until the neighbors were brought in to witness.

The swallow cannot proceed north without flying insects with which to fuel his flight. Warm weather is necessary for insects to penetrate the high martin-zone. So cause-linking-cause leads back to the weather. If the weather were identical by calendar dates year after year from the martin's point of departure in Brazil clear to my martin box in Austin, Texas, then I might have made a Texas Independence Day bird out of him. But the great storms which sweep across his migration route, destroying the high-flying insects for hundreds of miles, have no dependable schedule. Neither have the martins. Nature ignores the calendar; she approves approximations, however.

The so-called literature of escape with its growing popularity is in part a revolt against the tyranny of clocks. It is not labor that kills, but the small attritions of daily routine that wear us down. A month of days, a year of months, twenty years of months in the treadmill is the life that slays everything worthy the name of life.

A camping companion of mine insists on leaving watches at home when we go out for a week or two in the woods or by the seashore. If we forget, he gathers these instruments and locks them up. He maintains that the sun, moon, and stars are time guides, and makes quite an oration which I have listened to many times, about adjusting your life to the rhythm of nature.

Another philosophical person I know, finding his life bounded in the shallows and miseries of routine, broke away with the determination to do something quite irrational every so often. He has become, after a few years of this, not a mere classroom instructor, as he had been for thirty years before, but a man of affairs, with houses, lands, and other investments to look after, and has recovered, so he declares, a little of the old joy of living.

As I resumed my walk, the slow strokes of the axe began again. I was reminded of the huge clock that used to stand on our mantel shelf when I was a boy. If one noticed carefully, he could tell by the slowing up of the tick-tock when the clock needed rewinding. But no rewinding will accelerate the tick-tocking of these strokes I hear today in the quiet cedar brake.

With the lengthening of the span of human life, the problems of old age become increasingly difficult. There is more old age now than there ever was, and science promises in the immediate future an even greater supply. Increase in the proportion of the aged to the productive members of a society raises new economic and political questions, but the philosophical one is as old as civilization itself.

The ancient Greeks, worshipers of youth and fanatical cultists of the body beautiful, disliked to be reminded of the deterioration which the years bring even to the most conscientious practitioners. In their mythology the good and beautiful die young and are turned into gods, goddesses, stars, flowers, fountains, trees, and the like, in which transformation they are kept in a state of perpetual youth. But mythology aside, there were certain flesh-and-blood individuals in Plato's time who persisted in cultivating the body beautiful at an age when even the most faithful practice of its precepts failed to yield commensurate returns. The appearance of old men on the playing field and in the gymnasiums without benefit of clothing called forth from one of the speakers in the *Republic* critical comment, as follows:

> Yes, and the most ridiculous thing of all will be the sight of women naked in the palaestra, exercising with men, *especially when they get old;* they certainly will not be a vision of beauty, any more than *the wrinkled old men* who have *anything but an agreeable appearance* when they take to gymnastics—this, however, does not deter them. (Italics supplied)

Thus were these ancient Bernarr McFaddens castigated. Perhaps it is better to follow the Christian or Confucian, Buddhistic or Islamic faiths in which the old aspire only to spiritual beauty and leave exclusively to the young the palaestrae and bathing beaches where youth and beauty meet. And it might be well for the high priests of nudism, while that cult is still in its formative stages, to provide a special and private ritual for members of the faith after thirty-five.

From the Preacher, in Ecclesiastes, and Homer on down, literature has concerned itself with consolations intended to mitigate the miseries of declining years. The Preacher, after covering the grisly specter with a costly robe of rhetoric, jeweled with resplendent imagery, declares bluntly, "the conclusion of the whole matter; fear God and keep his commandments," since that is "the whole duty of man." Agamemnon consoles Nestor for the loss of physical prowess by reminding the patriarch of the pre-eminence he has attained in council.

When a group of young men twit the aged Sophocles, asking, doubtless, with an insinuating manner, "How does love suit with age, Sophocles—are you still the man you were?" "Peace," the aged poet replies, "most gladly have I escaped the thing of which you speak; I feel as if I had escaped from a mad and furious master." The speech of Cephalus, in which this passage occurs, contains many consolations more convincing than this one.

Seneca argues; Browning adjures us to "trust God, see all, nor be afraid." Fitzgerald, following Omar, is driven frankly to strong drink; Tennyson, to his milder wine. Whitman emits gusty lines, figuring old age in one poem as a rising and in another as a setting sun. He entitles his last trickle of poetry, some of it poor, but all of it hopeful, "Sands at Seventy."

As a matter not of philosophy but of actual practice, some of the island peoples of the Pacific and Roman aristocrats of glorious memory arrived at an identical solution—independently, of course, since there was no possible contact between these two cultures.

The savage islander nearing forty—they are a short-lived people—experiences the "sensation of mortality." Age, he feels, has laid its evil hand upon him. He's not the man he used to be. He meditates upon this new ailment for some time, and finally becomes convinced that he is really slipping, that there is no comeback, that he is permanently on the downward path.

It then becomes his duty to advise the headman of the village of this state of affairs and to suggest that invitations be issued to his funeral. The villagers receive the summons with joy and proceed through properly appointed committees to arrange the customary festivities. When the happy day dawns, the candidate for burial marches at the head of the column of merrymakers out into the woods, and there, after appropriate good-bys and mutual felicitations, he is placed in the bottom of an open grave. The dirt is heaved in, the festal throng dissolves; and the disease we call old age has received preventive treatment. These villages have discovered the fountain of perpetual youth: they remain forever young.

In Rome the philosophy was the same but more self-conscious, and more a private practice than a social institution. The aging aristocrat, balancing the pleasures against the pains of his present existence, decides with impartial detachment that life is no longer desirable. He thereupon issues invitations not indiscriminately to a whole community, but only to a group of his nearest and dearest friends, companions few but fit. They gather in his home at the appointed time and gravely discuss the ways of gods and men. They speak sententiously as the Romans of the great period did, each contributing reflections, earnest and dignified. The hour arrives, a slave holds the cup, the host opens a vein in his arm and slowly passes away, still participating, up to a certain point, in friendly conversation.

Montaigne tells the story of a Roman who was afflicted with a painful and apparently hopeless malady. He decided upon death by starvation, and issued invitations to a list of friends to drop in as convenient and converse with him during his final fast.

Starvation, however, chose to kill the disease before it did the patient, and the learned leeches pronounced him sound and well, needing only a gradual resumption of nourishment to restore him to full strength and vigor. This situation posed a question for which neither code nor precedent had an answer. After serious consultation with friends, he decided that the few years remaining to him would hardly justify retracing his steps from Death's door; so, continuing his fast, he entered in.

One rarely finds an animal in feral state suffering from sickness or old age. Life and death are here so nicely balanced that a feather out of place, a rheumatic stiffness in a joint, a motor reaction slowed down by a fraction of a second, or a dimmed vision means instant extinction. In a state of nature, nearly every individual animal must be in full possession of all his powers, mental and physical, to survive at all. No drunkenness or eating to excess is permitted. The sapsucker, drunk on fermented sap, falls an easy prey to the ever-watchful hawk, if indeed he does not dash himself to death against a limb with the usual overconfidence of inebriety. So also the robin, staggering about your lawn from overindulgence in chinaberries, is snapped up quickly by the harmful and unnecessary cat.

A sharp, unsentimental surgery obtains throughout the animate world. Mother Nature wants to see her creatures healthy and happy or not see them at all. It is only in domestication that man's physical ailments are conferred upon the lower animals.

Lingering illnesses and old age appear among herding animals wherever an exceptionally favorable environment produces a surplus over and above the number taken by the herd's predatory enemies. Buffalo hunters found aging bulls, which had been driven out of the herd, still surviving. J. W. Abert's *Journal* records meeting with an old buffalo bull, "which appeared reluctant to move out of our road. He looked old and was so gaunt that his skin hung upon him like wet drapery upon a skeleton."[1] I have heard that old

[1] *Guadal P'a,* The Journal of Lieutenant J. W. Abert, etc., with Introduction and notes by H. Bailey Carroll, The Panhandle-Plains Historical Society, Canyon, Texas, 1941, p. 93.

age appears also among the rabbit hordes of Australia. But these are the exceptions.

I once followed a distressful call through the woods for half an hour before finally identifying it. It was a sick mockingbird. When I finally got sight of him, he was sitting on a limb, tail down, wings loose at his sides, and head hung forward. The sound he made was nothing like anything I had ever heard come from a bird's throat before or since. I accounted for his persistence in that state by the fact that he is such a terrific fighter that his enemies want to be sure he is quite incapable of resistance before attacking him. I have heard also that lions in a natural state sometimes die of old age because of the fear in which they are held by other denizens of the forest.

Trees, on the other hand, as well as vegetable life generally, are subject to diseases which do not kill; they have warts, wens, cancerous growths, grotesque deformities, and come gradually to declining years with definite symptoms of senility, lingering on and on.

As I finally turned back toward my camp under the shadow troubled live oak, the sound of the cedar cutter's ax became fainter and fainter, until it seemed to be an echo loose in the lonely cedar brake. *Chop-tick, chop-tock,* steady, slow, and then a brief silence. Again, a dozen strokes or so and pause; until finally I could hear it no more.

Errata

PAGE

xv, line 9: FOR Loan READ Reference

xxii, line 8: FOR identation READ indentation

xxiii, line 12: FOR adjustible READ adjustable

28, line 7: FOR Epidonax READ *Empidonax*

29, line 26: FOR There is doubt READ There is no doubt

41, line 8: FOR better those READ better than those

42, line 11: FOR touches feet READ touches his feet

75, line 9: FOR severly READ severely

84, line 16: FOR "This Brave New World," READ "Brave New World"

87, line 15: FOR friends READ friend

96, line 26: FOR do this way READ do it this way

99, line 12: FOR Jes zactly READ Jes' zactly

102, line 8: FOR if it were READ as if it were

114, last line of footnote: TRANSFER Courtesy Museum of Zoology, University of Michigan TO LAST LINE OF PRECEDING PARAGRAPH

117, line 13: FOR *harvardii* READ *havardii*
line 21: FOR Quercus READ *Quercus*

119, line 3: FOR (*q. breviloba*) READ (*Q. breviloba*)
line 26, FOR Harvard's READ Havard's

121, line 29: FOR the one my bird was reclining READ the one where my bird was reclining
line 34: FOR other READ others

122, line 2: FOR Cow men READ Cowmen

134, lines 20 and 24: FOR *Ptilogonatidae* READ Ptilogonatidae

135, line 9: FOR Empidonax READ *Empidonax*

143, line 12 of footnote 3: FOR animals. READ animals."

190, line 2 of footnote 2: FOR folk belief long ago exploded READ folk belief, long ago exploded,

191, lines 9–10: FOR *Phalacocorax Mexicanus* READ *Phalacrocorax mexicanus*

196, line 21: FOR whites READ Whites

207, line 17: FOR McCullough READ McCulloch

216, line 6: FOR poular READ popular

228, line 32: FOR Laye READ Loye

229, line 31: FOR careful scientist READ a careful scientist

235, line 14: FOR droop- READ drupe-

240, lines 2, 8, 15: FOR Skoberg READ Skogberg

244, line 14: FOR where a READ where an

245, line 14: FOR tree or shrub READ a tree or shrub

280, line 34: FOR life oak READ live oak

The Author's Emendations

In the years following the first publication of *Adventures of a Texas Naturalist* Mr. Bedichek made various notes in the margins of his personal copy, reflecting constructive criticisms from his friends and some of his own second thoughts. Those marginal comments of greatest interest have been reproduced below. Francis H. Allen, who is referred to in the annotations, was a friend and fellow Texas naturalist.

(Passages replaced, deleted, or commented upon by Mr. Bedichek are italicized.)

4: "In periods of excessive rainfall the regurgitations of a dozen bloated rivers *spill over the continental shelf.*" Comment: "No."

41. "The *temporary capitol* burned in 1881." Correction: "First Capitol." "The great granite statehouse was completed in 188*3*." Correction: 1888.

43. "After two unsuccessful attempts to invade Austin, once in the *temporary capitol* in 1865, and again in the *new* capitol in 1883, these swallows waited another third of a century[1] before appearing *in force* under the new Congress Avenue bridge . . ." Corrections and comment: "First Capitol"; "granite"; "(1) Meantime street paving interfered [with] their supply of wet limestone mulch, much prized by them as building material."

53. "A game warden on the Aransas *Game* Refuge . . ." Correction: "Aransas National Wildlife Refuge."

54. "But the reduction to absurdity in the hunter-naturalist feud was reached some years ago in England where sportsmen demanded the extermination of martins and other swallows, because they ate mayflies, mosquitoes, and other insects and thus starved the trout to death!" Comment: "Some English review scoffed at this."

"Scientists have established beyond peradventure that the brown pelican's food consists chiefly . . . of non-game fish, but these birds are persecuted shamefully on the Texas coast, killed in flight for practice, and their nesting places destroyed. On Bird Island near Flower Bluff in 1932, I found nests broken up and pelican eggs scattered about so thickly that one could hardly walk along the beaches without stepping on them." Comment: "Investigate Allen's story concerning frenzy of these birds, when they break up their own nests."

56. ". . . the so-called 'Ducks Unlimited'." Comment: "See letter on this outfit in my file."

70. "Even the botanists, whose business it is to know the ways and wiles of vegetable life, were amazed to find growing in the *bomb-blasted* blocks of London one hundred twenty-six species of wild flowers never before recorded on or near those plots of soil." Note: "*op. cit.*, p. 82 hereof."

79. "*The wren which picks the alligator's teeth is immortal*; . . ." Comment: "Insert attached footnote. [1]It is the "service" feature of this that is folklore. There is a bird that pecks in and around the alligator's mouth for parasites or for whatever else he may find loose and nourishing'."

81. "Well do I remember the sense of companionship with which, a Texas norther howling about the barn, I settled down in a comfortable stall, my forehead pressed firmly into the flank of the great beast, to do the milking, talking soothingly to her as every good milkman does." Comment· "Now they use the radio."

105. ". . . every normal motion is torn asunder, . . ." Query: "?"

110. "Aubrey Beardsley used to eat a pound of raw meat before going to bed . . ." Revision: "There is a story that Aubrey Beardsley used to eat a pound of raw meat before going to bed . . ."

132. "The swift is *the only bird that flies with alternate wing-beats*; . . ." Comment: "Francis H. Allen questions this."

169. "Alexander Wilson carried the brains and entrails of a Carolina parakeet in his pocket 'until it became insufferable,' trying to find a cat to eat the mess in an effort to confirm or discredit the general belief that entrails and brains of the parakeet kill cats. . . . the parakeet is probably extinct and this bit of folklore now seems safe from experi-

mental attack. There are plenty of cats and plenty of cocklebur seed, but no entrails, and entrails may be as essential element of the mixture."

Note: "See conclusion of Alexander Wilson on Paraquet where he did feed entrails and brains to a cat, but bird had fed on *Indian corn* [itals Mr. Bedichek's] not cocklebur seed. So this story is embalmed, forever old forever new, like the figures on Keats' Grecian Urn."

170. "The frog . . . doubtless still wears a precious jewel in his head, . . ." Interpolation: "The frog . . . doubtless *like the toad* still wears . . ." Marginal note: "Toad. F. H. A."

175–176. "Since the wood duck nests in the hollow of a tree ten, thirty, or even fifty feet above the ground, the method of descent of the ducklings has been a matter of considerable controversy . . .

"The anatomist makes his contribution by observing that the wood duckling is hatched with long, sharp toenails, which would seem to indicate that nature knew that he would immediately have some climbing to do . . . . which would seem to anticipate some sort of fall, but whether from the nest or from the mother's back or beak is not indicated." Comment: "Add as footnote here that Guide I met in Saratoga, Texas, 'Rosier,' said *he saw* [itals Mr. Bedichek's] wood duck carrying y[oun]g down. A Mrs. Bruce Reid verified story, also."

191. "The pioneer stomach *stood for* almost anything . . ." Comment: "Colloq."

192. "On the other hand, palpable mistakes, a typographical error, mispronunciation or a fool translation, sometimes produce a good name. 'Redstart,' a corruption of *rothstert*, literally 'redtail,' is better than the original." Comment: "Stert in ME is *tail*. F. H. A. Yes. But 'red' not 'roth'; even in OS was 'rod'."

193. "The word 'stock' is held by some to apply to this dove because at one time it was believed to be of the stock of the domestic pigeon. According to another belief, it is a stock dove because it nests in 'stocks,' or trunks of trees." Comment: "F. H. A. questions this."

195. "There is a common *iris* called blue-eyed grass." Comment: "belongs to iris family, not an iris, strictly speaking. F. H. A."

"So the grass is 'blue-eyed' because the corolla, corresponding to the iris of the eye, is blue and the center, corresponding to the pupil, is yellow, *as in human beings—*" Correction: "as we call human beings from color of the *iris.*"

"Eula Whitehouse makes the following note about this plant: '. . . One of these plants was called "joe-pye weed" in honor of the Indian doctor, Joe Pye.' The scientific name is *Eupatorium compositifolium.*" Query: "The Joe Pye weed is *E. purplureum?*"

" 'Sand weed' is an excellent name because the plant grows better in the sand than in any other soil, . . ." Addendum: "Holds blowing sand."

196. "In Texas the accidents of history have brought four racial groups together—Whites, American Indians, Mexican Indians and Negroes." Comment: "These two Indian groups should be put together as 'Indians'."

197. "Folk estimates of national character are found, also, in folk names. We call the shrike a French mockingbird. Why?" Comment: "F. H. A.: 'Wilson says the Brown Thrasher is called a "French mocking bird" in Maryland, Va., etc.' "

202, n. 1. "An ingenious suggestion is that he does it to scare insects out of hiding, but I have never seen him apprehend an insect in this way." Comment: "Since this footnote, I have seen him scare up insects in this way and I believe that is generally his purpose. But I have seen him spread his wings on a blank wall where there were certainly no insects—maybe just habitual gesture."

213, continuation of n. 7, p. 212. "If any of the names given the mocker by early French settlers in Louisiana had stuck, *rossingol,* or *moqueur,* or *grand moqueur,* or *voix d' amour,* what a boon it would have been to poets!" Correction: " '*rossignol.*' F. H. A."

221. Sensory impressions are notoriously unreliable. Court testimony has proved frequently that no two eye- and ear-witnesses ever see and hear the same occurrence exactly alike, and laboratory tests confirm the finding. Messages from the objective world come to us gummed-up with prejudices, colored by suggestions, and confused with associated memories." Comment: "e.g., my own memory of opossum car-

rying y[oun]g on her back with their tails twisted around hers."

226. "George Finley Simmons credits the following interpretation of the barred owl's hoot to Stanley Clisby Arthur . . ." Comment: "Barred owl's hoot, just two phrases seldom if ever, longer."

230. " 'There is no sound, whether made by bird or beast about him, that he cannot imitate so clearly as to deceive everyone but himself,' says Neltje Blanchan . . ." Comment: "F. H. A. says *deception* not necessary to successful *mimicry.*"

237. "*Bradford Torrey,* not a naturalist but a poetic essayist with a keen and sympathetic eye, . . ." Re-evaluation: "Torrey was really a pretty good naturalist—ornithologist and Botanist—not simply an essayist."

237, n. 11. A quotation from A. C. Bent on Dr. Harold E. Edgerton's bird photography with use of intermittent flashes in a low-pressure tube. Comment: "In 'Flight of Birds' much better photography."

240. "*Skoberg,* a delightful *Minnesota Norwegian* with a strong interest in nature, . . ." Correction: "Skogberg, a delightful Michigan Swede . . ."

241. ". . . comprising eight genuses. . ." Correction: "F. H. A. 'genera'."

243, continuation of n. 2 from p. 242. "I have even read detailed reports of sexual manifestations induced by presenting stuffed specimens to imprisoned birds. . . . If one might go out into the woods with a sackful of stuffed specimens and secure the reactions described by tossing them out to healthy birds in their natural environment, I would follow such experiments with more patience." Comment: "They have now done just this. Note here experiments made by author to whom T. P. Harrison referred me."

245. "With these birds, building material is a problem of first importance, because they are dependent upon dead sticks with which to lay the foundations of their huge nests, and it takes a lot of sticks." Comment: "footnote here on McThennan [?] reservation in La. where dead sticks are hauled in by the truckload."

247. ". . . the very time when the migrating robin is *hard-put* to find anything at all to eat . . ." Comment: "not in dictionary."

killing of, 154–155; war of commercial interests on, 154–155; airplanes in killing of, 155; lovers of, 156; effect on, of sudden change of natural conditions, 157, 258. *See also* plant life; animal life

wild-life
— clubs: use of right-of-ways by, 23–24
— preserves: right-of-ways as, 12, 13, 23

wild
— steers: on Mount Livermore, 137
— turkeys. *See* turkeys, wild

Williams, M. L.: on mockingbird killing rattlesnake, 207–208

Wilson, Alexander: on Carolina parakeet, 169. *See also* emendations

The Wilson Bulletin: 182

windmill: and tank, 137–138

winds: erosion of soil by, 4; on prairies, 23; effect of, on petroglyphs, 124

Winner, Septimus: and "Listen to the Mockingbird," 226 n–227 n

winter wren: 121

wire, barbed: and horses, 157, 158

wire fences. *See* fences; fences, barbed-wire

wolf: trap for, 87; in balance of nature, 142; study of diet needed, 146; and jack rabbit, 159; dog suckled by, 161; learning by pup of, 161; suckled by dog, 161

wolves, red: and skunks, 127–128

wood
— doves, African: in Palestine, 162
— duck. *See* duck, wood
— duckling: 176, 177

woodpecker, golden-fronted: nesting box for, 260–261
—, pileated: 67–68
—, redheaded: 262–264; range of, 262, 263–264; and insects, 262–264; and automobiles, 263; and utility poles, 263; poles for, 264

woodpeckers: 194, 259, 263, 264

wood pewee: use of tails for balance, by, 135
—, western: feeding of, over pond, 134–135

woods near right-of-ways: 22

"Word out of the Sea, A": 214

words: from typographical errors, 192

Wordsworth, William: 139–140; on indiscriminate collecting, 58; quotation from, 84

work: and cedar cutter, 284, 286; salvation by, 286

World War I: golden eagle during, 150

wren: Inca dove compared to, 63; and alligator, 79; and mockingbird, 206; and utility poles, 263; value of, to trees, 264
—, Bewick: 121, 261; nesting facilities of, 260–261; perch of, 261
—, cactus: 121, 232; dummy nests of, 121
—, canyon: 121; in author's room, xxiii; nest of, in gourd, 261; song of, 261–262
—, Carolina: 121; movement of, into New England, 30; nest in sun helmet, 261
—, marsh: 121
—, rock: 121
—, Texas Bewick: 121
—, winter: 121

Wright, A. C.: on cardinals, 183

Yankee weed: 196

yaupon: 73–74, 76
—, evergreen: as hedge plant, 75
—, berry: 199

year, solar: swing in, 281

yellow-billed cuckoo: 239

yellow-breasted chat: 233

yellow buckeye: 74

yellow daisies: 60

Yellowstone: 117

yellow Texas star: 60

yoga detachment: 140

Yorick: 284

Yorkshire, England: indiscriminate collecting in, 58